D1590828

Jesus in his Lifetime

✠

Also by John Marsh

Amos and Micah

The Fulness of Time

Gospel of St John,
Pelican Commentary

History of the Synoptic Tradition
(Rudolf Bultmann)
(trans.)

New Testament Theology
(Ethelbert Stauffer)
(trans.)

A Year with the Bible

Jesus in his Lifetime

☩

JOHN MARSH

SIDGWICK & JACKSON
LONDON

First published in Great Britain in 1981
by Sidgwick and Jackson Limited

Copyright © 1981 John Marsh

ISBN 0 283 98638 7

Photoset in Baskerville by Robcroft Ltd, London
Printed in Great Britain by
The Garden City Press Limited
Letchworth, Hertfordshire SG6 1JS
for Sidgwick and Jackson Limited
1 Tavistock Chambers, Bloomsbury Way
London WC1A 2SG

To my wife
GLADYS
my friend of Friends
mother of children
true helpmeet and
fellow disciple
in appreciation
gratitude and love

Contents

*To the esteemed Faculty of Theology
in Duke University, North Carolina,
U.S.A.*

Greeting:

It was in 1958 that you honoured an obscure English teacher of theology in the University of Oxford by inviting him to deliver the Gray Lectures at your university. My memories of that visit, your ready hospitality, generous hearing and stimulating comment, have remained among the most treasured of my life.

The lectures were written and delivered, but they have not been published; largely due to the unending fascination of the theme which then attracted me –the probable theological and religious motives behind the compilation and arrangement of the gospels. In pursuing that theme I was led to many others, and it has seemed impossible to reduce the material to coherent order until now. This book is the product of reflection in retirement on the theme of the lectures I gave so long ago in Duke.

I trust that you can accept the book happily, and that it will not prove too unworthy a unit in the series of Gray Lectures. I cannot suppose that there will be no disagreement with at least some of the views I express; that is part – and a very valuable part – of being a theologian.

Finally, I would like to express my gratitude once more for the honour you paid me in both asking for, and listening to, the lectures.

John Marsh

Introduction

Thousands of books have been written about Jesus; surely all that can be said about him has already been said. Why write another?

The answer is threefold: first, like many before him this writer has felt constrained to offer the fruits of his study and discipleship in an act of personal gratitude to his Lord; second, at a time when the general intellectual climate seems set against religious belief the findings of Christian biblical and theological scholars have tended to reach the ordinary Christian in very sceptical, not to say negative, terms, and it has become a matter of urgency to try to bridge the gap between scholarly research and popular belief; third, it appears to the author that a study of Jesus has yet to be written which at one and the same time satisfyingly shows him both as deeply involved in the social, religious, political and even revolutionary movements of his time, and as the founder of a religion that is relevant to each and every political order of mankind, of whatever time or place.

No one book can hope to meet all these demands. The most that the present author can hope for is that his book will help to identify and elucidate the basic points at issue, and offer some useful beginning to a unified and comprehensive understanding of the total ministry of Jesus of Nazareth, historical founder of the Christian religion.

1

The Unavoidable Story

The fundamental basis of Christianity is not its doctrine, its philosophy, its worship or its morality, whether social or personal, but the story it tells about Jesus in his lifetime; from that story its doctrine, philosophy, worship and morality all derive their distinctive character. If it ever became impossible to tell that story with integrity, Christianity would cease to be. Yet it is precisely that impossibility that, in the view of many inside as well as outside the Church, faces it at the present time. The question is being put urgently, and must be answered honestly, "Can the story of Jesus in his lifetime be told with integrity to the typical 'twentieth century man'?" This book is one attempt to pose that question rightly, and to answer it truthfully.

☩   ☩   ☩

Difficulties:
Intellectual Perspectives

There are intellectual challenges to those who tell or listen to the story of Jesus in his lifetime. The story raises difficulties of its own, such as what, if anything, can be meant by calling Jesus the 'Son' of God. Moreover, the general intellectual climate of the West in the twentieth century differs enormously from that of the Near East in the first. Then men had a simple cosmology – a solid firmament above them, hell and the deep beneath, and their own 'terra firma' in between; but now they know themselves to be in a vast Einsteinian universe whose unit of measurement is not a mile, or even thousands of miles, but a 'light year', the distance travelled by light in one year, speeding at the rate of some 186,000 miles per second. Then demons and other sub- and super-human agencies were thought to be real elements in human experience, much as complexes and neuroses are today. The story of Jesus must sound strange to modern ears. How can a moderate man believe that Jesus possessed powers enabling him to turn gallons of water into wine, to feed upwards of five thousand people with five small loaves and two dried fishes, and to raise dead people to life – not to mention his birth of an alleged virgin mother or his own bodily resurrection? There are, it seems, far too many incredibles for honest credence.

✠   ✠   ✠

Difficulties:
Literary Perspectives

Biographical lack

Modern scholars have pointed out one incontrovertible and insuperable difficulty: the information about Jesus, contained almost exclusively in the four gospels, is quite inadequate for anything like a biography in the proper modern sense. The gospel narratives, covering no more than some four years of his life, leave many 'hidden' years, while those reported on are far from exhaustively treated. The material available is clearly inadequate as a basis of a biography; some would even hold it insufficient for any valid study or portrait of Jesus in his lifetime.

The original text

No book of the ancient world has been scrutinized more closely than the New Testament, and the gospels in particular. That rigorous examination has been, and continues to be, the work of Christian scholars. The gospels were written in Greek (though some scholars have pleaded in vain for an Aramaic original behind some sections), and it is gratifying for the modern reader of the Greek text to know that the rigorous textual labours of past scholars have provided him with a text that is definitely authentic. It is also gratifying to learn that no discovery so far of any part of the gospels in scrolls or papyri which ante-date the earliest complete manuscripts has caused scholars to lose any confidence in the general integrity of the now internationally accepted text of the New Testament. In this area at least modern man seems to have come as near as possible to Jesus in his lifetime.

Gospel sources

Some thirty years or so passed between the death of Jesus and the writing of the first gospel. Before the gospel was written the material it incorporated had been handed down by oral tradition. But however reliable that may properly be considered to be, it is not surprising that scholars have tried in one way or another to bridge that thirty-year gap. This first attempt to get behind the gospels themselves came to be known as 'source criticism'.

It is noticeable, even in reading an English translation of the gospels, that Matthew, Mark and Luke share a good deal of material that is almost identical verbally, a feature even more evident in the Greek text itself. The generally accepted explanation of this is that Mark's gospel was written first (though Roman Catholic scholars have mostly given priority to Matthew) and that Matthew and Luke used his gospel as a basic contribution to their own. In addition Matthew and Luke are thought to have used another source common to their two gospels, which came to be known as 'Q' (for 'Quelle', German for 'source') and contained the material of Jesus's teaching and that of John the Baptist. Finally there was a source special to Matthew, and one special to Luke, known as 'M' and 'L' respectively, each containing nativity stories and some special contributions to the Passion story. Two features of the first three gospels were thus disclosed: that they inevitably share very much the same outlook – for that reason they were called the 'synoptic' gospels; and that, particularly in the case of 'Q', it seemed very possible that the gospel reader had been brought nearer to Jesus in his lifetime (by some five or ten years) than had previously been critically possible to suppose.

The fourth gospel did not yield to any of these analyses. It was thought to be a less 'historical' and more 'spiritual' gospel. More recently it has been shown that it relies on a tradition about Jesus not very different from that which informed the synoptists, and on other sources for the great discourses in the gospel, for the 'signs' which are recorded, and for the impressive prologue with which it opens.

The 'forms' of the gospel narrative

While some scholars were thus tracing the synoptic gospels to their written sources, others were led to examine the development of the oral tradition itself. It became apparent that the gospel story was but one example of the way in which folk history, moral traditions, teachings, popular myths and fairy stories, in many languages and cultures all over the world, have been handed down orally and then fixed in a written document. The development of the gospels could thus be compared with that of other writings. It became clear that no gospel was a continuously written narrative, but rather a series of discrete items strung together in an order suiting the evangelist's concern at the time he wrote. Two results can be noted: it was now clearer than ever before that no gospel was intended to be a biography; and, for the first time, it became possible to discover why some particular story, incident or teaching had been incorporated in a gospel.

The paradoxical result was that this procedure, which took critics to a time before the written gospels had taken shape, left the gospel reader further away from Jesus in his lifetime than before. As the critics pointed out, the gospels were produced by and for a Church that was fighting for its life, and the situation which their contents primarily disclosed was not that in which Jesus himself worked, but that in which the early Church found itself as it contended with its opponents – Jews, followers of John the Baptist, and the whole weight of the Roman Empire. In that situation the Church tried to pass on to the contemporary believer the basic guidance for life that had first come from Jesus himself. While this may be too negative a conclusion from the evidence, it explains why so eminent a form critic ('form criticism' came to be the name of this particular scholarly discipline) as Professor R.H. Lightfoot could close his Bampton Lectures with the reflection that 'for all the inestimable value of the gospels, they yield us little more than a whisper of his voice; we trace in them but the outskirts of his ways'.

Editorial motives

Form critics dealt with the gospels by considering one by one the various component items out of which they were composed – pronouncement stories, miracle stories, parables, conflict stories and the like. Such an atomistic treatment may well have contributed to Professor Lightfoot's sense that the gospel wood could not be seen for the individual trees. It is therefore interesting to note a more recent rise in the study of the work of the 'redactors' or 'editors' who brought the gospels into their present form. This has certainly achieved a more synthetic and theological view of the gospels as a whole; but it is still difficult to detect any lessening of the gap disclosed by form criticism between the situation of the primitive Church and that of Jesus in his lifetime. Redactional criticism has failed to bridge that gap.

Non-Christian contributions

But it is not only New Testament criticism that makes Jesus seem inaccessible. Many other disciplines reinforce the ordinary Christian's apprehension that the gospels cannot be taken as a faithful portrait of Jesus in his lifetime. If the work of scholars in the history of religion is considered, it seems impossible any longer to envisage Jesus as the sole founder of the Christian Church, the one authoritative teacher of its people, the one source of its cultic and sacramental life, the one moral authority to be obeyed. Rather have many religious movements of the first century shared in producing the distinctive character of Christianity. Among these are Gnosticism, Jewish Rabbinism, the Mystery Religions and Stoicism. The discovery of the Dead Sea Scrolls, bringing new insights into the noncomformist sectarians of Judaism in Jesus's time, underlines anew the need to recognize many influences beside that of Jesus that shared formatively in the genesis of the Christian Church. The Jesus presented in the gospels as the sole founder of Christianity must be recognized, it is claimed, as having many features derived from other persons and movements. Along this road, as others, there appears to be no real access to Jesus in his lifetime.

The claims of Jesus

The final misgivings of the ordinary believer may well lie in what seems the demonstrated inaccessibility of the Jesus to whom he has been taught to pay all the honours of divinity. For Christian scholars, with commendable honesty, having studied the status, titles and dignity of Jesus, have concluded that in his lifetime Jesus never made for himself the exalted claims that were soon made for him after his death and resurrection. Thus he never stated that he was the Messiah, even though others so greeted him, and even though in the stress of his trial he may have admitted to Messiahship. Nor did he speak of himself as the 'Son of God', at any rate in the synoptic gospels (the fourth gospel is manifestly of a very different character from them); and even the title which he is reported to have used of himself, 'Son of Man', bears none of the characteristics of deity that the Church has ascribed to him in its doctrine. Again, in the synoptic gospels Jesus accepts the address 'Lord', but clearly not in the exalted theological sense found in Paul, who can write that 'to this end Christ died and lived again, that he might be Lord both of the dead and of the living' (Rom.14.9). So it appears that the Christ of the Church's faith is a being of an entirely different nature from Jesus in his lifetime. The former is still accessible to Christians in the life, discipline, cult, sacraments and morality of the Church; the latter is, and must remain, inaccessible.

A new beginning

Such conclusions can satisfy neither the simple believer nor the believing critic. Unless there be some identity between Jesus in his lifetime and the 'Christ of faith' Christianity remains rootless. That is basically why there has begun a 'New Quest' for the historical Jesus, notably initiated by disciples of the very scholars who had shown how impossible the old quest for 'Jesus in his lifetime' was. They have pointed out that what Jesus thought about himself, and made known, is not necessarily limited to the words that he spoke, but may also be clearly implied by things he did, such as forgiving sins (Mark 2.5), or offering table fellowship to religious and social outcasts (Mark 2.16). It is hoped that this book will be a further, if modest, contribution to the New Quest, for unless such a quest is found viable Christianity itself will become as inaccessible as Jesus in his lifetime is deemed by some to be.

Reconstruction:
The Beginnings

The form critics were right: the evangelists were not primarily concerned to pass on information about Jesus in his lifetime out of sheer historical interest, but rather to awaken, strengthen and spread the belief that the Jesus whom the Church worshipped was the universal Messiah (=Christ), the Son of God and saviour of the world. Admittedly the records of Jesus's teaching which they recorded relate to the tensions and rivalries between the primitive Church and both the official Judaism out of which it grew, and the reformist movement within that Judaism associated with the name of John the Baptist, which continued after Jesus's death (Acts 18.25-19.7). But those controversies were also a feature of Jesus's own ministry. He would never have been crucified had there been no controversy with the Jews; the relationships between the Baptist and Jesus's own disciples were competitive and controversial, as is clear from passages concerning fasting (Mark 2.18), the Messiahship of Jesus (Mat. 11.2ff.), the rivalry in prayer (Luke 11.1), and the attempt to secure Jewish recognition (John 4.1; 5.33-36; 10.40ff.). Such passages do not establish the words and events recorded in the gospels as precisely accurate accounts of Jesus in his lifetime; but their use in a continuing controversy with the Jews and the followers of John indicates that some not wholly dissimilar events and words characterized both the life of Jesus and the situation of the early Church. Form criticism may well be right to point out that in such passages there is always some disclosure of the situation of the primitive Church; but it is equally proper to suppose that there is also some disclosure of the situation of Jesus in his own lifetime.

Form critical scepticism has not gone unchallenged. Professor Dodd has shown that the parables can be seen to derive from Jesus's own historical situation (*The Parables of the Kingdom*, esp. ch. 4). Form critics need not be sceptics – and the evangelists may be held to furnish some reliable information about Jesus in his lifetime. Moreover, the quantity of it is more considerable than critical caution would at first admit.

Perspectives, distortion and reality

Man's spatial knowlege of the world about him is always distorted by perspective, though he has learned to compensate for it, and can know and deal with objects in space as they really are. Knowledge of historical persons and events is also subject to perspective and distortion, including, of course, knowledge about Jesus of Nazareth. Can such distortion be recognized for what it is, compensation be duly made, and Jesus be known 'as he really was' and/or 'is'?

Spatial distortion is at its worst when the observer is alongside the object viewed. Paradoxically the position that enables him to make accurate measurements of the object gives him the most distorted view of it. For example, a man standing at the foot of Nelson's column in Trafalgar Square in London could accurately measure the size of its base, but from that position would have a most distorted view of it were he to look up to the top. The further he went from the column, the less distorted it would appear, and the better it would be seen in its due proportions and in its relation to other objects round about. Temporal perspectives are much the same. To be an eye witness of a temporal event enables the observer to make accurate statements about what has taken place, but he cannot, at the moment of witnessing, see the event in its true proportions or in relation to other previous and subsequent temporal events. They will become the more apparent the further he is removed from the event. To use terms which I have used elsewhere (see my Penguin Commentary on St John's Gospel, pp. 11ff.), an eye witness is useful for determining what has taken place (the event as seen), but he is not on that account necessarily a reliable source of information as to what was going on in what has taken place (the event evaluated).

Temporal perspective can certainly change the 'look' of events. Public happenings and private experiences alike appear very different after a lapse of time. 'No news is as good as it sounds when you first hear it, and none so bad as when you first hear it' was a comforting and sobering reflection heard during the First World War. But things other than the lapse of time can affect how an event appears. Prejudice, whether sympathetic or hostile, can radically alter for an observer his judgment of what is going on, even if he experiences no alteration in his observation of what he sees taking place. Two modern newspapers can report precisely the same events as taking place, and yet differ so radically in their judgment as to what is going on that it is sometimes hard to realize that they are actually reporting the same incident. An example relevant to the gospel story can be used to reinforce the point. Jews and Christians would agree that what took place on . Good Friday was the crucifixion of Jesus of Nazareth; but the former would characteristically see this as the due punishment of an offender against the Jewish people and the Jewish law, while the latter would describe it as the vicarious, redemptive self-offering of an entirely innocent man. To the Jew the man from Nazareth would have seemed but a false Messiah, while to the Christian disciple, at any rate after three days, he would have been the divinely vindicated inaugurator of the imperishable kingdom of God.

But the most potent and far-reaching factor that can affect a man's perspective is the belief, peculiar to Christians, that God can and does act in what takes place. This does not relieve the believer from the burden of living in the world, with its immense diversity of competing and conflicting human purposes, but rather enables him to live in it more creatively and responsibly. It encourages him to seek, and enables him to find, in the life, death and resurrection of Jesus Christ, the overriding, unifying, redemptive and re-creative activity of God which, in the end, is what is going on in all that takes place. But the belief that God acts in history is repugnant to many historians, who maintain that history is the sphere of human action alone. Human actions can be observed, and testimony given to them; human agents can be questioned and tested: but an invisible God cannot in the nature of things be observed in action, and testimony to his deeds is therefore unobtainable. Neither can God be questioned or tested. An historian with integrity, it is therefore argued, must reject the suggestion that God acts in human history.

Such considerations are forceful and impressive, but they are cogent only in relation to the sphere of 'what takes place'; it is there alone that observation and testimony are available and relevant. If it is affirmed that though the action of God cannot be seen in the area of 'what takes place', it can nevertheless be discerned in the sphere of 'what goes on', new possibilities arise. It is no longer necessary, in order to affirm a divine action in history, that some human witness should 'see' God at work. It is not in a 'view' of what takes place, but in a 'review', that divine action becomes discernible. If on this basis some series of divine actions is affirmed, it would be natural to suppose that it would exhibit features consistent with and significant of the nature and purpose of God.

The four gospels were undoubtedly intended to record certain acts of God. It is interesting to note that they cannot be understood without some recognition of the distinction between 'what takes place' and 'what goes on', nor without constantly remembering that no assertion that God has acted can properly be made on a 'view' but only on a 'review' of what has taken place. The available evidence shows that immediately after the crucifixion the disciples reacted to their 'view' of what had taken place with bewilderment, fear and foreboding (Mark 16.11, 13, 14; Luke 24.11, 18-26; John 20.19). That reaction quickly and radically changed. The form critics are entirely right in what they say about this: not a word of the gospels would have been written from any temporal perspective had not the disciples come to believe that the Jesus who had been crucified on a certain Friday was raised from the dead on the following Sunday, to become once more the living centre and leader of the fellowship he had initiated 'in his lifetime'.

The evangelists wrote a remembered and compiled story, and each incident recorded is liable to some distortion, not mainly because of the interval between event and record (this was not so serious a difficulty in a time of fixed oral traditions) but much more because of the disciples' belief in the resurrection. The fundamental question, however, is not how great the distortion is, but whether the distortion enables the viewer to acquire a truer knowledge both of the object itself, and of its relationship to other objects. Does the Easter perspective enable men to know more truly Jesus in his lifetime?

Two illustrations, one historical, the other musical, may offer some help. Written history is sometimes defined and even justified as being the means of letting men know precisely 'what took place' on a certain past occasion (*'wie es eigentlich geschehen war'*). This is not so much false as inadequate, for it describes but part, and the lesser one, of the historian's full task, the annalistic; while the second and much more important part is interpretative. An annalist records 'what takes place' each year, without any explicit evaluation of the events concerned. Such accounts are manifestly far from true history, which requires not only a reliable account of 'what took place', but in addition as clear an indication as possible of 'what was going on'. Consider one illustration from British history. One annalist could have described the scene at the signing of the Magna Carta by King John on the island of Runnymede on 15 June 1215 so well that a court painter could later portray the event on canvas so vividly that anyone who had been present on the day would at once exclaim, 'That's just how it was.' Yet neither annalist nor painter would really convey to others what was actually going on at Runnymede that day. Only when the long story of the fight for individual freedom before and after Magna Carta is told can Runnymede disclose its meaning, and the annalistic description be transformed into history.

The musical illustration may also help. When one listens to a new piece of music for the first time one does not really hear it. All the notes of the composition may be properly played, the various themes and counter-themes accurately rendered, but it is not until a second performance that the listener can knowingly hear what the composer is really doing as he announces his first theme, and hear that, and all the other musical devices, in relation to the composition as an aesthetic whole. The second hearing revealingly establishes for the hearer what the first really states, and demonstrates that the character of each part is both dependent on and contributory to the whole. The parts together make up the whole, and the whole gives to each part a character arising in that situation and no other, since it is acquired from that place in the sounded whole. Played on its own, the single note or chord will always sound the same, but in different musical contexts it will receive and reveal new and distinctive qualities. It may well be that the story of Jesus in his lifetime cannot be told until it is retold.

New Testament scholars have warned the gospels reader that the story of Jesus in his lifetime has been profoundly affected by its post-resurrection perspective, with consequent distortion. But such a 'review' of the story of Jesus may well disclose more of the actual truth about his pre-resurrection life than could have been discerned by any observer at the time. Indeed there are signs in the gospels that the evangelists were themselves aware of this. John certainly was. At the end of his account of the cleansing of the Temple, he reports a saying of Jesus and a scripture that he quoted; he then adds that 'after his resurrection his disciples recalled what he had said, and they believed the scripture and the words that Jesus had spoken' (John 2.22; cp. also 7.39; 13. 7, 19). This is but one example of a common human experience, when some moving event recalls forgotten things to mind, and gives significance to happenings that have hitherto seemed unimportant. That same awareness is found in the synoptic gospels. Each records the story of the Transfiguration; Matthew and Mark close it with Jesus's injunction that the disciples should not 'tell anyone what they had seen until the Son of Man had risen from the dead' (Mark 9.9; Mat. 17. 9), while Luke makes the same point by saying that 'the disciples kept silence at that time and told nobody anything of what they had seen' (Luke 9. 36). Whatever else this may mean, it signifies at least that the event known as the Transfiguration was more recognized for what it was after the resurrection than it was before.

Modern scholars have rightly asked how much reliable information about Jesus in his lifetime can be expected from gospels written mainly for non-historical purposes. The evangelists again seem almost to have anticipated the question. John wrote at the end of his narrative, 'Jesus did many other signs in the presence of his disciples [i.e. in his lifetime], which are not written in this book; but these are written that you may believe that Jesus [the Jesus of history, Jesus in his lifetime] is the Christ [=Messiah], the Son of God, and that believing you may have life in his name' (John 20. 30f). The synoptists make the same point in their own way. Mark heads his gospel: 'The beginning of the gospel of Jesus Christ, the Son of God' (Mark 1. 1), thus informing the reader that such an exalted person is the subject of his narrative. Matthew and Luke each tell a nativity story that leaves their readers in no doubt that the Jesus who was born in Bethlehem of Mary was by nature and origin a very extraordinary being. This is also the burden of Peter's preaching on the day of Pentecost, recorded in Acts: 'Let all the house of Israel therefore know assuredly that God has made him [Jesus in his lifetime] both Lord and Christ, this Jesus [the Authorized Version has 'this same Jesus'] whom you crucified.' The identification may create difficulties, but it was certainly made by the evangelists and preachers of the primitive Church, and accepted by the company of the faithful.

But this does not bridge the embarrassing gap disclosed by the critics who point out the difference between what the evangelists say that Jesus taught about himself, and what they intended to teach others about him. It is not difficult to sympathize with modern man's reluctance to accept the identification offered by the evangelists. Yet it would not be far-fetched to suggest that John's narratives of Jesus's appearances to the disciples after the resurrection are given in their particular form at least in part to show that the person who so visited them was in fact none other than the Jesus of Cana and Capernaum, of Galilee, Samaria and Judea, of Bethany and Jerusalem, the man who was crucified at Golgotha and buried in Joseph's tomb. Such an identification receives verification from those who witnessed both his miracles and his appearances after his resurrection. The experience of Thomas is particularly instructive. He was absent on the first Easter Sunday when Jesus appeared to the disciples as a group. He was unable to accept their evidence, and said that he would not believe their story unless he could see for himself, and touch the nail wounds with his fingers and put his hand in the wound in his side. But when Jesus appeared again the following Sunday and offered Thomas the confirmation he had demanded, Thomas simply and believingly adored his 'Lord' and his 'God' (John 20.28). Jesus responded with a question and a comment. The question must have made Thomas ask himself about the real basis of his adoration for his Lord, for Jesus asked, 'Have you believed because you have seen me?'; and his comment must have prevented Thomas making any quick or easy answer, for Jesus said, 'Blessed are those who have not seen and yet believe' – and they include those who accept the apostolic testimony as authoritative and authentic.

✠   ✠   ✠

Reconstruction: History

There are manifest difficulties both for ordinary readers and for professional historians in the story that the evangelists tell about Jesus in his lifetime. It is important to distinguish clearly between what they say took place, and what they say was going on in what took place. This is not the same as to distinguish between facts and interpretation of facts, for 'what goes on' goes on in the very realm of 'what takes place', and is either equally fact or sheer falsity. The evidence for the one differs from that required for the other, but both belong to actual history. One requires eye-witness and contemporary record; while the other, apart from some special insight, requires time for 're-view' and judgment. This is of considerable importance in the evaluation of the gospel narratives.

History and the Old Testament

The evangelists did not write history in a literary vacuum, but in a well-established tradition, that of the Old Testament. In spite of many stories of supernatural phenomena, epiphanies of the divine, records of miracles and a very distinct political-religious bias, the Old Testament makes a considerable contribution both to the knowledge of what took place, and to the discernment of what went on, in the period of history which it spans. From the beginning the Old Testament authors wrote in the belief that God was at work in Jewish history, while later they recognized that he was at work in the history of all the peoples of the earth. Nor was his activity confined to the world of men, for his sovereignty extended to the whole of creation, animate and inanimate, terrestrial, subterrestrial and celestial alike. In this the Old Testament writers differed greatly from many modern authors, who believe that history is simply and solely the sphere of human action. The Old Testament history includes not only what takes place in the world of men, but also what takes place in the order of nature, for all this takes place as God acts to achieve his universal purpose.

For the Old Testament, in the words of Hebrews (Heb. 1. 1), it was 'in many and various ways' that 'God spoke to our fathers'. A dream could be a communication from him (Gen. 20.3; 31.11, 24; 1 Kings 3.5). Visual images (Judges 2.1; Num. 22.24; 1 Chron. 21.18; Isa. 1.1; 6.1), auditory images (Jer. 1.4; Ezek. 6.1; Hos. 1.1) and ecstatic inspiration (1 Sam. 10.10) could disclose his purpose. A 'chance' junction of events could mark his intervention in history, like the east wind that turned the sea into dry land at the Exodus from Egypt (Exod. 14.21). Even a 'pagan' myth could be used to affirm that Israel's God, who acted in history, was the same God who had created the world (Gen. 1.1-2. 3). God 'spoke' through prophets from Moses to Malachi, acted through leaders from Noah to Nehemiah, through kings from Saul to Zedekiah, through priests from Eli to Ezra. Finally, to the Old Testament historians God's activity in history was discernible in a pattern of events that reflected the 'classic' intervention at the Exodus, a theme which inspires 2 Isaiah (e.g. Isa. 43.16-21).

But if God was so perpetually active in history, why had he not already achieved his universal purpose? Two points are made very clearly: first, no recipient of a divine word could be a wholly adequate channel of communication between God and his people. Isaiah put this very powerfully: 'I am a man of unclean lips, and I dwell in the midst of a people of unclean lips' (Isa. 6.5). Moreover, there were false prophets as well as true, bad kings as well as good, evil priests as well as faithful – and even true prophets could agonize about their calling (Isa. 6.5; Jer. 20.7). Second, Israel never ceased to be in some measure a rebellious people (Deut. 9.7; Isa. 1.23; 30.9; 65.2; Jer. 5.23; Ezek. 2.3). So while God remained in overall control of history, the fulfilment of his universal purpose was repeatedly frustrated by the rebelliousness of the very people he had called to further his purposes both for themselves and for the whole of mankind.

The God who acts

The Old Testament belief that God acts in history began with the parochial view that he had done so in their history and on their behalf (cf. Exod. 15.21; Judges 5.3, 11). Such simple, parochial, triumphalist views had, in the light of history, to be either abandoned or modified to include experiences other than military victory and economic prosperity. It was the genius of Hebrew religious insight that it successfully took the latter course, and came to articulate how and why God could apparently forget or abandon his people. God was seen to be dealing with his people on a basis of moral retribution. Moral disobedience or religious infidelity (the two are never disconnected in the teaching of the prophets) were equally subject to divine retribution – an understanding of history embodied both in Deuteronomy and in the framework of the book of Judges. But even that principle proved inadequate to sustain continuing belief in God's sovereign historical activity. A new element was added: the conviction that the God who acted in and through and for his 'chosen' people, in fact acted on the same principle of moral retribution in his dealings with other peoples (cf. Amos 1.3, 6, 9, 11, 13; 2.1). In consequence God became a worldwide sovereign: 'Your maker is your husband; and the Holy One of Israel is your redeemer, the God of the whole earth he is called' (Isa. 54.5). God could combine both weal and woe for his people, even bringing them out of 'political death' of defeat and exile into a new national life (cf. Isa. 53, esp. vv. 10-12; Ezek. 37) in a universal community of nations. So it appeared that in God's historical activity his use of moral retribution was not carried to the point of a final frustration of his purpose. There was another way to achieve this purpose, in spite of man's disobedience, a way that was articulated in Isaiah 53, and realized historically in the story of Jesus. Finally, if God was to be unreservedly trustworthy he must be sovereign not only over Israel and the other nations of the earth, but also over the non-human world, else perchance some element of nature might be able to frustrate the ends he sought through his activity in history.

The Creator God

Belief in God as creator seems to derive from Israel's contacts with Babylon. There the captive Israelites encountered a religion which recognized two deities contending for control of the natural and historical orders. The heavenly bodies, as sources of light, were deemed to exercise some control over human destiny. Astrology was then theology. Such thinking was embodied for the Babylonians in a creation myth that explained weal and woe as reflections of the struggle between the god of light and the god of darkness. The priestly writers of Genesis 1 used that myth to state their quite different faith, nailing their monotheism to a literary mast. There were not two gods, or more, but only one creator God, himself the source of light. There were no 'minor deities' in planets and stars, but only the one sovereign disposer of the destinies of men. The 'seven days' of creation belong to Babylonian myth; the one God belongs to the monotheism of Israel. Hebrew theology of creation had moved a long way forward from its earlier formulation in Genesis 2, as had its theology of history from its earlier understanding of God, which saw him as little more than a totem deity of the Hebrew confederacy of tribes.

God was in Christ

The New Testament writers generally, and the evangelists in particular, worked with the same general understanding of history and used the same historiographical tools which the Old Testament had forged. They sought to show that in Jesus God had acted anew, and finally, to recreate his world. The evangelists display a notable progression in their definition of the scope of what God did through Jesus in his lifetime. Mark's narrative begins with the activity of John the Baptist, which heralded that of Jesus, and which Mark saw as embodying in an actual historical setting a situation intuitively seen by Old Testament prophets. It is as if he had said, 'The story I have to tell does not begin with Jesus himself, or even with John the Baptist, but is really the final chapter of a story that was definitively outlined by the prophets! Matthew, who picks up Mark's narrative at this point for his own reproduction, prefaces it with a genealogy of Jesus that traces his descent back to Abraham, which is his way of saying, 'Here begins the history of the new Israel, of which Abraham is still the temporal beginning, but of which Jesus is the creative origin and head.' Luke also uses Mark's gospel at this same point, but his genealogy traces Jesus's ancestry back as far as Adam, which is his way of saying, 'Here begins a new humanity, of which Adam is still physically "father", but of which Jesus is the creative origin and head.' Finally John, not so reliant on the text of Mark as Matthew and Luke, follows the priestly writers of Genesis 1 and sets the story of Jesus in its place in God's creative purpose: 'In the beginning was the Word . . . and the Word became flesh', which is his way of saying, 'Here begins the story of the new creation, of which the first creation remains the temporal beginning, but of which Jesus is the creative origin and head.'

What took place

The gospels contain many statements of what took place, e.g. 'Jesus went journeying from town to town and village to village' (Luke 8.1). But even such statements may also act as clues as to what was going on. When Matthew reports that Jesus 'went up on the mountain' (Mat. 5.1) he is not only recording something that took place, but also indicating what was going on. For he is linking Jesus with Moses, who 'went up on a mountain' to receive from God the law that he passed on to the Old Israel: 'It was said to the men of old . . . but I say to you' (Mat. 5.21, etc.). But he also indicates how the new situation surpasses the old, for the law is now given on Jesus's authority, and to an Israel that is not left on the plain, but which goes 'up on the mountain' with him. Jesus and his disciples are already a new corporate body.

What went on

Many an Old Testament text, prophetic oracle, historical event or person is used to illuminate some event in the life of Jesus. Matthew thus reports Jesus's explanation of his teaching in parables: 'This is why I speak to them in parables; for they look without seeing, and listen without hearing or understanding. There is a prophecy of Isaiah which is being fulfilled for them: 'You may hear and hear, but you will never understand; you may look and look, but you will never see. For this people's mind has become gross; their ears are dulled and their eyes closed. Otherwise their eyes might see, their ears hear and their mind understand, and then they might turn again and I would heal them. But happy are your [the disciples'] eyes, because they see, and your ears because they hear' (Mat. 13.14-16). Such a prophecy could be repeated in any situation in which parabolic reaching failed to enlighten its hearers. But the word 'fulfilled' means much more than just 'repeated': it means 'repeated, and embodied once and for all in an historical situation'. Isaiah's situation can be repeated indefinitely, whenever God's word is spoken by a man, from Isaiah himself to the sermon by the preacher of the gospel today. But all such occasions are but reflections of that time when God himself moved among men and spoke his word himself ('but I say to you'). 'Fulfilment' is one means by which the unique character of the situation of Jesus is indicated by the evangelists.

Taking place and going on

One incident reported in all four gospels can be profitably studied, the so-called 'Triumphal Entry' into Jerusalem, the original 'Palm Sunday', described in Mark 11.1-10, and parallels. The story tells how Jesus entered Jerusalem riding on an ass, accompanied by a crowd of excited and enthusiastic Passover pilgrims. Matthew alone states that 'this took place to fulfil what was spoken by the prophet, saying, "Tell the daughter of Zion, behold your king is coming to you, humble and mounted on an ass, and on a colt, the foal of an ass."' Even had Matthew not made that comment, it would have been made by some New Testament scholar. But Matthew has exposed one of the means by which the evangelists tried to indicate what was going on in what took place.

Clearly Jesus meant to ride into Jerusalem in conformity with the oracle from Zechariah 9. But that was no stilted attempt to 'act out' some scriptural prescription, but rather a means of telling the disciples, the Galilean pilgrims to the Passover, the Jerusalem crowd and the authorities that his first message of the coming of the kingdom of God was still the centre of his message and of his own personal office and destiny.

The oracle from Zechariah continues: 'I will cut off the chariot from Ephraim and the war horse from Jerusalem; and the battle bow shall be cut off, and he shall command peace to the nations; his dominion shall be from sea to sea, and from the River to the ends of the earth.' Jesus was serving notice to all that he was not the military Messiah of popular expectation; he would not head a rebellion against Rome, as Zealots and others hoped and even planned. His way to a universal kingdom was to be entirely peaceful. (Horses were the 'military transports' of the day; donkeys were for civilian usage.) He may not have been in the modern sense a 'pacifist'; but he was against any use of military power to eject Rome.

The story gives other indications of what was going on. The disciples and the crowds spread garments on the road before Jesus, gathered branches from the trees, and greeted him with shouts of 'Hosanna to the Son of David'. In these three ways they were telling Jesus that he would have to resort to force if he were to be accepted as the Messiah. The spreading of garments repeated (and fulfilled) the actions of Jehu's supporters when he began his ruthless and bloody extermination of the whole house of Ahab (2 Kings 9.13). The gathering of branches (palm branches, says John) repeated (and fulfilled) the action of the crowds in welcoming Simon Maccabeus as he rode into Jerusalem, a military victor, in 152 B.C. 'Son of David' was a title often given to the expected Messiah, but a Messiah who would be a military leader and restore Israel's political fortunes. So, with great economy of words, the evangelists indicate both what was taking place and what was going on.

Typology

This sample of gospel historiography is doubly interesting: first, it shows that what some scholars have done in interpreting the gospels, i.e. noting fulfilments of the Old Testament in the life of Jesus, was done by the evangelists themselves; second, it provides two other allusive references to the Old Testament, of the sort that have become known as 'typological'.

Typology has largely been written off by honest modern scholars for being an antiquated, unscientific and unhistorical device. It does not treat historical narrative as history but as a kind of 'spot the hidden text' game, in which the important thing is neither what took place nor what went on, but to what extent, for example, an Old Testament background can be detected. Yet properly used and understood typology remains a valuable and modern tool for understanding history.

Suppose a third world war erupts, and Russian troops quickly overrun Western Europe, reaching the Channel ports of Belgium and France. Suppose the British then mount a rescue operation for their stranded troops, and with a flotilla of small boats bring back thousands of men to their home shores. The newspapers would certainly use banner headlines to announce 'Another Dunkirk', and the public would thereby learn both what was taking place, and what the journalists believed was 'going on'. So in biblical typology. When Matthew referred to Zechariah's prophecy in his Palm Sunday story, he was inserting a 'banner headline' to let his readers know at once what was taking place and what was going on. For what Zechariah had said about the advent of Jerusalem's king to his city was now taking place as Jesus entered the capital on a donkey. But the point of the headline was not to inform the gospel reader that Jesus rode on a donkey, but to enable him to see what kind of kingship was being announced and inaugurated. And it is important to note that it was Jesus himself who provided the material for the banner headlines!

So typology, properly understood, is a useful tool of historical perception. It does not claim or require that history repeats itself, but in its biblical use it acknowledges that where God acts there will be recognizable disclosures of his operation. Above all, it does not remove the reader from the historical occasion under review, as an allegorical interpretation does, but rather offers him a tool which can help him understand what is really going on.

Typology is not confined to scripture (cf. above on the 'Exodus' pattern of God's action, p.24). But the New Testament has one distinguishing characteristic: it discloses not just a 'repetition' but a 'fulfilment' of a previous event. The return of the Jews from Babylon may repeat typologically the Exodus from Egypt under Moses, but that could not exhaust the possibilities of repetition. Some modern Zionists see the establishment of Israel as a modern state in precisely that light. But when, as in Matthew's gospel, the Exodus is used typologically to disclose what was going on in the life of Jesus, more is claimed than that the Exodus is being repeated. The suggestion is that God has at last, once and for all, beyond all possibility of frustration, irreversibly established his universal salvation or kingship in the actual history of mankind. Fulfilment, not repetition, is the substance of New Testament typology. To see that the Exodus is fulfilled in Jesus is much more than to recognize parallels in two events of different times; it is to affirm that all that was intended in and through the first Exodus has been achieved in the new and final 'Exodus' in Jesus Christ. Naturally that claim can be disputed and denied; what cannot really be denied is the usefulness of typology in providing a recognizable basis to that claim.

A resurgence of typology is not without its dangers. It is easy to become more concerned with the identification of types than with the understanding of the history that the types were meant to disclose. Moreover, some types used by the evangelists have been greatly modified by later theology in the Church, especially in such debates as those of Nicaea and Chalcedon. The title 'Son of God' no longer conveys its original biblical meaning to the modern ear, but reflects the theological and metaphysical positions of the orthodox at two great Councils of the Church. It may well be that what the later theologians thought to be the implications of calling Jesus the 'Son of God' properly developed Christian doctrine, but these were not part of the original meaning of the Old Testament title. It is therefore important to determine what such terms meant to the evangelists who used them. Such de-theologizing and re-biblicizing are a necessary prelude to the needful restatement of Christian doctrine in the modern world.

Eschatology

In the lifetime of Jesus the Jews believed, as many still do today, that their history was an unfinished story awaiting its final chapter. The Messiah, they believed, was about to come and accomplish his mission. Then evil would be abolished and God's universal, beneficent and unending reign would begin. But the Christianity which grew out of the life and mission of Jesus believed that the last chapter was already being written, for Jesus was identified as the Messiah who, by his life, death and resurrection, had brought into the historical order the final and unending reign of God. Judaism thought, and still thinks of, history as the area of the penultimate, to be followed in due course by the ultimate. By contrast Christianity saw history as the area of the penultimate into which, paradoxically but actually, the ultimate had already come. In John's words 'the Word became flesh'. Small wonder that the two faiths generated quite different ideas of the historical, and particularly of the 'eschatological', i.e. what is, or will be, the 'end' of history, the 'end' of all things'.

The Jews looked forward to a day in history when the new order would have begun: 'The wolf shall dwell with the lamb, and the leopard shall lie down with the kid, and the calf and the lion and the fatling together, and a little child shall lead them. . . . In that day the root of Jesse (the expected Davidic Messiah) shall stand as an ensign to the peoples; him shall the nations seek, and his dwelling shall be glorious' (Isa. 11.6,10). Not only men, but the whole animate order would, under the Messiah, enter on the final 'eschatological' order.

There are various expressions in the New Testament concerning this final order. It is generally held that it will be creation-wide in its scope, and not confined to humanity (Rom. 8.20ff.; Eph. 1.10; Col. 1.20). But the really puzzling thing is the evident equivocality of belief about the time of the end. There are sayings in the gospels (Mark 1.15; Mat. 12.28; Luke 11.20) and epistles alike (Col. 1. 19f.; Eph. 1.17-22) which suggest that the arrival of the final kingdom of God was the good news that Jesus, and possibly John the Baptist (Mat. 3.2, cf. below, p.109) proclaimed. But other passages suggest that 'the end is not yet' (Mark 13.7; cf. 1 Cor. 15.20-25; 1 Thess. 4.15ff; 2 Thess. 2.2). And Christian eschatology is still undecided. Professor Dodd has propounded a 'realized' eschatology, the belief that the substance and truth of Jesus's own message was that the kingdom of God had arrived with his coming. This has not found universal acceptance (what theological position ever has?), being rejected by most continental scholars, who prefer to think in terms of an 'inaugurated' eschatology, in which the final kingdom is deemed to have begun, but needs time to be brought to its full consummation.

The difficulty in accepting a 'realized' eschatology is clearly the undeniable and effective presence of evil in the world. Had the final and perfect divine order been established, surely evil could not continue to flourish. So, however clearly Jesus may on occasion have stated that the kingdom of God had arrived (and scholars have sometimes underlined the paucity of such sayings), a compromise has had to be made in the face of continuing evil. Can it be that Jesus, having already inaugurated his kingdom, will, at a time not yet reached, bring his work to its felicitous conclusion? This will be further examined in subsequent sections.

Reconstruction: Recovering the Story

Problems: mainly chronological

How long did Jesus's ministry last?

The sources for recovering the story of Jesus are still predominantly the four gospels. This of itself poses difficulties, since they offer conflicting evidence on certain points. Four chronological points are worthy of discussion.

The first concerns the length of Jesus's ministry. The synoptists refer to one Passover only, when Jesus was crucified, which seems to limit his ministry to a little less than a year. John, however, tells of three Passovers (2.13; 6.4; 11.55), and possibly a fourth (5.1), leaving room for a ministry of two to four years.

Yet the synoptists give hints of a ministry longer than one year, and of more than one visit to Jerusalem. Jesus could hardly have arranged for the loan of a donkey (Mark 11.2) and the use of an 'upper room' for his Passover meal had he not visited the city before. More than one Passover is implied in the story of the feeding of the five thousand, where Mark reports that Jesus told the crowds to sit down 'on the green grass' (Mark 6.39). In Palestine the grass is green for only a very short period, between mid-March and mid-May, the period within which the Passover falls. John's statement that 'there was much grass in the place' (John 6.10) confirms Mark's report. As it is highly improbable that the feeding of the five thousand took place in the same year that Jesus was crucified at Passover time, it would seem likely it took place at least twelve months before Jesus died.

The synoptists tell of a dispute between Jesus and the Pharisees about the disciples' misconduct on a certain Sabbath, when they plucked corn in a field and ate it (Mark 2.23f). But corn did not ripen until some weeks after Passover time, which means that this dispute followed the Passover in whatever year it took place. It is highly unlikely that it followed the feeding of the five thousand, because this incident is reported with others that took place while John the Baptist was alive, whereas the feeding of the five thousand took place after his execution, so it must have occurred the previous year. This means that the synoptic record requires a period of very nearly two full years, without allowing for Jesus's baptism, his temptation, or the early preaching of the kingdom in Galilee.

Some further indirect evidence is worth consideration. In Palestine the whole winter is a time of rain. Hence it is highly improbable that Jesus would have begun any sustained period of preaching during those three months, and very probable that he would have done so once the dry season had begun. It is equally probable that if his disciples shared in any preaching campaign they would have been called together around the beginning of the dry season.

There are three recorded 'summonings' of the disciples. The first occurred when he invited certain individual disciples to 'follow him' and so become 'fishers of men' (Mark 1.16-20). It was not till after that that Jesus began his public ministry in Galilee. The second 'summoning' was when he called to himself 'the men he wanted', and 'appointed twelve to be with him, and to be sent out to preach, and to have authority to cast out demons' (Mark 3.14f.). The third took place while Jesus was on a tour of the villages of Galilee, when he 'called the twelve to him, and began to send them out two by two' (Mark 6.7). It would be difficult, indeed quite wrong, to read any strict chronological sequence into Mark's narrative, but the way in which he and the other evangelists tell their story leaves open the clear possibility that the ministry of Jesus lasted for more than the one year that has often been taken to be implied; instead it seems it could have extended into three dry seasons. This is a defensible approximation to the Johannine narrative, with its mention of three Passovers; and, if the view be right that the fourth gospel really demands a Passover between those recorded in 2.13 and 6.4, then both the synoptists and John give space for three summers in the ministry of Jesus.

No reconsideration of John is likely to reduce Jesus's ministry to one year. It is therefore possible, even probable, that the public ministry of Jesus lasted for three years and spanned four Passovers.

Did the activity of Jesus and John the Baptist overlap?

The evidence from John and the synoptists again conflicts. Mark states explicitly that 'after John had been arrested, Jesus came into Galilee proclaiming the Gospel of God' (Mark 1.14). Matthew agrees (Mat. 4.12), and Luke, though not explicitly, implies the same (Luke 3.19f; 4.1f., 14). But John's story is very different. He tells how John saw Jesus and hailed him as the 'Lamb of God' (John 1.29). The next day, John continues, he saw Jesus and repeated his identification, at which two of his disciples (one of whom was Andrew) followed Jesus (John 1.35ff., 40). The day after that Jesus decided to go into Galilee (John 1.43), and later on still he and his disciples 'went into the land of Judea; there he remained with them and baptized. John was also baptizing at Aenon near Salim . . . John had not yet been put in prison' (John 3.22ff.). This, John states, caused a report to reach the Pharisees that 'Jesus is winning and baptizing more disciples than John' (John 4.1).

On the face of it the stories are irreconcilable. But John's record gives a possible background to that knowledge of Judea and Jerusalem that has been seen to be implied by some features of Mark's story (see below, pp. 115-120). Moreover, such parallel activity of Jesus and John may well explain the willingness of Andrew and Peter (and possibly James and John) to respond to Jesus's call to 'follow him' reported in the synoptic story as the first encounter between Jesus and those disciples. So it may be concluded that the activity of John and Jesus did overlap for a while.

It is also interesting to reflect that Jesus and John, though not strictly cousins, were in some way related, and that the two families were known to visit (Luke 1.40). Such contacts would have enabled Jesus to know something of the Essene-Qumran style of life, whose disciplines and sacramental practices seem to have influenced both John and Jesus.

Was the Temple cleansing at the beginning or the end of Jesus's Ministry?
On this point there is also divergence between the synoptists and John. The former place the cleansing early in the last week of Jesus's life (Mark 11.1, 11f., 15-19), while John includes it in Jesus's first visit to Jerusalem near the beginning of his ministry (John 2.12-22). It would be irresponsibly easy to plead that since neither account can be shown indubitably to be in error, Jesus must have cleansed the Temple twice, for it is most unlikely that such a double disturbance would have left no trace in any of the gospels. It is equally difficult to determine if either dating is accurate, for the gospels do not string disparate incidents on to a thread of chronological order but rather so arrange their sequences that the theological significance of each occasion and of the whole ministry can best be displayed and understood. The primary aim is to indicate what was going on in all that took place.

Mark explains Jesus's action by quoting scripture: 'My house shall be called a house of prayer for all nations. But you have made it a den of robbers' (Mark 11.17; cf. Isa. 56.7; Jer. 7.11). Gentiles, on penalty of death, were not permitted beyond the Court of the Gentiles. Money-changers operated within the Temple precincts because the Jews had negotiated a concession permitting them to use Jewish coins for the purchase of whatever was needed for the Temple rites. So Jesus was protesting not so much at the 'commerce' taking place as against Israel's religious nationalism, her failure to undertake what her great prophets had demanded, a universal mission for her God. Against that failure the continuing practice of traditional ritual availed nothing. The Jerusalem authorities were understandably aggrieved.

John relates that Jesus expelled the sellers of sheep, oxen and pigeons, thus emphasizing not only the need to replace nationalism in religion with a true universalism, but also the need to renounce a sacrificial system in favour of a truly spiritual worship. Once the Jewish sacrifice of animals ceased, the commerce in the Temple would disappear. When Jesus was asked for his authority for his action, he answered, 'Destroy this temple, and in three days I will raise it up' (John 2.19). John thus indicated what was going on in this incident: Jesus was offering men, in and through his own self-sacrifice, which had to be a once-and-for-all offering, a new and spiritual 'temple' of 'place' or 'manner' in which God could be worshipped universally.

So both John and the synoptists affirm that the narrow nationalism of the Jews should be replaced by a new universalism (as indeed second Isaiah (chs. 40-55), Jonah and Ruth had pleaded in the Old Testament), free from sacrificial rituals, enabling men to worship God 'in spirit and in truth'. But why is the incident so differently placed? It is inevitably disappointing for a modern historian to learn that there are no proper historiographical grounds for resolving the difference between John and the synoptists, but the simple believer need suffer no such embarrassment. In his timing Mark showed that the issue played an important, even a decisive part (Mark 11.18) in determining the fate of Jesus; while John's earlier placing is meant to testify that the issue did not arise fortuitously at the end of the ministry, but was inherent in the attitude of Jesus from the very start. Moreover, in John's account there is an 'end interest', for the saying about destroying the Temple quoted at his trial was uttered here. Both traditions bear witness to the conviction that to write history is more than to catalogue events in a precise chronological sequence.

Was the Last Supper a Passover meal?

John makes it quite plain that the Last Supper could not have been a Passover meal, because he reports that during Jesus's trial the Jews would not enter the Praetorium to watch the proceedings before Pilate 'so that they might not be defiled but might eat the Passover' (John 18.28). That concurs with his timing of the crucifixion on the day of preparation for the Passover, when the Passover lambs were slain – a very 'theological' timing for a gospel that begins with John the Baptist's testimony, 'Look, there is the lamb of God; it is he who takes away the sin of the world' (John 1.29).

The synoptists state otherwise. Mark says that 'on the first day of unleavened bread, when the Passover lambs were being slaughtered, his disciples said to him, "Where would you like us to go and prepare for your Passover supper?"' (Mark 14.21).

The conflict of evidence is plain, and has been the subject of considerable, but by no means unanimous, discussion. There are three types of solution; one supports the synoptic chronology, another supports the Johannine, and a third shows how both traditions are assilimable with the facts. Of the solutions offered, the best, in the view of the present writer, is of the third type, one advanced by Mlle A. Jaubert (*La Date de la Cène*, Paris, 1957). She traced the difference between the two dates to the use of two calendars, one solar, used by the Jerusalem authorities, the other lunar, adopted by the Qumran sect and some others. The solar calendar put Passover day on a different day of the week each year, while the lunar calendar had the Passover always on the same day of the week, a Tuesday. If Jesus used the lunar calendar the differences from the 'official' Passover would be accounted for; this would have the advantage of giving more time (perhaps even more than enough) for the various 'hearings' before the Sanhedrin, Herod and Pilate. It would also give an intriguing example of the influence of sectarian life on Jesus and his disciples, possibly through John the Baptist. But attractive though Mlle Jaubert's suggestions are, there are difficulties which appear insurmountable, not least the question as to how Jesus could have got a Passover lamb slaughtered on a Tuesday in Jerusalem. Anything like an 'unofficial' slaughter is improbable before 70 A.D. and the fall of Jerusalem. It is equally improbable that such an alternative celebration of the Passover by Jesus and the Twelve would have been either suppressed or forgotten by the time the gospels were written.

So, after a further review of the discussion that many scholars have entered, the present writer still prefers his comments in his Penguin Commentary on St John:

> What the two different chronologies have in common is not just the eating of a meal and the crucifixion of Jesus, which for some unknown reason they place at different chronological points. What is also common is the reference to the Passover, and the consequent setting of the death of Jesus in a paschal perspective. Whether the paschal significance of the death of Jesus is brought out by means of the story of the Last Supper, or by incidents recorded by John at the crucifixion, as Jesus, like a true Passover lamb, was left with unbroken legs; what matters is that the paschal theology is made available to the Church, so the Christians might be able to understand what God did in giving his Son to die for the world. But why should John offer the Church a perspective different from that of the synoptists? The present writer's guess is that it was linked with the eucharistic experience of the Church. The Eucharist was, and still is, a rite to be performed 'in memory of' Christ. But what occasion is remembered? Is it the first eucharist after the resurrection, when in a mysterious trinity of wonder, doubt and joy, the earliest disciples were admitted to a new and indestructible communion and communication with their Lord? Is it the Last Supper where before the passion and death Jesus pre-enacted his self-offering for men? Is it the actual event of crucifixion and death itself? It would seem that both John and the synoptists share in the inheritance of the first eucharist. The one whom they remember does not come from it, for he came to it. That being so, it appears that the Synoptists have chosen to see the eucharist as the re-enactment of the Last Supper, its pre-enactment; while John sees it as the representation of the act itself. And this is quite in keeping with his whole attitude to history and eschatology. He so writes his story that God, in his coming to men, is not something still to be enacted, but something which happened once for all when Jesus was crucified and so glorified.

The conclusion to be drawn from all this is that it is

important for the modern reader to be aware of the differences between modern historiography and that of the evangelists. It is not the case that the first records of Jesus were written down as modern historiography would suppose and require, in a chronologically accurate order, and that later John made some important corrections for sound chronological reasons. Rather the very first order is as theological as the last; and while chronological questions may quite properly be raised, it must always be remembered that chronology was itself a theological tool in the hands of the evangelists. Difficult as it is for the modern reader to realize, there are more important things, even about chronology, than correct chronological order. It is more important to understand why John can say that Jesus's hour has come (John 12, 23; 13.1; 17.1) than to determine with irrefutable accuracy the date of the month on which it came!

Problems: mainly interpretative

The differences between John and the synoptists are not confined to chronology; they are interpretative as well. John's profound hymn to the divine creative Word who became flesh in Jesus Christ (John 1.1-5, 10-14) is a much more theological introduction to his gospel then Mark's brief opening, or 'title', 'Here begins the gospel of Jesus Christ the Son of God' (Mark 1.1). And that first impression is reinforced even in the first chapter. In Mark there are occasions on which unclean spirits cried out that Jesus was the Son of God (Mark 1.24; 3.11; 5.7), but it is not until Mark 8 that there is any human testimony to that effect, when Peter answered Jesus's question, 'Who do you say that I am?', with the affirmation, 'You are the Messiah' (Mark 8.29). But in the very first chapter of John it is recorded that John the Baptist saw Jesus coming towards him, and exclaimed, 'Look, there is the Lamb of God; it is he who takes away the sin of the world' (John 1.29). On the next day, when he repeated the statement, two of his disciples (one being Andrew) left his company and joined that of Jesus. The same chapter ends with Nathanael saying to Jesus, 'You are the Son of God; you are the king of Israel' (John 1.49).

If all this is taken as accurate chronology there is certainly some discrepancy, if not acute contradiction, between John and the synoptists. But it would be wrong to accept that conclusion without much more careful examination. It must not be forgotten that Mark

quite consciously started his gospel with the heading 'Here begins
the gospel of Jesus Christ [Messiah] the Son of God', which reveals
his theological 'bias', and that as early as chapter 2 he relates how
some scribes in Capernaum realized that Jesus could not forgive
sins, as he was claiming to do, unless he were of more than human
status and dignity (Mark 2.7). Later in the same chapter Jesus speaks
of himself as 'the bridegroom' (come to claim his 'bride' Israel), an
indubitable if covert reference to his crucifixion. It is worth
recalling what Hoskyns and Davey said in their commentary on the
fourth gospel: 'The true understanding of the history of Jesus . . .
cuts right across the chronological understanding of history. For
this reason . . . it has to be detached from its chronological context
and narrated non-historically, since only so can justice be done to
its theological significance' (Hoskyns and Davey, *The Fourth Gospel*,
p.126).

So for neither synoptists nor John is chronological accuracy the
most important concern of the historian. That is why John can place
the Temple cleansing at a very different point in Jesus's ministry
from the synoptists. That is also why the synoptists can differ among
themselves in their timing of events. Take, for example, the
narratives of the preaching in the synagogue at Nazareth, and of the
calling of Peter and Andrew. In Mark, Peter and Andrew were called
by Jesus immediately he came into Galilee from his encounter with
Satan in the wilderness, and began to proclaim that 'The time has
come; the kingdom of God is upon you; repent and believe the
gospel' (Mark 1.15). The immediate response of Peter and Andrew
to Jesus's call is meant to show that the recent victor over Satan
commanded at once the allegiance and obedience of those endowed
with the insight to perceive his true status and function, however
dimly. Having thus recorded the beginning of a new community of
a new Israel, Mark proceeds with the story of Jesus and relates
healings (including a fever, leprosy, paralysis, physical disability,
demon possession, haemorrhage and even death), disputes with
the authorities, the calling of other disciples, and his teaching in
parables. Only then does Mark tell about the preaching in
Nazareth, and then only in outline. But Luke puts the preaching in
Nazareth, recounted more fully and dramatically, at the very
beginning of Jesus's work in Galilee, as he came from his encounter
with Satan in the wilderness, and not till that story is told does Luke
resume his use of Mark's story of 'what Jesus did in the presence of
his disciples'. There is no way of determining whether Mark or Luke

(or neither!) offers the correct chronology; what is clear is that in re-arranging Mark's order Luke is indicating that the authority of Jesus did not lie simply in the content of the message he brought –that 'the time had come' and that the 'kingdom of God had come upon' men – but rather in the fact that the kingdom of God was centred in his own person and activity. 'The spirit of the Lord is upon me,' he claimed, and this quotation from scripture is followed by the explicit statement that 'Today in your very hearing this text has come true' (Luke 4.18,21). Luke's interpretative concern is as plain as his chronological dislocation: it is more important to indicate what was going on than simply to record what was taking place, or when.

The placing of incidents in a context is thus one pointer to their interpretation. Another and more important series of indications concerns what is said about Jesus himself. In the gospels he is given various titles; each is given and subsequently used to help under-stand and interpret his person and his work. Modern scholars have rightly recognized some difficulties in the traditional handling of the titles. The Councils of Nicaea and Chalcedon in the fourth and fifth centuries spelt out, in terms of a theological metaphysic, what it meant to call Jesus 'Son of God'. It is not surprising that the findings of those Councils have largely determined what Christian inter-preters have said about that and other titles given to Jesus in the gospels. But doctrine should not determine interpretation; rather should interpretation undergird doctrine. Each title used has its own history, and it is important to recover the meaning the titles had at the time the evangelists used them. Such a study needs to be mainly focussed on three questions: What did Jesus think and teach himself? What did his contemporaries, disciples and others think about him? What did the early Church come to think about him, and why?

The Son of God

The effect of the Councils of Nicaea and Chalcedon has been to make this term applicable to Jesus exclusively. In him alone there was, and in him alone could there be, the union of manhood and deity that entitles Jesus to be called Son of God. But in the time of Jesus the title was in more general use, both in Judaism and in other religions and cultures. In Egypt, Babylon and Assyria it had been customary to believe that kings were 'begotten' by gods, while in Rome the emperor was known as *'divi filius'* – son of God. Such ascriptions of divinity may approximate to the later notion of the divine right of kings, but they neither embody nor generate the meaning of the title as it came to be defined in the great Councils of the Church. In Hellenism a wonder-worker was called a 'divine man', though this was but the recognition of a 'charismatic' personality. The Qumran community called its members 'children of God', as well as children of light, truth, righteousness and grace. None of these, however, offers a real parallel to or origin of the use of the title in the developed language of the Church.

In Old Testament Judaism, as elsewhere, the title 'son of God' was used of individual persons, though on its own distinctive basis. Three times it is applied to a king; in 2 Samuel 7.14 God says of Solomon, 'I will be his father, and he shall be my son'; in Psalm 2.7, with clear reference to a king's enthronement, it is said, 'You are my son, this day I become your father' (cf. also Ps. 89.26f.). So for Israel a king was not 'begotten' by God. But since the language of the Psalm is that customarily used for the adoption of a child, enthronement appears to be the point at which the rule of a monarch receives proper legal status under God. This implies that the king himself must observe, and ensure that his people follow, the will and commandments of God. This was the basis of the authority of the prophet in Israel – he was the 'voice' of God to exhort king and people alike to constant obedience to his will, and to warn of the dangers of disobedience.

Another distinctive Hebrew use of the term 'son of God' is found in its application to the people as a whole. Moses was told to say to Pharaoh that 'Israel is my first-born son' (Exod. 4.22) a usage paralleled when the people cried out, 'Thou, Lord, art our father (Isa. 63.16). But such language is more than metaphorical or metaphysical; it is also thoroughly historical, indicating what the prophets discerned in Israel's history. Hosea declared, 'When Israel was a boy, I loved him; I called my son out of Egypt' (Hos. 11.1; cf. Deut. 1.31; 32.6f.). This understanding of Israel's history enters into the oracles of the prophets (e.g. Isa. 43.6; 63.8; Jer. 3.4, 19, 22; 31.9, 20), the records of Deuteronomy (Deut. 14.1; 18.5; 32.18), the narratives of the historical books (Exod. 4.22; Num. 11.12) and the poetry of the Psalms (Ps. 34.11; 82.6; 149.2). Yet it never conveyed the idea of physical paternity, a point which was made both by Malachi (Mal. 2.10f.) and, satirically, by Jeremiah (Jer. 2.26f). Rather God's fatherhood meant two things for Israel: first, that in her origin, history and destiny alike God, as father, was supreme, and Israel, as son, entirely dependent and subordinate. Second, all Israel's history, ups and downs alike, flowed from the attitude and action of God, his love, his guardian care, his chastisement, forgiveness and mercy. The history of Israel could never be told simply in terms of 'crime and punishment'; hence the call of prophet after prophet for God's people to 'return' to him, when repentance would meet with mercy, forgiveness and restoration, not only in the realm of the spirit, but in the material life and fortunes of the historical order.

There is a further use in the Old Testament of the term 'son(s) of God', in which the sons are members of the divine court, and known as 'heavenly beings' or even, in the New English Bible translation, as 'gods'. In origin such figures were probably the gods of defeated nations, whose gods were thus depicted as lesser beings than the true God whom Israel worshipped as her defender. 'Who is like the Lord in the court of heaven, like God who is dreaded among the assembled ones, great and terrible above all who stand about him? (Ps. 89.6f.). The heavenly court is the place of divine planning and decision, pictured in Job 1.6 and 2.1. But other than heavenly beings could stand in that court, for it is the burden of Jeremiah's complaint against the false prophets that they have not 'stood in the council of the Lord' (Jer. 23.18, 22), as a true prophet should. Amos reflects this conviction in his certainty that 'the Lord does nothing without revealing his secret [=council] to his servants the prophets' (Amos 3.7). It is even the privilege of pious Israelites to know that 'the secret of the Lord is with them that fear him' (Ps. 25.14). And Eliphaz can ask Job, 'Do you listen in God's secret council?' (Job 15.8), which is not wholly senseless, for Job later expresses a longing for those past days when 'the secret of God was upon my tent, when the Almighty was yet with me' (Job 29.4f). So even if this range of meanings gives pride of place to heavenly beings, it also has a place for human figures in the divine council.

It can be said in conclusion that the world contemporary with Jesus, in both Hellenistic and Palestinian Judaism, as also in Jewish apocalyptic literature, uses the title 'son of God' only in reference to Israel as a whole or to pious Israelites. Not even the figure of the Messiah is called 'son of God' save when a Messianic passage is quoted, such as 2 Samuel 7.14 or Psalm 2,7. The title was undoubtedly current; but its meaning as developed by the Church was still in the future.

Son of God in the gospels

Luke and John both record occasions when Jesus was called 'son of Joseph' (Luke 4.22; John 1.45; 6.42). His mother is known in all four gospels. No interpretation of the title 'Son of God' can be properly entertained that would in any way contradict the human parentage (however that be judged) attested by the gospels. There is, as already noted (p.16), no clear evidence that Jesus ever called himself 'Son of God'; but that does not mean that there is no evidence of his awareness of some special relationship with God, or that he made no attempt to let others know about that relationship. Indeed the contrary is the case.

One of the most astounding things in the religion that the gospels describe is that God is called by the name 'Father'. This is not to say that other peoples, the Jews included, did not do this themselves. What is distinctive about the gospels is that Jesus seems to have originated the quite surprising use of a word for God that comes straight from the close intimacies of human family life. 'Abba' means and is usually translated as 'Father', but its more accurate counterpart in English would be 'Daddy'. This is the word Jesus used in his agonizing prayer in Gethsemane (Mark 14.36), though there can be little doubt that its use did not start there. Did Jesus then have some sense of a special relationship with God? Are there indications of that in the gospels?

The first instance of Jesus's use of 'Father' for God is in the story of his visit to Jerusalem with his parents when he became a *bar mitzvah*, a son of the Law. When the Passover feast was over, the family returned to Nazareth with other Galilean pilgrims. But at the end of the first day's journey Mary and Joseph missed Jesus, and returned to Jerusalem to find him. They found him in the Temple, and in their anxiety reproached him. He responded by asking, 'Did you not know that I must be in my Father's house?' (Luke 2.49). This indicates that he had already come to sense that his responsibility to the 'Father' of Israel was his major responsibility, and that it had already acquired some special significance for his life ahead. This would not have been an improbable effect on a sensitive young man of what must have been an outstanding religious experience, rather like a confirmation followed by a eucharist to a devout adolescent today.

The next emergence of the Son-Father relationship was at Jesus's baptism. Elsewhere (below, pp.109, 112) it will be argued that when John called for repentance he was calling for a repentance of all who had kept Israel from being a just and righteous society and a true and missionary people of God in the world. That is why, when Jesus came for baptism and John hesitated, Jesus persisted. He too was a member of the unfaithful people of God, and so stood in need of sharing both the repentance and the baptism. He was baptized, and as he came up out of the water three things happened: the heavens opened, the Spirit descended like a dove, and a voice was heard which said, 'You are [or 'This is . . .] my beloved Son; on you [or 'him'] my favour rests' (Mark 1.10f.; Luke 3.22f.; Mat. 3.16f.). What would these words have meant to Jesus at the time?

First, the words should not be interpreted apart from the two other constants in the baptismal story, the opening of the heavens and the descent of the Spirit 'like a dove'. These may well be part of the post-resurrection perspective, bringing perhaps some distortion of 'what took place'. But they also perform the important function of indicating what was going on at the baptism of Jesus. The heavens opening was an indication, through its evocation of Isaiah 64.1, that at last God, the Father of Israel (Isa. 64.8), had come down in power to vindicate his people, despite their waywardness – a very proper insight into the meaning of a baptism for the remission of sins. The Spirit descended 'like a dove' upon Jesus, which implied that he was possessed of the spirit of Jonah ('Jonah' being the Hebrew word for 'dove'). As Jonah was the one Hebrew prophet who undertook, though reluctantly, a mission to the Gentiles, the descent of the dove meant that Jesus would himself take God's salvation to the Gentiles (cf. the same theme in Simeon's song in Luke 2.32).

The voice said, 'You are my Son; my favour rests on you.' To be God's son in the context of an Israelite repentance-baptism is to be the individual in whom a new 'son' or 'people' or 'Israel' of God is established, much as Solomon was the one individual in whom the old Israel had been established long before. 'Son' is a noun in the singular, but 'sonship', in the context of Hebrew history, has a corporate meaning: the whole people was God's 'son'. So when Jesus is declared to be the Son of God, it is as the creative centre of a new Son or people or Israel of God. He is not Son in a purely individual capacity, but in an individual-corporate role in and through which God's people would find its final embodiment in human history. Those who joined themselves to the new people of God proclaimed by Jesus would become Son with him in the community that he creatively gathered round him. To have God's favour rest on one is to be assured that whatever work is done for God, and however much it may demand of the doer, it will not be allowed to be fruitless. It is not surprising that Jesus felt he had to retreat into the wilderness to ponder on what might lie ahead.

When Jesus returned from his testing in the desert, he proclaimed good news from God: 'The time has come. The kingdom of God has arrived.* Repent and believe the good news' (Mark 1.15). This is an understandable outcome of the baptismal experience, for it begins the expansion of the 'individual' embodiment of sonship into its corporate form comprising the community of those who followed Jesus. Sonship was a relationship into which others were invited to enter. In the Sermon on the Mount Jesus taught his followers to call God 'Father': they were, by their following of Jesus to be incorporated into the life of the new son of God centred in him. In that life of the new son they were to accept, with Jesus, the Law that God had given to the old Israel, but to keep it as members of a new community that for the first time in history would use the Law as God had originally intended (cf. below, pp. 74, 133). Similarly, in his appointment of the Twelve Jesus showed his followers that the new son or people of God would be continuous with the old people of God with its twelve tribal patriarchs, and yet discontinuous from it, for it was, even during Jesus's lifetime, able and ready to share its benefits with those who were not the racial descendants of Abraham.

Jesus had accepted from John a baptism for the forgiveness of sins. In a crowded house in Capernaum early in his ministry he healed a severely paralysed man, though he first made it plain that the basic and primary benefit that the new Israel would bestow was forgiveness (Mark 2.5). The already suspicious authorities at once condemned this as blasphemous, since it was God's prerogative alone to forgive sins. They rightly saw that if Jesus could validly forgive sins, then his word in the house at Capernaum would have been God's word, his action God's action. God would have been at work in him and through him. Yet, in spite of their evident religious shock, that idea was not in principle an unacceptable one; it was part of their own theological tradition that God had acted in and through the old people or son of God. So the central issue of the New Testament is raised: has God decided in Jesus and the community of Jesus to provide himself by his own activity with a new son or people in whom and through whom he will act

---

* For a justification of this translation see below, p127.

ineluctably to achieve his beneficent purpose for his world? (cf. also John 5.19-23; 8.27-29; 10.37f.; 2 Cor. 5.19).

The Son of Man

The evangelists report a number of occasions on which Jesus referred to himself as the 'Son of Man', but never record any other person so referring to him. It might seem that with this title the reader of the gospels can step right back to the days when Jesus was alive. But matters are nothing like so simple as that! The term 'Son of Man' has a number of meanings: the Son of Man has authority on earth (Mark 2.10); he is destined to suffer and die (Mark 9.12, 31); and his coming is still expected (Mark 8.38; Mat. 24.27, 30). Problems of interpretation abound; and in the background there is the difficulty already noted – and carefully examined in particular reference to this title in a monumental work by Professor Todt – that the resurrection perspective may have produced some distortions of what actually took place. Jesus, Professor Todt holds, was identified with the coming Son of Man in the period after the resurrection. He says: 'In consequence of this post-Easter identification of Jesus with the coming Son of Man, the designation Son of Man could be applied in a new way, namely to Jesus on earth, in the sayings concerning his activity and suffering. But even in this post-Easter application only Jesus himself was allowed to utter the name "Son of Man"' (Todt, *The Son of Man in the Synoptic Tradition* p. 327).

Three assumptions can safely be made about the evangelists' use of 'Son of Man'. First, they would have known, as Jesus would have known, that in its Hebrew form 'Son of Adam' (Authorised Version has 'Son of Man') it was the characteristic term used by God to address Ezekiel. There is no clear indication that Jesus ever quoted Ezekiel, but it is intriguing to reflect that by this title Ezekiel was directed to stand (rather than to be prostrate) before God (Ezek. 2.1); was sent as a messenger to Israel (Ezek. 2.3), and was said to dwell in a rebellious house (Ezek. 12.2, cf. Mark 8.38). He was to let Jerusalem know her abominations (Ezek. 16.2, cf. Mark 11.15ff.); to speak against the shepherds (= rulers) of Israel (Ezek. 34.2, cf. Mat. 15.14); and to be the agent by whom an Israel no better than a scattered skeleton would be brought back to new, articulate life (Ezek. 37.10, cf. Luke 18.30). All this forms an interesting outline of much of Jesus's own mission, and may well merit more notice than it has so far received.

Second, the evangelists, and most probably Jesus himself, knew

the term in Jewish apocalyptic (Daniel, Ethiopian Enoch and 4
Ezra), in which the Son of Man was a heavenly being who would
descend to judge the world at the last day.

Third, the evangelists had the advantage of writing their narratives
with the revealing hindsight of the resurrection. The result may well
have been some distortions or anachronisms, one of which, in the
view of many critics, is the pre-resurrection assertion that the Son of
Man would rise 'on the third' day (Mark 8.31). But they also had the
advantage of knowing that Jesus had a highly sensitive, creative and
discerningly prescient mind. It would be rash in the extreme to
suppose that he made no distinctive contribution to the use of the
title 'Son of Man', or that, in the alchemy of his mind, the leaden
prose of apocalyptic writing was not transformed into a golden
treasury of poetry. It would likewise be foolish to think that from his
first appearance in Galilee on the morrow of the arrest of John the
Baptist he would not have been aware of the inevitable suspicion,
hostility and danger from the authorities, or that towards the end he
would have remained blind to the possibility, not to say probability,
of death by crucifixion. And this may be added: if Herod could
think of Jesus as John the Baptist risen from the dead (Mark 6.14, 16),
it would not have been impossible for Jesus to have believed that in
the person of one of his disciples, if not in his own, he might 'rise
again' to renew his mission. And if the Twelve could have supposed,
on the same basis, that one of them might become 'Jesus risen from
the dead' after Jesus's death, that would explain, perhaps more
satisfactorily than in any other way, why to the very end (at the Last
Supper even, (Luke 22.24)) they argued about who would be the
greatest in the kingdom of God.

It is generally accepted that Matthew and Luke used the text of
Mark as one source for their gospels. It is also widely accepted that
they owe to another source, 'Q', the many passages which they have
additionally in common, and that 'Q' may be the earliest source of
information about Jesus. Professor Todt holds that in no saying in
'Q' is Jesus identified with the coming Son of Man, whom,
nevertheless, Jesus promised would come. Hence no one during
his earthly ministry would have recognized 'Son of Man' as a self-
designation of Jesus. It was the post-resurrection community that
first took that step, enabling the title to be applied to Jesus as he
suffered and died.

The case argued seems impregnably strong – but it is not clear
that every reference to a 'coming' of the 'Son of Man' is to figure who
will come to earth after the resurrection. The critical instance is

Jesus's answer to the High Priest at his trial. Both prosecutor and prisoner knew that the trial was a life and death issue for Jesus. The High Priest, baffled by his failure to secure adequate testimony to secure a verdict, asked Jesus, 'Are you the Messiah, the Son of the Blessed?' Jesus replied, 'I am; and you will see the Son of Man seated at the right hand of God, and coming with the clouds of heaven' (Mark 14.62). Jesus was quoting Daniel 7.13, and it is important to notice the language and the metaphor that the prophet used. The Son of Man, he says, will come 'with the clouds of heaven', not 'on them'. That is, he will be going from earth to heaven, and not from heaven to earth. For he will travel as an ambassador of his people to a royal court to be 'presented' to the all-sovereign, to secure for his people the support and friendship of the great king. The Old Testament commentators confirm that the language of the section is precisely that of an ambassador presenting his credentials to a royal court. The Son of Man is a successful ambassador, for he is given a universal and imperishable kingdom, which is later (Dan. 7.18) identified as that of the 'saints of the Most High'. A textual emendation leaves it possible, but still difficult, to avoid the imagery of ambassadorial presentation at court, and to substitute an earthward instead of a heavenward journey for the Son of Man. But the proper reading leaves the dramatic intensity in the narrative of the trial of Jesus.

The High Priest has really put Jesus in a position where he must either deny his Messianic status, or face a penalty of death. In his reply Jesus makes it clear that though he knows his admission will bring about his death, he will not on that account be deprived of the end of his work which he desires: the secure establishment by divine power of a universal and unending kingdom. For, to use Daniel's phraseology, he would be presented to the 'Ancient of Days', and receive at his hands 'the kingdom', which he will possess 'for ever and ever'. He is not saying, 'Kill me, and I shall return to earth as the Son of Man identified in Jewish apocalyptic,' but 'Kill me, and I shall return to God in heaven, and reign from there for ever'. The New Testament sequence of cross, death, resurrection and ascension accords thoroughly with this. It is moreover not very far from the inspired insight of the fourth gospel, that the crucifixion was itself the hour 'for the Son of Man to be glorified' (John 12.23). The question arises whether other sayings about the Son of Man may not properly be understood in similar terms.

Matthew's gospel provides an apt example, for it not only uses the title more often than any other gospel, but offers interesting clues to its significance for Jesus. Matthew indicates clearly that at the basis of Jesus's teaching and action was a conviction that the final kingdom of Heaven had arrived. The end of 'this present age' had been reached. He tells how Jesus was moved to pity at the sight of people 'harassed and helpless' like 'sheep without a shepherd' (Mat. 9.36). He then said to his disciples, 'The harvest is plentiful, but the labourers are few; pray therefore the Lord of the harvest to send out labourers into his harvest' (Mat. 9.37). But 'Harvest' is the stock figure for 'the end of the age', as Matthew himself states (Mat. 13.39). So the disciples are themselves 'reapers' in the divine harvest (they are called 'angels' or, otherwise translating the Greek, 'messengers' in 13.39), whose work is precisely to separate the citizens of the old age from those of the new – a truly 'eschatological' task. They separate the wheat from the tares (13.41), or, in a piscatorial metaphor, good fish from bad (13.49). So the end of the age does not come as the last moment of a chronological series, but at any and every moment when a man enters the kingdom of Heaven in repentance and belief in the good news. The Kingdom comes in the person and mission of Jesus and his community.

Matthew's other allusions to the Son of Man allow this interpretation. Jesus told his disciples when he sent them out on a mission (its precise chronological location is unascertainable), 'Before you have gone through all the towns of Israel the Son of Man will have come' (10.23); and at another indeterminate moment he announced, 'There are some standing here who will not taste of death before they have seen the Son of Man coming in his kingdom' (16.28). Was he mistaken, as many have supposed? Not if he believed that, whatever opposition might arise, or however his own person were affected, he would emerge as victor, acknowledged as the inaugurator of the kingdom of Heaven on earth. At Caesarea Philippi he asked his disciples 'Whom do men say that the Son of Man is?' He learned from their answers that no one had identified him with the popularly expected Son of Man described in Jewish apocalyptic – but why should they? He had not come 'on the clouds of heaven' with 'angels and heavenly splendour'. It was clearly not yet the great day of judgment. But he also learned that Peter recognized him as the Messiah, and, more, as the 'Son of the living God' (Mat. 16.16), which Jesus declared to be a God-given insight. He then began to teach that the Son of Man would suffer and die, so shocking a thought for a true Jew that Peter immediately protested. Clearly the disciples were not ready for the great transformation that he was to make in the concept of the Son of Man.

Can that transformation be positively related to passages like Matthew 19.28, where 'the Son of Man is seated on his throne in heavenly splendour' with his followers seated with him, 'judging the tribes of Israel'? Jesus is really saying that in the new creation (i.e. the new kingdom of Heaven that has arrived) Jesus and his disciples will be the ones who discern and decide who is admitted to or excluded from the kingdom – precisely in the manner of the parables cited (p. 50). For Jesus neither the Messiah nor the Son of Man was a solitary figure; the Messiah cannot be the Messiah or function as such without the people of the Messiah; and the Son of Man is the ambassador for the saints of the Most High. The heavenly splendour is wrongly conceived if it is related to royal courts on earth. Solomon had that sort of glory; but 'a greater than Solomon is here!' (cf. Mat. 12, 42; 6.29).

In a traditionally colourful apocalyptic passage Jesus said that 'the sun will be darkened, the moon will not give her light, the stars will fall from the sky, the celestial powers will be shaken. Then will appear in heaven the sign that heralds the Son of Man. All the peoples of the world will make lamentation, and they will see the Son of Man coming on the clouds of heaven with great power and glory. With a trumpet blast he will send out his angels, and they will gather his chosen from the four winds, from the farthest bounds of heaven on every side' (Mat. 24.29-31). This almost purely Jewish passage has received its post-Easter transformation from Matthew in being placed before the story of the crucifixion, so that his readers can see that the darkness, the earthquake and the rent Temple veil were signs that the Son of Man had come. (The sending out of his 'angels' or 'messengers' follows in ch. 28.) To interpret such apocalyptic literally makes it deadly unenlightening prose; to see it as an already imaginative insight into the final realities of life now being enacted and revealed in the tragic history of the crucifixion and the triumphal history of the resurrection is to make the imagery exciting and imaginative poetry. It is to know Jesus's own incomparably revealing poetic mind.

So for Matthew, as for Jesus himself, the Son of Man was a figure on earth. That is why Jesus could speak of himself and his disciples 'judging the twelve tribes of Israel' (Mat. 19.24); and why he can say, 'Whenever the Son of Man comes in his glory and all the angels with him . . . he will separate men into two groups' (Mat. 25.31f.). This repeats the function announced in 19.24, though here the final 'eschatological' separation of wheat from darnel, good fish from bad, is not based on verbal affirmations, or even on conscious following of Jesus, but on the service given to or withheld from those in need.

Matthew's creatively revealing narratives of the Son of Man find their natural climax in the last five verses of the gospel, even though the title is not applied to him there. Jesus appears to the eleven after his resurrection. In terms of Matthew 26.64 he has already gone with 'the clouds of heaven' and been 'presented' to the Ancient of Days, and received from him a universal and imperishable kingdom for the people of the saints of the Most High. When he came to the disciples they worshipped him, though 'some were doubtful' (Mat. 28.17). What Jesus said to them befits the Son of Man who had been presented to the Ancient of Days: 'Full authority in heaven and earth has been committed to me. Go forth therefore and make all nations my disciples; baptize men everywhere in the name of the Father and the Son and the Holy Spirit, and teach them to observe all that I have commanded you. And be assured, I am always with you to the end of time' (Mat. 27.18ff.).

The Son of Man had thus finished his task, met his destiny and gone, to use a Johannine phrase, 'to the Father', there to be given his universal and imperishable kingdom. He exercized full authority. But the heavenly seat of that authority did not spell separation from his followers, as if the heavenly kingdom could only follow chronologically upon the end of all earthly kingdoms. The kingdom had already been established in this world, and was still there in the community of his followers, of which he was still the centre and the essence. He was no longer 'Son of Man' – that task had been performed – but he who had been the 'Son of Man' was for ever one with and in them as they were sent, his 'messengers' ('angels'), to the four corners of the earth (Mat. 24.31). Similarly John finished his gospel by telling how Jesus on the evening of the first Easter day visited his disciples, breathed his spirit on them and said, 'As the Father sent me, even so I send you' (John 20.21). The community continues his work, doing so because he is with them and in them.

For Judaism the Son of Man was a supernatural figure who had yet to descend from heaven to be the universal judge on the last day. For Jesus the Son of Man had already appeared on earth, and in his ministry exercized the true eschatological judgment, as within the present chronological order with his disciples he separated out the wheat from the darnel. Son of Man is not itself a creedal title, offering some ready metaphysical suggestion about the divine status and nature of Jesus; but it is not wholly irrelevant to the questions concerning what the Church must think about its founder.

Messiah

'Messiah' is the most used title of Jesus, though in its Greek form 'Christ' rather than its Hebrew form 'Messiah'. 'Christ' has become virtually a surname for Jesus, who has been called Jesus Christ from the very early days of the Church.

'Messiah' or 'Christ' means 'anointed'. In the Old Testament it was used first of Saul, who was anointed by Samuel, and became known as 'the Lord's anointed'. The title implied that the king had been anointed by God's authorized representative; but later it was used of non-Hebrew kings (e.g. Cyrus, Isa. 45.1) and of prophets (1 Kings 19.16; Isa. 61.1) and priests (1 Chron. 29.22) also.

Anointing a person meant that he received God's spirit as an abiding gift; it bestowed a sacredness which made his person inviolable (1 Sam. 24.6). He was brought under the special care of God, and consecrated to the special duties assigned to him. Yet the name 'Messiah' could still be used even if, as with Cyrus and the patriarchs (Ps. 105.15), there could have been no anointing ceremony. The work done and the gifts displayed justified the use of the title for such *de facto* Messiahs.

The kingly associations of the title linked it inevitably with national prestige. If Israel's God were the supreme God, then his people must be seen to be the supreme people. In adversity they believed that prosperity would speedily be restored; and when Israel's inferiority became prolonged the Jews began to look for a Messiah who would bring them to their anticipated destiny. Into such a world of Jewish religious, political and military Messianism Jesus was born. His people had experienced two abortive Messianic risings under Theudas and Judas of Galilee (Acts 5.36f.). It is therefore not surprising to read that when John the Baptist drew his crowds on the banks of the Jordan 'the people were on the tiptoe of expectation, all wondering about John, whether he was perhaps the Messiah' (Luke 3.15).

To that there is an amazing contrast: though the gospels were written that their readers might believe that Jesus is Messiah, the Son of God' (John 20.31), they do not record of Jesus, as they do of

John, that the crowds wondered whether he was the Messiah. Indeed, before Peter's inspired assertion at Caeserea Philippi it was only the demon-possessed, 'out of their right mind', who 'knew him' (Mark 1.34) or addressed him as Messiah (Luke 4.41), and he would not let them publicize what they knew. In that same period two blind men (Mat. 9.27) and a Canaanite woman (Mat. 15.22) – inadequate witnesses for any Jewish court! – called him by the more politically Messianic title of 'Son of David'. Even after Jesus had attracted large crowds and fed five thousand people miraculously (Mark 6.35-44), and his disciples had conducted a successful travelling mission (Mark 6.7), there is no hint that anyone suspected that he was the Messiah. He was thought to be John the Baptist, Elijah or one of the prophets come back to life, a 'herald' of the Messiah, but not the Messiah himself (Mark 8.28). It was Peter who first voiced the conviction that he was in fact the Messiah (Mark 8.29), at which Jesus charged the Twelve not to tell anyone about him. He then went on to teach about the Son of Man, that he must suffer rejection, and death, and rise from the dead. Peter, who evidently had very different ideas about the destiny of the Son of Man and of the Messiah, expostulated strongly – and Jesus heard in what he said the enticement of Satan, the adversary (Mark 8.30-33).

After Peter's confession of Jesus's Messiahship there is still little indication of any public perception or proclamation. At one point Jesus told his disciples that 'if anyone gives you a cup of water to drink because you are followers of the Messiah, that man assuredly will not go unrewarded' (Mark 9.41). But this was no public utterance, but a word to the disciples that, because they were the Messiah's men, and so sharing in God's ultimate favour to the Messiah, those who helped them would help him and so see the due reward of their action – the reign of the Messiah established.

On another occasion Jesus addressed both crowd and disciples (Mat. 23.8ff.). In their life together they were not to use titles like 'Rabbi' (there is really only one Teacher), or 'Father' (there is only one Father – in heaven), or Master or Messiah. This constitutes no claim by Jesus to be the Messiah – though it is followed by teaching about the greatness of service, which reflects the pattern of life that Jesus envisaged for the Son of Man (Mark 10.45).

In the apocalyptic passages of Mark and Matthew Jesus foretells the coming of false Messiahs (Mark 13.21f.; Mat. 24.5, 23f.). False Messiahs had already appeared (Acts 5.36f.); and while it is entirely probable that this saying (like the two previous ones) was preserved, fashioned and published by and for the post-resurrection community, it is also probable that they were all linked with actual situations in the life of Jesus himself. If so, they would have warned the disciples that his claim to Messiahship would not pass unchallenged by persons or events, to the severe testing of their loyalty and faith.

The final uses of the title 'Messiah' come in the narrative of the trial and crucifixion. At his trial before the Sanhedrin the High Priest asked Jesus, 'Are you the Messiah, the Son of the Blessed One?' Jesus answered 'I am', and then went on to speak of the imminent arrival of the Son of Man in heaven, where he would receive from God his universal and imperishable kingdom. Yet, though Jesus deliberately changed the basis of discourse, the trial and events following continued to be based on his alleged Messiahship. Jesus was sent to Pilate for examination on the charges that 'We found this man subverting our nation, opposing the payment of taxes to Caesar, and claiming to be Messiah, a king' (Luke 23.2). The choice put to the crowd as to which prisoner should be released at the feast was between Barabbas and Jesus Messiah (Mat. 27.17). Those who mocked him as he hung on the cross said, 'Let the Messiah, the king of Israel, come down now from the cross. If we see that, we shall believe' (Mark 15.32). And the brigand who had been crucified alongside Jesus said, 'Are you not the Messiah? Save yourself and us' (Luke 23.39).

It is noteworthy that it was not until after the resurrection that any evangelist records a systematic attempt by Jesus to explain to the disciples what was involved in being the Messiah (Luke 24.26, 46).

What has the fourth gospel to contribute to a study of the title 'Messiah'? Its first five references to the Messiah come from its narratives about John the Baptist. The Jerusalem authorities sent a deputation to interrogate John, and he began by telling them, 'I am not the Messiah' (John 1.17, 3.28). 'But if you are not the Messiah, nor Elijah, nor the prophet, why then are you baptizing?' they asked. John replied that his baptism was symbolic, using water; but that the one to come would offer real baptism in the Spirit. When John hailed Jesus as the Lamb of God, two of his disciples began to follow Jesus, and one of them, Andrew, fetched his brother Simon Peter with the news, 'We have found the Messiah' (John 1.41). This judgment would have been derived from John and his expectations, but these were to prove inadequate for him confidently to discern whether Jesus was the Messiah or not (Mat. 11.2; Luke 7.19). When the Samaritan woman told Jesus that she knew the Messiah was coming, and he replied 'I am he', the occasion was a private conversation and, from the woman's point of view, about a Samaritan Messiah; it was by no means a public claim to be the expected Jewish Messianic deliverer. For the rest, the references in John are mostly in accounts of disputes about the Messiah and his status (4.29; 7. 26-42 [six times]; 10.24; 12.34). There is also a report that the Jewish authorities had 'already agreed that anyone who acknowledged Jesus as Messiah should be banned from the Synagogue'. This is evidently more a 'Jewish' than a developed 'Christian' dogmatic formulation; so there is less need than some believe to suppose that no such order was ever made in Jesus's lifetime, or that, as others believe, the statement is a clear instance of a post-resurrection perspective. The most positive use of the title comes from the lips of Martha, after Jesus had returned to Bethany four days after her brother had died. Picking up her reference to her brother's rising 'on the last day', Jesus said that he was himself the resurrection and the life. He asked if she believed this. Martha replied, 'Lord, I do. I know that you are the Messiah, the Son of God who was to come into the world' (John 11.27). This is indeed a very different conception from that of popular Jewish Messianism of the time, but it is still a long way from the suffering, dying and rising Messiah that came to be the object of the Church's belief and worship. Beyond that the fourth gospel records only that in his great prayer Jesus said, 'This is eternal life; to know thee who alone art truly God, and Jesus Messiah whom thou hast sent' (John 17.3). So, while the fourth gospel gives no evidence of a Messianic secret, it offers no evidence of any open proclamation that Jesus was the Messiah.

But this reticence contrasts sharply with the rest of the New Testament. At Pentecost Peter told how Jesus had been raised by God and exalted to his right hand, and had received the Spirit from the Father (cf. John 1.33; 7.39). He continued, 'Let all Israel then accept as certain that God has made this Jesus, whom you crucified, both Lord and Messiah (Acts 2.36). 'Messiah' is used frequently in Acts, as in the other books of the New Testament. The open claim that Jesus was the Messiah followed his death and resurrection, and is thus a post-Easter insight of the Church. This is aptly illustrated in the creedal passage with which Paul begins his letter to the Romans. The good news, affirmed Paul, is about God's Son, who

by physical descent was of David's lineage
by the Holy Spirit was the Son of God with power and
by resurrection from the dead was Jesus Messiah our Lord.

(Rom. 1.3f.)

This refers to three moments in the gospel story of Jesus: his birth, establishing his Davidic descent; his baptism, where he received the Holy Spirit, establishing him as the incorporation of the new Israel; and his resurrection, establishing him as Messiah and Lord.

What conclusion is to be drawn from this rather inconclusive evidence? That the Messiahship of Jesus was entirely a post-Easter insight of the Church, whose evangelists sought to endow it with his authority by making it an element, albeit a secret one, in the life and consciousness of Jesus himself? Some scholars would so infer. Bultmann says of Peter's confession at Caesarea Philippi that 'it is to be characterized as legend . . . a literary device . . . the disciples represent the Church, and the passages give expression to the specific judgement which the Church had about Jesus, in distinction from those outside' (Bultmann, *The History of the Synoptic Tradition*, pp.257ff.). But what does such a conclusion imply for the gospel reader's knowledge of what took place in the lifetime of Jesus? The best construction to put on such a judgment as Bultmann's is that the 'legendary formulation' was a means of letting the gospel reader know what was going on in what actually took place. This might mean that though Jesus was actually the Messiah, he was unaware of it – and that is not an unknown sort of experience for a man to have.

But the further point is worth raising, whether, in the review of Jesus's life after the resurrection, there were not disclosed incidents which compelled the community, its evangelists and others concerned in forming and transmitting the traditions about Jesus to recognize that this or that saying or action could only properly be understood on the assumption that Jesus already knew that he was indeed the Messiah, even if it proved to be a somewhat different Messiah from that of popular Jewish expectation. Indeed it would be very surprising indeed if the founder of a new religion out of Judaism had not formed his own quite new ideas as to what the office of Messiah meant. Certainly Jesus's own actions would have suggested to the popular mind that he was claiming or affirming his Messiahship when he sought to form a new Israel, or when he cited works that he had done as evidence that he was 'the one who was to come' (Mat. 11.2ff.). It may well be that Jesus made no explicit verbal claim to be the Messiah, but his actions may well have spoken, to those with 'ears to hear', more loudly than any words could have done. Hence a number of modern scholars such as Günther Bornkamm have seen in Jesus's actions a much more positive and theological witness to himself than Bultmann and his contemporaries could derive from his words alone.

The evangelists have done their job so well that the story they tell has a certain historical 'feel' about it. It is worth reviewing it again as if it were. The synoptists were sure that there was a real secrecy: that Jesus was aware of his Messiahship, but kept it a secret. If a reason for that be sought it can be found naturally in an understandably commendable prudence. Jesus began his work at the sensitive time when John the Baptist's had finished. John had called for a new Israel, repenting of its past failures to be a true people of God, and ready for a new relationship to both God and man. Many wondered if he was the Messiah. But he was arrested and imprisoned. Had Jesus appeared as the Messiah he would only have brought like action against himself. But he was not the Messiah of the popular imagination. That is clear from many words (e.g. Mat. 5.41) and actions (e.g. Mark 11.1-10). He sought no military leadership. He was silent about his Messiahship –though once the disciples began to penetrate his 'incognito' he started to modify their popular preconceptions about the Messiah, and taught them about the suffering Son of Man. But old ideas die slowly; the disciples continued to search for the chief place in his kingdom (Mark 10.37-45), and even at the Last Supper they discussed who was the greatest (Luke 22.24). Even after the resurrection they asked Jesus if he was going to restore a political kingdom to Israel (Acts 1.6). He replied significantly that they must wait for the gift of the Spirit, when they would become his witnesses – as he after the gift of the Spirit at his baptism had witnessed to the arrival of the kingdom. But if those so close to him as the disciples had for so long so greatly misunderstood his claims, how much more would those whose roots remained firmly in the popular traditions of Judaism understand?

The Messianic secret did two things: first, the Jewish authorities were prevented from obtaining any direct evidence of a Messianic claim and so from taking any early legal action against him; and, second, it prevented the crowds from reacting to any claim he might overtly have made in such a way as to lead them to move against him. Yet he spoke and acted 'Messiahship' in various oblique ways: in appointing twelve 'patriarchs' for the new Israel; in offering the new Israel a new 'law'; in citing his teaching and healing as scriptural fulfilment showing that he was 'the one who was to come'; and, most clearly, in his entry into Jerusalem on Palm Sunday as its true and Messianic king, in obvious and public fulfilment of a prophecy from Zechariah – though even there neither the crowds nor his disciples understood what his actions stated about his distinctive style of Messiahship (see above, p.28f).

The question arises: could the evangelists actually have discerned in Jesus's words and deeds a Messianic significance of which he was himself unaware? If they did, then they showed more discernment in their reporting of what took place than Jesus did as he spoke and acted. That is not an impossible relationship to exist between a biographer and the subject of his biography, for rarely do actors in the drama of history realize the full implications of their participation. It is not difficult to suppose that Jesus himself did not apprehend the full significance of his words and deeds during his lifetime; but it is almost impossible to suppose that on Palm Sunday he rode into Jerusalem as Zechariah's royal Messiah without knowing very well what sort of claim – and claimant – that action disclosed.

The Messiahship of Jesus offers an instructive contrast with that of Judaism and the Old Testament. The original 'Messiah' was the one anointed king of God's people, receiving God's spirit on appointment to his kingly duties. Thus he came under God's special care, which made his person inviolable. Judaism anticipated a Messiah from the house of David to achieve political independence once more for Israel, to restore its past glories, and to make it the supreme people on earth, as Israel's God was supreme in heaven. All this is transformed in the story of Jesus. He received his 'anointing' at his baptism, where he received the Spirit (Mark 1.10), and was declared to be in God's special regard (Mark 1.11). It is significant that Luke reports that Jesus's baptism took place 'during a general baptism of the people', i.e. the Messiah is identified with the people of the Messiah, and they are anointed and dedicated to the Messianic task together. The synoptic gospels are unanimous in telling that Jesus went from his baptism to his testing in the wilderness, from which he came into Galilee proclaiming, 'The time has come; the kingdom of God has arrived; repent, and believe the Gospel.' The Messiah-king had come, and the new Israel had been born. But the new was not as the old; for the Messiah did not come to secure or restore political independence, but to establish a community in whose order men would be delivered together from the captivity of wrongdoing and sin. The kingdom of the new Messiah was worldwide; for, as Simeon sang of him in the Temple, God had prepared in him a deliverance in full view of all the nations, 'a light that will be a revelation to the heathen, and glory to thy people Israel' (Luke 2.32).

The title 'Messiah' has both individual and corporate connotations. There can be no king without subjects and no Messiah without a community of the Messiah. It is relevant to recall that Jesus performed no Messianic work, nor spoke any Messianic words, save 'in the presence of his disciples', i.e. his community. Matthew even shows that in his teaching ministry the corporate reality is basic; Moses went up on to the mountain alone to receive from God the law for the ordering of Israel's life; when Jesus went up on the mountain, his disciples went with him. The Messiah and his community were one when with the authority of the God who spoke to Moses he spoke the new law of love to guide the life of the new Israel of God.

Finally, the inviolability of the Messiah's person also underwent transformation. Jesus knew that even under threat of execution he was fundamentally 'safe' (Mat. 26.53, 64; John 18.36; 19.11). In the eyes of 'the world' this new Messiah-king would come to a tragic end, and die. But, as Jesus made clear to the High Priest, even that inescapable tragedy would be but the way to heavenly triumph, and lead to his universal and unending reign. And, as Matthew saw when he recorded Peter's confession of Jesus's Messiaship, the Messiah's community was inviolable in and with him: 'on this rock I will build my church [community] and the powers of death shall never conquer it' (Mat. 16.18).

In Jesus's day a Messianic claim was political dynamite. Hence the concern as well as hope of the Jewish authorities whenever a Messianic claimant appeared; and hence too Jesus's own reserve in using the title, or allowing it to be used of himself. Yet it was the richest, most inclusive of all the concepts linked to Israel's hopes for the future, in which politics, religion, morals, law and justice, even the natural order itself, would be so transformed that no strife or evil would remain (e.g. Isa. 11.1-9; 65.17-25). No wonder that Jesus used it, weaving into it the tragic note that anticipates bliss but only as that which lies beyond bane, and is deepened thereby because the Messiah, the victor, has himself tasted the bane.

Son of David

The Messianic title 'Son of David' is almost a sub-title for 'Messiah'. It appears fourteen times in the gospels, and is once used genealogically of Mary's husband Joseph (Mat. 1.20). The title expresses the national memory of David who, though rebuked and disciplined for disobedience by God's prophets, was nevertheless honoured in tradition as an upright, righteous and obedient servant of God, and even, in Rabbinic writings, as a fervent student of the Law. Because his hands were stained with blood (so 1 Chron. 28.3) he was not permitted to build the Temple, but the privilege was granted to Solomon, his son. David was promised, 'Your family shall be established and your kingdom shall stand for all time in my sight, and your throne shall be established for ever' (2 Sam. 7.16). It was natural, if not inevitable, that in times of political eclipse Jewish hopes should focus on the terms of that promise, and expect some deliverer in a 'son' or descendant of David.

Two modifications were operative by the time of Jesus. First, Israel's Messianic expectations were more fully awaited. The Qumran community looked for an Aaronic or Levitical Messiah,* responsible for the religious community as such; he would accompany the Israelite Messiah (Son of David), though, in view of his responsibilities, he would be superior to him. (It is interesting that John the Baptist's mother was of Aaronic descent (Luke 1.5). A 'prophetic' Messiah was also anticipated, fulfilling the promise given to Moses, 'I will raise up for them a prophet like you, one of their own race, and I will put my words into his mouth. He shall

---

* Aaronic and Zadokits Priesthood: Priesthood in Judaism was hereditary, confined to male members of the tribe of Levi, though not all male members of the tribe actually served as priests. There was a time when Priest and Levite were used synonymously (Deut. 18.1), though the priestly office itself came to be restricted to the descendants of Aaron, who was a grandson of Levi. History saw further developments. In David's time the priest Abiathar (descended from Itharam, one of Aaron's sons conspired with Adonijah and Joab to usurp the throne of David. The plot was discovered and David dismissed Abiathar, replacing him with Zadok (a descendant of Eleazar, the other son of Aaron). Thus, when Solomon built the temple in Jerusalem, it was naturally the Zadokite priesthood that assumed charge of the sanctuary and its worship. (cf. 1 Kings 1.5-53; 2.35). By the time of Ezekiel the priesthood in general was giving the prophet cause for considerable complaint, and he proposed that only priests of the guild of Zadok should hold priestly office. But that still left many duties for the assistants to the priests to perform in the temple, and these assistants were 'Levites'. By New Testament times the number of priests had become so great that it was necessary to form a rota of twenty-four 'orders' or 'guilds' to allow everybody regular appearances at the Temple.

convey all my commands to them . . . ' (Deut. 18.18f.; cf. Acts 3.22-26). The second modification was that more emphasis had come to be placed on the nature of the Messiah than on the person of the Messiah himself.

The title 'Son of David' is used in the gospels mostly as a way of asking for help, especially from those who were virtual outcasts. The Canaanite woman seeking help for her possessed daughter was treated as an Israelite, though she herself recognized that her fortune was no more than that of a dog eating food dropped from the family table (Mark 7.28f.). Others who sought help were blind men (Mark 10.47), who were also healed. It is recorded also that 'in the temple blind men . . . came to him, and he healed them' (Mat. 21.14), though by a law of David blind men were not allowed there (2 Sam. 5.8, esp. the Greek Septuaguit text). Such cries for help were far from political. They show that even the Davidic Messiah was more than a military leader. Jesus's healings were real evidence to some of his contemporaries that a Davidic Messianic age had dawned (for example, see, the story of blind Bartimaeus, Mark 10.46-52).

In Mark 12.35ff., as also in Matthew and Luke, there is a discussion about 'Son of David' as a Messianic title. The Jews based it on the promise to David (2 Sam. 7.13-16) that his throne and his kingdom would be established forever. But Jesus pointed out that David, the presumed author of the Psalms, had himself said, under the inspiration of the Spirit, 'The Lord said to my lord, "Sit at my right hand until I put your enemies under your feet."' He then asked, 'If David himself calls him "Lord", how can he also be David's son?' This discussion took place after Palm Sunday, when Jesus had been greeted by the crowds with the double acclamation: 'Blessings on him who comes in the name of the Lord! Blessings on the coming of our father David!' Those shouts were a contradiction of the enacted prophecy of the arrival of a peaceful king to his waiting city (see above, p.28). So now he wished to point out that though he might be acclaimed as the bringer of the Davidic kingdom he would not be a political, military Messiah. He would not reign from an earthly throne over a kingdom he had conquered by military might (John 18.36), but would exercize his universal saving sovereignty from a heavenly throne, at the 'right hand' of God, which is the place of truly ultimate authority and power. This is not an isolated saying, for the theme was restated to the High Priest at the trial, when Jesus declared that 'from now on you will see the Son of Man seated at the right hand of God'. This was a new conception of the king-Messiah, and evidently much in Jesus's mind in the last days of his ministry. Yet it must not be seen as removing the idea that the Messianic age or kingdom of God had already arrived in his own coming, or that after death Jesus would still be the effective head of that kingdom. He would not only be the exalted Messiah at the seat of heavenly power, but would be with his disciples to the end of time (Mat. 28.20). This was not stated in so many words as Jesus quoted Daniel to the High Priest, but it can reasonably be supposed to have been the implication of the heavenly journey of the Son of Man to receive his universal and everlasting kingdom.

So it is plain that though Jesus did not, so far as the available evidence goes, call himself 'Son of David', he did understand its political-military significance, and he rejected it. He could respond to it as a cry for help, for such a plea recognized more of the general benefits of the Messianic kingdom. That notion also Jesus radically reinterpreted, more radically than even modern critics have supposed. Bultmann has written: 'Neither in the earliest Church nor anywhere in the New Testament is Jesus looked back upon as a deed of God by which – as by Abraham, Moses or David – he showed "mercy" upon the People. Of course not! For Jesus's importance as Messiah-Son-of-Man lies not at all in what he did in the past, but entirely in what is expected of him for the future. And once this expectation is fulfilled by the eschatological drama, that event will never become, like the crossing of the Red Sea, a past to which one could look back thankfully, drawing confidence from it, but it will be God's last deed of all, by which he puts history to an end' (Bultmann, *Theology of the New Testament*, I p.36). But the earliest Church did look back on what Jesus did, and draw confidence from it, as the Church still does. At every eucharist bread is broken and wine poured out 'in memory of him'; and something done once and for all (Rom. 6.10; Heb. 7.27; 9.12; 10.10) is the basic reality of a repeated sacramental sign.

The decisive question concerns the final, the eschatological drama. Is it, as Bultmann and many moderns believe, something still to be enacted, when God 'puts an end to history'? Or has history already had its end put to it? Jesus himself and the evangelists have their own views. Jesus sees his condemnation to death not as the way to ignominious defeat, but as the road to final and heavenly victory, which will seat him in heaven with full authority and power

(Mark 14.62). The evangelists, in reporting what took place at that time, preface their narrative of the crucifixion with material from Jewish apocalyptic, precisely in order that their readers may be led to discern what was going on in what took place there and then. It was really the 'eschatological drama', so much the focus of Jewish apocalyptic. This understanding of the crucifixion and what ensued means that the end of history had come while history itself was still in process. The 'end' had appeared in the middle, and quite new ways of thinking were called for. The 'end' (the *'eschaton'*) began when Jesus first announced its arrival: 'The time has come. The kingdom of God is here' (Mark 1.15). Like any phenomenon on earth, the kingdom was subject to attack (Mat. 11.12), but it remained eternally secure, and the gates of hell could not prevail against it (Mat. 16.18). From his knowledge of what Israel had done to her prophets (Mat. 5.11f.), and from his own experience of following John the Baptist, Jesus knew that his mission was critically dangerous. Yet he approached the threatened end with an extra-ordinary confidence: 'From now on you will see the Son of Man seated at the right hand of God.' His crucifixion would not be just another event in history receding into temporal distance with passing years; rather would it remain as the real and living centre of history itself, the one point where eternity touched time, and redeemed it from its all-encompassing transience. So for every Christian in his own present, the coming of Jesus-Messiah-Son of God-Son of David is neither something past nor solely a hope for the future; it is something which has brought past, present and future together in a new creative whole. In that perspective Dr Dodd's words about the eucharist are more than pertinent: 'Past, present, and future are indissolubly united in the sacrament. It may be regarded as a dramatization of the advent of the Lord, which is *at once* [italics are Dodd's] His remembered coming in humiliation and His desired coming in glory, both realized in His true presence in the Sacrament' (Dodd, *The Apostolic Preaching and its Developments*, p.234). To that need be added only that according to John the moment of Jesus's glorification was at the cross (John 12.23; 13.31f.; 17.1).

Lord

A quick glance through the Authorized Version of the New Testament is enough to show that the title 'Lord' is often applied to Jesus. Outside the gospels he is 'Jesus Christ, our Lord'; he is called

'Lord of the living and the dead' (Rom. 14.9), and even 'king of kings and Lord of lords' (1 Tim. 6.15; Rev. 17.14). In the Authorized Version it seems from the gospels that the same title was often used both to address Jesus and to talk about him. But that impression is false.

'Lord' translates a Greek word 'kyrios', which is used of the relationship between one particular person and certain other persons, or between that person and his own 'properties'. In this way a master was said to be the 'lord' of his slaves, a property owner of his stewards, a landlord of his tenants. What that relationship implied is revealed when the word is transferred to indicate the man's relationship to his property: a farmer is 'lord' of his harvest, a vineyard owner of his produce. His property is completely 'at his disposal'; he can do with it what he will. When Christians call Jesus their 'Lord', they mean, among other things, that they are wholly at his disposal, and that he has the full right to ask of them whatever he will.

There is an interesting complication. Before the gospels were written the word 'kyrios' had been used by a group of scholars in translating the Old Testament into Greek. How could they translate the Hebrew name for God, which the Jews thought too sacred to be spoken? They used 'kyrios'. So when the evangelists used that same word from a contemporary social context, it easily attracted to itself a new theological meaning. This was not entirely a misfortune, for in the rest of the New Testament Jesus was being called 'Lord' in a more than social sense. But the gospels themselves show little of any such tendency.

The gospels often use the word 'kyrios' when someone asks Jesus for help. In every case it would be natural and sufficient to translate 'kyrios' in such a context by 'sir', which, in English, like 'kyrios' in Greek, can be used both as a polite form of address, and as a title of dignity of status, that of a knight. 'Kyrios' is also used in speaking about Jesus, and even the closest scrutiny of the gospels suggests that there are few, if any objections to translating it as 'Master' or 'Teacher' in such contexts. There are borderline cases. Jesus once asked, 'Why do you keep calling me "Lord, Lord" and never do what I tell you?' (Luke 6.46). This perhaps suggests that Jesus was already becoming aware that his claims could only be properly met if they were given a priority rightly accorded to the divine. On another occasion Jesus healed a man possessed by a demon, who then wanted to travel round with Jesus and his company. But Jesus told him, 'Go home to your own folk and tell them what the Lord in his mercy has done for you' (Mark 5.19). Jesus was evidently using the terms in which men were already speaking of him, as 'Master'; but on this occasion he could have been hinting that such terms meant more than men had yet perceived. But even if, as seems more probable, there was no ascription of divinity to Jesus in his lifetime, such passages remain pointers to what was going on in that life; those who spoke of him or addressed him as 'Lord' were in fact being theologically prophetic as well as presently polite!

As 'kyrios' came into the biblical vocabulary as the Greek form of the awesome, unpronounced Hebrew name for God, it was not charged with any specifically Jewish content from Hebrew history or theology, as were other terms like Son of God, Son of Man, Messiah and Son of David. No other term was so useful for speaking of Jesus to Greeks and other Gentiles, and Paul made much use of it in his letters and speeches (Acts 20. 19, 21, 24, 28, 35). Significantly, the earliest Christian creed is not, as might be expected, 'Jesus is the Son of God' or 'Jesus is the Messiah', but simply 'Jesus is Lord'.

When did Jesus come to be, or to be called, 'Lord'. The hesitation of scholars to think that it was during his own lifetime is incontrovertibly consistent with scripture. As quoted above, Paul affirms in the opening verses of Romans: The gospel of God is about his Son, who

by physical descent was of David's lineage,
by the Holy Spirit was Son of God with power, and
by the resurrection from the dead was Jesus Messiah and Lord.
(Rom. 1.3f.)

Again, Paul wrote: 'If on your lips is the confession, "Jesus is Lord", and in your heart the faith that God raised him from the dead, then you will find salvation' (Rom. 10.9). Finally, Peter in his Pentecostal speech closed with these words: 'Let all Israel then accept as certain that God has made this Jesus, whom you crucified, both Lord and Messiah' (Acts 2.36).

The resurrection was a decisive turning point. But was it a turning point in man's knowledge of Jesus, or in his actual status, function and dignity? Was Jesus Son of God, Son of Man, Messiah, Son of David, Lord, before the resurrection, and only seen to be such in the light of it? or did he become these things only when he was raised from the dead? It is undeniably scriptural to take the former view. Firstly, it does not contradict what Peter and Paul said about God making Jesus Messiah and Lord by the resurrection from the dead. If in his life he had not manifested the qualities of the titles he came to bear, he could never have been acclaimed as such even after rising from the dead; as Jesus himself said, 'If they do not listen to Moses and the prophets they will pay no heed even if someone should rise from the dead' (Luke 16.31). Secondly, it is plainly the teaching of scripture that it was precisely the very Jesus who was crucified who was now the exalted Messiah and Lord (Acts 2.36).

The answer to the question whether Jesus was called 'Lord' in the theological sense of that term during his lifetime is almost certainly 'No'. Even after the resurrection he was not always so acclaimed. 'They worshipped him; but some doubted,' reports Matthew (Mat. 28.17); 'Jesus himself came up and walked along with them; but something kept them from seeing who it was' (Luke 24.16); Mary at the empty tomb thought that Jesus was the gardener (John 20.15). But there was also a quite new reaction: some did worship him (Mat. 28.17). The disciples who recognized him at Emmaus in his breaking of the bread returned to Jerusalem to hear the others saying that 'the Lord has risen' – and if that were still equivalent to 'the Master has risen', it could only be so with a new and theological meaning of 'Master'. When Jesus addressed Mary by her name as she stood by the tomb, she called him 'Rabbouni' (=my Master); but a week later doubting Thomas, faced with the presence of the risen Jesus and the sight of his wounds, cried out 'My Lord and my God' (John 20.28). Here the title 'Lord' has absorbed a new and divine meaning. Even if these post-Easter records are a reading back of the convictions of the primitive Christian community, they clearly support the critical view that it was only in the light of the resurrection that Jesus could be really seen as 'Lord' – or Son of God, Son of Man, Messiah or Son of David – in the way the Christian Church has come to honour him. The titles reflect his life's activity, which was that of a new and permanent Israel or 'son' of God, who has become the substance and life of his unending kingdom.

Reconstruction:
The World to which Jesus Came

As many people in the twentieth century have painfully learned, it is no enviable lot to live in an occupied country. But that was the lifelong experience of Jesus. Yet for him, and for every loyal Jew, the unavoidable problems of occupation were given a deeper dimension by their profound religious conviction that the God who had called them into being as a nation, and chosen them to be his special people on earth, had promised them Palestine as their own land forever. That that promised land had become an occupied territory was at one and the same time a theological paradox and a political problem.

The paradox was not new. It had been with the Hebrew people in one form or another ever since the fall of Samaria (722 B.C.) and the destruction of Jerusalem (586 B.C.). It persisted in spite of the return from the Babylonian exile (485 B.C.), which brought neither the political independence nor the territorial extent of the nostalgically idealized kingdom of David. It assumed a new vitality during the time of Alexander the Great, when an urbane Hellenist culture was carried all over the world. This produced two characteristic reactions among the Jews: some, belonging for the most part to the landed aristocracy and the wealthy upper echelons of the priesthood, saw an opportunity for cultural advance along with the preservation of their own prestige, privilege and power. For them Judaism had either to adapt or perish. Others held fanatically that no concession should be made that would in any way infringe upon or embarrass the religious faith and practice of Israel. Jews must remain faithful to the God who had called them, and given them the Law as the sole rule for their life.

Palestine, Rome and the Herods

After the death of Alexander the Great (333 B.C.) his eastern empire was divided between Egypt and Syria. Palestine passed to Egypt. But in 198 B.C. the Syrian king Antiochus III (223-187 B.C.) annexed it to his empire, though it was not until the reign of his son Antiochus IV (175-163 B.C.) that the full effects of this were seen.

The progressive Hellenists of Judaism worked with their new overlords to Hellenize the state, and a number of projects were begun. These roused the opposition of the anti-Hellenists, and eventually brought Antiochus IV to Jerusalem to settle the matter and force Hellenization upon his Jewish subjects. But when, in 167 B.C., he grossly desecrated the Temple, the furnace of revolt was kindled, and under the leadership of Mattathias the successful Maccabean rebellion was begun. Against extraordinary odds, and more than once favoured by what must have seemed a providential fortune, the Maccabees entirely changed the situation of the Jews. They achieved independence, assumed the office of High Priest, and exercized the power of government, without immediately claiming the title of 'king'. These were stirring, heroic days, long treasured in the national memory. The day when Simon Maccabeus rode into Jerusalem as the conqueror of Israel's foes (141 B.C.) 'with the waving of palm branches, with lutes, cymbals, and zithers, with hymns and songs' was never forgotten. It was significantly re-enacted by the crowd when Jesus rode into Jerusalem on Palm Sunday (see pp.28,185ff.).

The fortunes of the Maccabean dynasty varied. They lost their strict independence when John Hyrcanus I had to pay tribute to Antiochus VII (138-129 B.C.). But by a 'favourable providence' they were able, under Alexander Jannaeus (103-76 B.C.), to extend their borders until it seemed as if they had at last restored the idealized kingdom of David. But the end was not yet.

The problem of Hellenization persisted. Throughout the period the landed aristocracy had remained pro-Hellenist, and had retained their places on the national Council ('Sanhedrin' it came to be called). But when Alexander Jannaeus's widow Salome ascended the throne (76 B.C.) she found it necessary to foster relationships with the rising 'Pharisees', who embodied in a predominantly lay movement the spirit and traditions of the 'pious ones' who had fought so signally and successfully under Mattathias in 167 B.C. With their support she appointed her son Hyrcanus as High Priest. But on her death in 67 B.C. his brother Aristobulus, with the help of the Sadducees, seized both the High Priesthood and the throne. His tenure proved brief. Rome had come to world power, and was presently engaged in securing the safety of her eastern territories. Pompey was sent to deal with the situation, and in the course of his mission he came to Jerusalem in 63 B.C. He reinstated Hyrcanus as High Priest, and made him 'tetrarch' of the Jewish kingdom,

comprising Judea, Idumea, Galilee and Perea, with responsibility
to the Roman Governor of Syria. The dream of Jewish independence
was over, and those Jews – not a few – who thought political
independence a necessary basis for a truly Jewish way of life had to
face a future that looked as harsh politically as it seemed unpalatable
religiously.

Pompey could make decisions about the government and
administration of the Jewish kingdom, but events and personalities
were to have the last word. In the years following Pompey's visit, it
was the Idumean king Antipater who finally emerged as the
imperial appointment to the tetrarchy of Judea. When he died in 42
B.C. his two sons, Phasael and Herod, were appointed tetrarchs to
succeed him. Troubles soon came to them. In 40 B.C. the Parthians
invaded Syria, and the Jewish aristocracy, in anti-Roman oppor-
tunism, welcomed a Parthian force to Jerusalem. Phasael was killed;
Herod fled. Hyrcanus was ousted from the High Priesthood, and
his nephew Antiochus made both High Priest and king. This
produced a predictable reaction from Rome. A campaign was
initiated under Herod, which resulted in the capture of Jerusalem.
Herod entered upon his reign as king of the Jews in 37 B.C., and it
proved to be eventful, ruthless and not wholly unsuccessful. He
recognized his insecurity, and sought to remedy it. Thus he
massacred forty-five of the seventy-one members of the Sanhedrin;
reserved to himself the right to appoint the High Priest; 'eliminated'
survivors of the Maccabean dynasty; and built a chain of forts and
garrisons throughout his territory and on its borders. In such ways
he managed to achieve a period remarkably free (for the times) from
invasion and insurrection; to which he added, as the crown of his
architectural ambitions and operations, a rebuilt Temple of great
magnificence, symbolic of the fact that though he was very 'pro-
Hellenist' he was not insensitive to the piety of the Jews he
governed.

But his ruthlessness, based on his insecurity, found tragic
expression in his family relationships. His eldest son, Antipater,
reported that two younger brothers, Alexander and Aristobulus,
were plotting against their father. Herod had them executed, only
to find that Antipater himself was equally guilty. He too was
removed! It is against such a background that the story of the
massacre of children in Bethlehem (Mat. 2.16ff.) assumes a terrible
credibility.

Herod died in 4 B.C. His kingdom was divided into three

tetrarchies, to be governed by three of his sons. Judea, Samaria and Idumea went to Archelaus; Antipas received Galilee and Perea; while the territory north-east of Galilee was allocated to Philip. These dispositions were not entirely popular, and for a time there was considerable ferment. Josephus, the Jewish historian, reported that there were 'ten thousand disorders' in Judea, specifically mentioning a group of ex-Herodian soldiers, a rising at Sepphoris in Galilee under Judas, son of Hezekiah, whose rising had been suppressed by Herod the Great, and another rising in Perea led by a slave named Simon. The discontent was the basis of two petitions to the Emperor, who finally removed Archelaus from his tetrarchy and placed Judea under direct rule from Rome, locally embodied in the person of a Procurator, with an official residence on the coast at Caesarea, and facilities for visits to Jerusalem when occasion required. This was the Judea of the ministry of Jesus, and Pontius Pilate was its Procurator from 27 to 34 A.D.

The tetrarchy of Galilee and Perea was governed by Antipas, who practised some self-encouragement by adding the title 'Herod' to his name, thus becoming the Herod mentioned in the gospel story of Jesus's ministry. His matrimonial affairs were unlikely to please his Jewish religious subjects. John the Baptist made that plain, and suffered imprisonment and death for his pains. Antipas proved an unpopular ruler, and was deposed and sent to Gaul in 39 A.D.

Philip, who received the north-eastern territories, was by far the best of the brothers in office. He built up the life of his tetrarchy, and, like his father, carried out a large programme of building, including the towns of Caesarea Philippi and Bethsaida Julias. He died, not unlamented, in 34 A.D.

Such, all too briefly, was the history of the Jewish people that had left its mark on the physical boundaries, the political hopes and the religious expectations of the Palestine into which Jesus was born. Josephus wrote that the Jews of the time had four 'philosophies' among them. That is far too academic a word to convey what these movements were. 'Party' is too political. 'Movement' is perhaps the best term, though it remains more important to understand than to find an apt name. Each of the four movements owed its origin and its continuing purpose to the revolt of the Maccabees against the desecration of the Temple by Antiochus Epiphanes IV in 167 B.C. Jewish reaction then, as it would be now, was at one and the same time religious, political and cultural. Every Jew wanted to live in a Jewish society where peace would ensure freedom to worship God in their traditional way. But each of the four movements had its own ideas of realizing that brave dream.

Sadducees

First, the Sadducees, who comprised the Priesthood and the landed aristocracy, constituting the centre of Jewish wealth and power. They combined nationwide influence with an operational base in Jerusalem. They exercized virtual control of the Sanhedrin or Great Council of the nation, for, though they were in a numerical minority, the presidency was vested in the High Priest, who could count on the support of the priests and the aristocrats. The opposition of scribes and Pharisees was divided and relatively ineffective. The Sadducees used their power to secure for the nation, as for themselves, as good and sound a basis as possible on which a new start could be made when the day of liberation at last arrived. They negotiated some important elements of autonomy: they were given responsibility for the Temple and its worship; the Sanhedrin was granted the administration of justice, save for cases involving the death penalty. The Sadducees emphasized the religious duty of obedience to the Law, which for them meant the divine Law revealed to Moses and contained in the written scriptures of the first five books of the Old Testament. This attitude inclined them to be literalist, inflexible and conservative. They had no place for the new ideas stemming from Persian religion, which were spreading at the time, such as belief in angels or in resurrection. For them God was removed from all evil, and each individual man was free to make his own moral choices and to control his destiny. Hence the nation's future must be their own work, and in that light they saw their 'concordat' with Rome. They were still truly heirs of those Hellenizers who were ready to deal with Antiochus IV in 167 B.C. Yet, like other Jews of the time, they sensed that the times were apocalyptic: the promised Messiah might well be near. They meant to be well placed if and when he came.

The Sadducees were too Hellenist, too collaborationist, to be narrowly nationalist. Yet without their religiously convinced and politically adept powers of negotiation, which secured such useful measures of autonomy from Rome, the national lot would have been much harder than it was, and the outlook much less hopeful. They exhibited, as Josephus records, a good deal of the arrogance and self-centredness of an aristocratic and priestly hierarchy, and were certainly not the popular idols of the masses; nevertheless, whatever their defects, they made the preservation of a good deal of traditional Jewish life a reality in a not very promising situation.

Pharisees

If in the Palestine of Jesus's day the Sadducees represented the tradition of the Hellenizers, the Pharisees, the second movement or 'philosophy' considered by Josephus, were the successors to those 'Hasidim' or 'pious ones', mostly laymen, who had supported the armed religious revolt under Mattathias. Down the years they continued to provide an opposition to the Sadducees, and from the time of John Hyrcanus, and particularly in the reigns of Alexander Jannaeus and his widow Salome, they were sufficiently coherent to become a political ally of the royal house. Their name, really a nickname, meant 'separated', though of itself it offers no clue as to what they were separated from. Clearly they had a deep zeal for the Law, and their wearing of phylacteries (small leather boxes containing Hebrew texts) and long tassels to their cloaks made them stand out as easily recognizable aspirants to a piety not easily accessible to ordinary men.

The Pharisees were certainly separate from the Sadducees, with their own influence on national life. While the Sadducees, because of their wealth, priestly status, control of the Temple, domination of the Sanhedrin, and readiness to negotiate with the alien occupiers, exercized their power at the centre, Jerusalem, the influence of the Pharisees was more felt in the rural areas of Judea, and in the other tetrarchies of the Jewish kingdom. Here they controlled the synagogues in each town, where weekly services were held, and the scriptures read and expounded, and where Jewish children were educated. This was a less dramatic exercize of power, but it was far-reaching and more durable than that of the Sadducees, who disappeared after the Jewish war of 70 A.D.

The Pharisees were exclusive in their nationalism, jealous for the preservation of the Jewish way of life. With the Sadducees they accepted the divine authority of the Law revealed to Moses as recorded in scripture; but they supplemented this with what they called 'the Tradition of the Elders', an oral tradition by which the written Law, not relevant to the many new circumstances of life in first century Palestine, was brought up to date and kept as a guide of authority to contemporary man. So the Pharisees tried to make obedience to the Law easier and more generally accepted. In two ways they failed: first came the paradoxical consequence that the very device calculated to make respect for and obedience to the Law easier and more general actually achieved the precise opposite. There were some 613 'commandments of the Law' applicable to daily contemporary living; this was far too many for the ordinary man to take in. Second, even among the Pharisaic interpreters of the Law there were considerable differences of interpretation. Two schools of thought were in conflict, one with a stricter interpretation associated with the name of Shammai, the other more lenient and associated with Hillel. Pharisaic emphasis on the Law was rooted in the conviction that obedience to it was part of Israel's duty under the covenant which God had made with his people. Disobedience inevitably and rightly brought punishment; the Pharisees saw the Roman occupation itself as a punishment for national sins. Only complete obedience to God's Law could pave the way for that promised divine intervention which would inaugurate the new Israel in the imperishable glory of the Messianic age.

So the Pharisees waited with the Sadducees and others in apocalyptic expectancy and their own law-abiding hope for the coming of 'the day'. When it dawned many of them would be ready, like the 'pious ones' in 167 B.C., to take up arms against the oppressor. This meant that they were interested in any apparent Messianic symptoms in Jewish life (cf. John 1.19, 24). If they were not actual political activists, they were political optimists, expecting an ultimate future (which might begin very soon) in which the final reign of God would be universally and irrevocably established.

⸺he gospels seem to leave their readers with an inescapably bad impression of the Pharisees. Certainly a long-surviving anti-Pharisee and anti-Jewish attitude in the Christian Church has made it difficult to review the gospel evidence impartially. Doubtless the controversies between the early Church and Judaism which continued long after the death and resurrection of Jesus account for much of the critical tenor of the evangelists. But it would be quite wrong to suppose that there was no controversy in Jesus's own lifetime. On the contrary, Jesus made his own call to a strict observance of the Law (Mat. 5.17-20), but he also claimed that the Law required 'fulfilment' rather than the 'supplementation' proposed and taught by the Pharisees. What fulfilment meant he explained in the Sermon on the Mount (see below, pp.131-8) – but the Pharisees found that his practice of fulfilling the Law was, in their view, simply breaking it (Mark 3.1ff.). Yet he had friends and disciples among the Pharisees, such as Nicodemus (John 3.1; 19.39), and possibly also Joseph of Arimathea (Mark 15.43). He was as ready to sit at table with them as he was with any other fellow –Jew (Luke 7.36; 11.37; 14.1). Such evidence should lead to a less partial judgment of the Pharisees. Even Matthew 23 can and ought to be seen, not as seven curses on hated opponents, but as seven woeful conditions of those who know that the Law needs accommodating to new conditions of life, but refuse to penetrate to its depth, adding pettifogging regulation to pettifogging regulation until all respect for the Law is destroyed, and human life tragically impoverished. The 'Woes' on the Pharisees are nothing but the counterpart of the 'Beatitudes' on the citizens of the kingdom of Heaven in the Sermon on the Mount; they indicate the entirely different situation of those who choose to remain under the Law from those who, with Jesus, seek its fulfilment. 'The Law came by Moses; grace and truth came through Jesus Christ' (John 1.17). Jesus knew the Law was an indispensable aid to man; but it could only properly serve its function in the realm of grace and truth.

It is thus possible to recognize the depth and importance of the conflict that the Pharisees had with Jesus and at the same time to commend the great moral and spiritual contribution they made, not only to the Jewish people, but to the whole civilized world. They talked much about the Law; but they also spoke much of God's love. They sought his help, and his pardon, and looked for his reign. They were ready to serve him in bad times and in good, and to crown their service, if need be, with their lives. It is not surprising that the differences between such leaders and Jesus should be profound, and open to misunderstanding by those unable to appreciate their depth and gravity.

Zealots

So much for the 'philosophies' as Josephus calls them, of the two 'establishment' parties in the Jewish state. They held in common the belief that the only legitimate and true ruler of Israel was God himself, but they had very different attitudes to the Roman power that was usurping that divine prerogative. There were also two non-establishment or non-conformist philosophies or movements, each with its own reaction to the situation in which the Jewish people found themselves.

First of these was that of the Zealots, who can be called political activists in contrast to the Pharisees who were political quietists and the Sadducees who were political diplomats. If God was the true king of Israel, then, claimed the Zealots, his subjects must fight for him and resist any human usurper. Josephus reports that Judas of Galilee began the movement when in 6 A.D. a census was ordered in preparation for turning Judea from a tetrarchy to a province under direct Roman rule. But that is more a tribute to Judas than a fact of history, for the story of such resistance goes back at least as far as the bands of Jews who came to support Mattathias against Antiochus in 167 B.C. (1 Macc. 2.29-44). But at the time of the census Judas of Galilee did raise a (Messianic?) revolt.

In the nature of things the Zealot phenomenon had an inter-mittent rather than a continuous public history. Resistance flared up at particular crises, but the embers were kept alive in between by the bands of devoted Jews who were always ready for action. The best modern parallel of them is the formation in occupied or oppressed territories of rural and urban guerillas, who are always in existence, ready for any emergency, and somehow make some sort of a livelihood in various ways. Josephus's favourite word for a Zealot was 'robber' or 'brigand'. The name 'Zealot' indicates the true religious fervour which inspired Zealot activity, while the term 'robber' or 'brigand' (or even better 'Jewish guerilla') suggests the form of activity which the Zealots followed.

The Greek word for 'robber' comes from a word meaning 'booty makers'; and the term was first used of foreign soldiers. But the Jewish guerillas really made their 'livelihood' by obtaining booty. They waylaid travellers and robbed them (Luke 10.30), raided selected targets, robbed persons in the street, and resorted to other forms of predatory violence. The word 'robber' illuminates those passages in the gospels where it is found. The (evident) Jew who 'fell in with robbers' (Luke 10.30) was one of their victims, who had evidently put up some resistance to the loss of his goods, or he would not have been left 'half dead'. Jesus accused the Jewish authorities of turning the Temple in Jerusalem into a 'robbers' den', a guerilla headquarters where the 'robbers' shared out their spoils. Jesus may well have been intentionally commenting on the profitable trading carried on within the Temple precincts, but to accuse the authorities of turning the Temple into a brigand headquarters was a much more serious matter. The clue is given in the passage from scripture which Jesus quoted: 'Does not scripture

say, "My house shall be called a house of prayer for all the nations?"
But you have made it a robbers' cave' (Mark 11.17). This can only
mean that the Jewish authorities had treated the gifts that God had
intended to be shared with all nations as if they were robbers' booty,
to be shared out among themselves in their 'cave'. So Jesus showed
that he accepted the teachings of Second Isaiah (chs. 40-55), Jonah
and Ruth, among Old Testament books, rather than the restrictive
nationalism that had derived from the work of Ezra and Nehemiah.

In the story of the Passion the evangelists record that when Judas
and the armed band came out to arrest Jesus he asked, 'Have you
come out against me as against a robber, with swords and clubs to
capture me?' (Mark 14.48). He added that the fact that he taught
openly in the Temple every day sufficed to show that he was no
brigand or guerilla. Finally at his crucifixion the titulus fastened to
the cross indicated that he was condemned as a 'robber' or
'guerilla', for it read 'Jesus of Nazareth, King of the Jews' – which
implied that the convicted man was a 'Zealot', 'robber' or 'brigand'.
Perhaps the strangest irony was that Jesus was crucified between
two robbers (indicating that he was but another?), while the person
the crowd chose to be set free rather than Jesus was Barabbas, and
'Barabbas was a robber'.

Yet it has to be admitted that to those hostile to Jesus certain
things about him could have suggested that he was a 'Zealot'. He
not only proclaimed that God alone should be the one ruler of
Israel; he preached the good news that his reign had already begun.
He went about with a band of disciples, as many other Zealots did.
And the act of cleansing the Temple must have suggested to
officialdom that a Zealot rising was neither improbable nor distant.
How near, and yet how far, from the real truth!

Essenes

For his fourth philosophy or sect of the Jews Josephus chose a
group known as the Essenes. The name probably derives from a
word meaning 'the pious ones', which serves to recall those 'pious
ones' who supported Mattathias in his revolt. The movement
certainly seems to have originated about the middle of the second
century B.C., possibly with those who seceded from the Temple
with the ill-fated Onias III. Josephus reports that the Essenes were
radically opposed to the Sadducees' theocratic bureaucracy in
Jerusalem, objecting to the Temple cult and its animal sacrifices,

and to the adaptation or supplementation of the Law by the Pharisees. They therefore left the areas under easy surveillance from Jerusalem and settled in the desert country west of the Dead Sea. Here they lived as an ascetic, monastic community, with a life style appropriate to the new Israel, to 'prepare the way of the Lord' (Isa. 40.3; Mark 1.3). Their community comprised both priests and laymen. Priests were not allowed to marry, though they did adopt children; lay members could marry. They lived in strict obedience to the Law, and, instead of the animal sacrifices of the Temple, they practised purificatory baptisms or lustrations to purge away the stain of sin. They required entrants to the community to undergo a three-year probation, and to surrender all personal property upon entry; they held all things in common (cp. Acts 4.32). Josephus reports that they had members in 'every city' from the north of Samaria to the south of Judea, so they were able to exert a considerable influence upon contemporary life. Much more has become known about one such community since the discovery of the Dead Sea Scrolls at Khirbet Qumran. Reviewing the life of the community helps one grasp more fully the social and religious environment in which Jesus worked and spoke.

The Qumran community was another group of Jews who deliberately rejected the leadership of the aristocratic bureaucracy in Jerusalem; they lived in the desert west of the Dead Sea. They were also part of the quite wide movement for lustration or baptism, which sought a way to moral and ritual purity other than that provided by the Temple and its (animal) sacrificial system. It was moreover a community of priests and laymen, though its priests were Zadokite, i.e. of Aaronic descent (see footnote, p.61). The movement was strongly and narrowly nationalist; they exceeded even the Pharisees in patriotic zeal.

The priests exercized the legal and juridical functions of the community, which had as its general governing body a General Assembly (cp. Acts 6.2; 15.12), which admitted new members, prescribed punishments for rule-breakers, and re-admitted properly penitent offenders. A two-year probation was required of all applicants to the community, and, as with the Essenes, all private property had to be surrendered upon entry. The community was strictly hierarchical, each member owing obedience to his immediate superior. The Law was, of course, their rule of life; and arrangements were made for its study 'day and night' (Ps. 1.2). There was a common meal, open to full members only, at which the bread and wine received priestly blessing. There were frequent lustrations or 'baptisms', by which members could keep themselves morally and ritually pure. The sect also used a lunar calendar rather than the solar one followed by the establishment.

The community looked out on the times in apocalyptic expectation. It saw in the world two spirits at war – the spirit of light or good, and the spirit of darkness or evil (Belial). They looked forward to the coming of two Messiahs, an Aaronic Messiah, a priestly figure, and an Israelite Messiah, a figure of Davidic descent, the former having precedence over the latter. The end of all things seemed imminent. When it came it would bring a war of cosmic dimensions, for which their carefully nurtured moral and ritual purity would render them proper participants. The salvation ensuing from that war would establish the righteous in eternal bliss, with a new heaven and a new earth (Isa. 65.17; 66.22; 2 Pet. 3.13; Rev. 21.1); a new Jerusalem (Isa. 65.18; Rev. 3.12; 21.2); and a new perfect manhood for the redeemed (Isa. 55.3; Jer. 31.33f.; Ezek. 37.26ff.).

From this brief review it is clear that the Qumran and Essene communities offered to the Jews of the time a way of living under Rome, as distinct from that of the establishment in Jerusalem as from that of the other dissenting movement, the Zealots. They declined any 'deal' with Rome, brooked no 'easing' of the Law, and rejected the initiation of military action. They lived, so they believed, the Law-abiding life that God demanded, and so waited for the day when by his intervention, in the arrival of the Messiahs, the final conflict would begin. They kept themselves in every way prepared and ready to join that battle, knowing that the end would be a world remade forever by their faithful God. But this alternative was not just a pious imagining in monastic retreat, but an active missionary crusade in all the Jewish tetrarchies as well. The Qumran community, like the Essene, had lay members in all the major centres of population, spreading its ideas, and gaining recruits for the community. Luke states that John the Baptist was 'in the desert' until the day of his public appearance – which probably implies that he was in touch with some community or communities similar to the Qumran – or even the Qumran itself. As will become clear, there is a good deal of similarity between the Qumran sect, its practice and teaching, and that of John the Baptist, and even of Jesus himself.

The defiance of despair

One ingredient in the Qumran recipe for Jewish life under Roman occupation needs special mention: the apocalyptic ideas which increasingly affected sectarian and public opinion, and received literary expression in the first and second centuries B.C. and A.D. Jesus and his company may never have seen the literature itself, but there is much to suggest that its ideas had a significant influence on them.

Apocalyptic was related to the particular political and religious situation of the Jews of Palestine. Their position, though not desperate, could understandably induce despair. The nation chosen by the one true God to be his own special people, to which he had made many promises of a glorious future through the prophets, now found itself in the humiliating position of an occupied territory, governed, oppressed and taxed by an apparently irresistible world Gentile power. Had God's arm been shortened that it could no longer save (Isa. 50.2)? Or was Israel still paying dearly for national sins (Isa. 59.2-15)? And if that were so, would there not come a time when all her penalties had been paid (Isa. 40.2)? There was no reassuring answer to be found to such questions, either in a review of the recent past, or in an assessment of the possibilities of the foreseeable or even more distant future. Was there any message for God's people that could defy or destroy an otherwise unavoidable despair? Apocalyptic gave the inspired and inspiring answer.

An apocalypse is literally an 'uncovering'. For the encouragement and hope of the Jews the apocalyptists uncovered the future – not simply the immediate future, which seemed dark, nor even the more distant future, which was inevitably uncertain, but the ultimate future, when God would have settled all his accounts, both with Israel and with all the Gentile nations, and would establish his final, universal and indestructible order in true prosperity, piety, justice and peace. In that final assertion of divine authority Israel would be given her promised primacy among the nations. The apocalyptists developed their own imaginative and powerful ways of communicating how that would be done.

They used the simple device of pseudonymity, putting into the mouth of some known and trusted figure from the past a series of predictions. To the contemporary Jew some of the predictions would have appeared to be, what in fact they really were, accurate enough narratives of what had brought Judaism to its present plight, and he would therefore have been encouraged to believe that any further predictions would prove equally reliable in fulfilment. Such names as Daniel, Baruch, Moses, the Twelve Patriarchs, Esdras and Zephaniah were all used in this way. One of the most influential of them was First or Ethiopian Enoch, which was certainly in some sort of circulation in Jesus's time, and which left its mark on his thought and teaching. A brief resumé of the work will be useful.

The author ascribes his book to Enoch, the long-lived ancient who 'walked with God' for 365 years, and then 'was seen no more, because God had taken him away' (Gen. 5.24), so making him a very credible witness to the divine will and purpose that his predictions were to disclose. The whole history of Israel, from the 'fall of the angels' (Gen. 6.1f.) to the Maccabean revolt (1 Macc. 2.1 etc.) would then have appeared to be pure prediction from the lips of Enoch – a very considerable commendation of his reliability! After this follows a dream vision of Enoch, and an account of his journeys through the earth and the underworld of Sheol. Then come the three Similitudes of Enoch (chs. 37 – 61). The first similitude tells of the final judgment, when all sinners will be expelled, and a lasting inheritance provided for the righteous under the Elect One of Righteousness and Faith. The second similitude predicts a new heaven and a new earth, with the Elect One enthroned in glory. Then the Son of Man appears, described in much the same way as in Daniel 7.14 (see p.49) and said to have been named 'before the sun and the stars were created'. Here too is foretold the resurrection of the dead, who will be judged by the Elect One. The third similitude gives details of the final judgment of the saints and of the wicked. In the next section (chs. 72-82) there is a discussion, significant in view of Enoch's age of 365 years at his 'translation', of questions of astronomy and the calendar. There follows (chs. 83-90), in the form of dream visions, a brief review (though really a 'preview' from Enoch's perspective) of world history, from the fall of the angels (Gen. 6.1f.) to the Maccabean revolt, concluding (ch. 90) with a vision of the new Jerusalem that is still to come. This section displays another general feature of apocalyptic writing, the use of imagery calculated to be intelligible to the intended reader, but harmlessly meaningless to an 'outsider', especially an enemy or an oppressor. Finally (chs. 91-105), Enoch advises his children in a summary exhortation:

When they write down truthfully all my words in their languages, and do not change or minish aught from my words, but write them all down truthfully – all that I first testified concerning them, then, I know another mystery, that books shall be given to the righteous and the wise to become a cause of joy and uprightness and much wisdom. And to them shall the books be given, and they shall believe in them and rejoice over them, and then shall all the righteous who have learnt therefrom all the paths of righteousness be recompensed. . . . For I and My Son will be united with them for ever in the paths of uprightness in their lives; and ye shall have peace: rejoice, ye children of uprightness. Amen (1 Enoch 104.11f.; 105.2).

Every Jew found the apocalyptic message heartening. God was still in complete control of the world – how else could Enoch have predicted all history from the fall of the angels to the present time? The assurance that God would soon bring the present age to an end and inaugurate the final age of righteousness and peace meant that the fortunes of Israel were on the brink of final restoration. Such an assurance, with the confident expectation of a Messianic deliverance, no doubt confirmed the Sadducees in their attempts to secure meanwhile the best possible deal for the nation and its political and religious institutions. The Pharisees would have found support for their concern to bring the whole nation to immediate full obedience to the Law, and to prepare to recognize the Messiah when he came, and support him in the inevitable war of liberation that would restore to Israel her destined primacy among the nations. The Zealots would certainly have seen themselves as the 'advance guard' of the new order, infiltrating into the old, and beginning in it the Messianic task of making God's enemies their 'footstool' (cf. Mark 12.36). But the Qumran and desert communities generally interpreted apocalyptic differently, finding in it the basis and support for a twofold policy: to live, even within the present age, the obedient life of the age to come, in the holiness and righteousness of a reformed non-sacrificial religion; and to be prepared when the Messiah arrived to do battle with and for him against his enemies. Pacifist they certainly were for the present; but they were ready for fierce and fanatical conflict in the Messianic future.

Miscellaneous movements

Scribes

In the Old Testament, as in the Near East generally, a scribe was either a copyist (Baruch in Jer. 31.4) or, as even in the New Testament (Acts 19.35), an important civil servant, often the equivalent of a modern Secretary of State (cf. Seraiah, 2 Sam. 8.17). It is therefore significant that this high title was given to Ezra, who was called 'a scribe learned in the Law of Moses' (Ezra 7.6). Ezra was a priest, but his scribal duties lay in the study and exposition of the Law, and in delivering judgments on that basis of it. In such ways the scribes made their considerable contribution to Jewish life.

They had a noble history. In the Maccabean revolt they made up a delegation that approached Alcimus and Bacchides to ask for justice. They met with a friendly reception, only to have sixty of their number treacherously massacred. In Jesus's day they were respected as those who pursued the highest activity possible to man, the study and exposition of the Law, and its application to human life. Scribes had no official position, but were voluntarily given authority, sitting 'in Moses' seat'(the place of authority) in the synagogues. They were a 'closed order', for admission demanded training and ordination. They received no monetary reward for their scribal services, and many of them had to earn their livelihood by practising some other trade, just as Paul, himself once a scribe, earned his livelihood as a tent maker during his ministries to the Christian Church (Acts 20.34; 1 Thess. 2.9; 2 Thess. 3.8). Their task was said to be 'to put a fence around the Law', i.e. to enable every Jew to live within the Law, without need or excuse to act 'outside it' and so transgress. This inevitably required additions and modifications (see above, pp. 73f), and the scribes were responsible for the development of the oral tradition. They were thus by no means die-hard conservatives, but men ready to move forward with the times, and meet the new demands of the age. The lack of a central scribal authority meant that differences arose on a number of points; in the time of Jesus these were focussed in the differences between the two scribal schools of Shammai (the more rigorous) and Hillel (the more lenient and accommodating).

Matthew and Luke often couple scribes and Pharisees together, and there is no doubt that their collaboration was very close, and their joint influence considerable. Yet Luke presents Jesus as making some distinction in their responsibilities for the religious situation of the Judaism he knew. He recognized the scribes as that part of the Jewish establishment concerned with theology and religious training (Luke 11.45-52), and the Pharisees as those whose concern it was that religion should not only be accepted but publicly seen to be so (Luke 11.39-42, 44). The real tragedy for Judaism was that the two groups combined to jeopardize the very thing they wanted to preserve.

But it must not be supposed that all Jesus's relations with the scribes and Pharisees were negative and critical. He was ready to accept invitations to dine with Pharisees (Luke 7.36; 11.37; 14.1), and at least one consulted him on a very positive enquiry (Nicodemus, John 3.1). Joseph of Arimethea (Mat. 27.57) was a member of the Sanhedrin, and either a Pharisee or a scribe. Matthew tells of a scribe who professed his readiness to follow Jesus (Mat. 8.19), and even if that offer did not prove fruitful it seems that Jesus recognized that some scribes became 'learners in the kingdom of Heaven' (Mat. 13.52). And Mark tells of the scribe who answered Jesus so 'wisely' that Jesus said to him, 'You are not far from the kingdom of God' (Mark 12.34). It would be strange indeed had the emergence of a new teacher such as Jesus produced no conflict with the establishment; it would have been stranger still had that conflict not raised all the fundamental issues of religion, or had it not continued after the death of Jesus between Judaism and the Christian Church.

Herodians

Very little is known about the Herodians, but they were evidently strong and influential enough for the Pharisees to think an alliance with them on certain issues worthwhile. Their name suggests that they were politically rather than religiously orientated; the most probable explanation is that they worked for a return from government by procurator to government by an Herodian king, presumably Herod Antipas. That would be consistent both with the few references to them in the gospels, and with the fourth century A.D. report that they believed Herod to be the Messiah.

Galileans

Little is known of the Galileans, save what Josephus has to tell. They were, he says, of an extreme Pharisaic outlook, and originated at the rising led by Judas of Galilee in 6 A.D. Jesus was then a growing adolescent, and would have known something of the penalties that were exacted from the rebels. Josephus says of them that 'they have an inviolable attachment to liberty; and they say that God is to be their only ruler and Lord. They also do not value [have no fear of] dying any kinds of death, nor indeed do they heed the deaths of their relations and friends, nor can any such fear make them call any man "Lord"' (Jospehus, Ant. 18.1.6).

The New Testament has a clear reference to one of them, the founder, Judas of Galilee, cited by Gamaliel in his plea for the Apostles before the Sanhedrin (Acts 5.37). In every other instance the word 'Galilean' could have no more than a simple geographical implication. But Luke could be referring to these extremists when he tells of news reaching Jesus concerning Galileans whose blood Pilate had mixed with their sacrifices. The presence of such men in the Temple could well have occasioned sufficient disturbance for Pilate to have intervened savagely with his troops. One other possible reference to them may be found in John, when he reports that Jesus came to Galilee and 'the Galileans welcomed him, having seen all that he had done in Jerusalem at the feast, for they too had gone to the feast' (John 4.45). Does this refer to a band of 'Galileans', who could evidently cause trouble in the Temple themselves, and who, having been in Jerusalem when Jesus cleansed the Temple (according to John's chronology), now wanted to give him an allies' welcome, hoping that they might find in him a powerful recruit for their guerilla movement?

Economic, social and religious stratification

Finally, in a review of the world into which Jesus came, it is appropriate to look beyond the various movements of Judaism to those 'unphilosophic' citizens who failed to identify themselves with any of the groups so far examined.

It has been said of the Palestine of Jesus's time that it was, like many another eastern country, a land of the very rich and the very poor. That may be as much information as one phrase can convey, but it by no means gives a full or balanced picture of the Jewish society of the time.

When Jesus sent a message to John the Baptist in answer to his question as to whether Jesus was 'the one who was to come', he ended with the surprising words, 'and the poor are hearing the good news' (Mat. 11.5). The 'poor' certainly included a large part of Judaism, but they were spread over a fairly wide range of economic circumstances. They included, for example, the artisan class, who would often be the owners of small family businesses – 'petits entrepreneurs' – just as Joseph owned the carpenter's business in Nazareth. There would not have been dire poverty in such a home; but when Jesus's parents attended the Temple for his 'presentation', they offered the alternative sacrifice open to the poor – two pigeons instead of a lamb and a pigeon (Lev. 12.6-8; Luke 2.22ff.). These same considerations would also apply to the four Galilean fishermen who left their family businesses to follow Jesus and become part of his community.

But poorer people there were. The peasants farmed strips of land from which they derived but an exiguous livelihood; the land was not very fertile, and there were rents, taxes and tithes to be paid. Life was very hard for them. There were also the unskilled labourers, the sort of men who are the subject of Matthew's parable of the workers in the vineyard (Mat. 20.1-16). They provided the reservoir of the unemployed, who could be hired by the day at whatever wage proved negotiable – usually low. Then there were the outcasts, who had no real standing in Jewish society, or place in its economy. It is instructive to classify them in terms relative to a modern 'welfare state': the physically and mentally handicapped, i.e. the blind, the crippled, the lame and the deformed, the leper, the 'possessed' and the lunatic; the 'Quislings', i.e. those who worked for the Roman occupying power, among them particularly the tax officials; the racially or religiously undesirable, the Samaritans, Gentiles and half-Jews; and the orphans. For all these, so much assisted in a modern welfare state, life was very hard, and poverty dire. Inevitably there was much begging (Mark 10.46; John 9.8); Luke tells a story of one unfortunate poor man who was carried to the house of a rich man in the hope that he might receive some of the scraps of food that were thrown away (Luke 16.20). Yet, as still today, begging was an embarrassing shame to the economically secure (Luke 16.3).

There is no evidence that the poor had any organized movement to resist the established economic order, but it is clear that they were as eager as any to welcome the appearance of the Messiah and his kingdom of peace and plenty. They were very different from the poor of later Europe who, in the toils of a newly developing industrial society, lost touch with their ancestors' religion; they were still, within their limits (inadequate, though, for the Pharisees) loyal Jews, and as devout as their circumstances allowed. They were hardly susceptible to a call for economic rebellion; but they did understand the promise of a Messiah and his bountiful rule.

The people of the land

This is a classification rather than a group of people, of religious rather than social origin. Originally the term was applied to the populace, the citizenry, the 'people', in a quite neutral sense (Gen. 23.7; 42.6; 2 Kings 11.14; 21.24), but from the time of Ezra, the phrase acquired a derogatory meaning. The exiles who returned from Babylon to Jerusalem to rebuild the city and the Temple were opposed and hindered in their work by the people they found in the land on their return, who showed no concern for the Temple or for the religion it served, nor any respect for the Law which was so sacred to Israel. So 'people of the land' came to be used disparagingly of anyone who did not know, or study, or care for, the Law. To be a good Jew it was necessary to obey the Law; to obey it meant to know it; and to know it meant studying it. But such study was hardly practicable for the many groups of the 'poor' as such. The time and energy taken up in eking out the most meagre of livelihoods left them with little energy and no motivation for the official demands of piety. It is this situation which may well be the background of Jesus's word to John the Baptist that 'the poor were hearing the good news'. He may well have been speaking of the 'people of the land' rather than simply of the economically poor.

'People of the land' were found in all sections of the community, among the wealthy as among the indigent poor; among the artisans (Jesus and his disciples included), as well as the unemployed. Being poor was not in itself an evil; but to be ignorant of, untutored in or indifferent to the Law was to invite – and receive – the wholesale condemnation of all Law-loving Jews. For such 'poor' people of the land there was no hope in Judaism, for they were not admissible entrants to the Messianic kingdom. The good news that Jesus brought them was that the kingdom was already here, and that they could enter it forthwith, in true repentance for national and individual sins, and in trustful acceptance of the forgiveness of God. This could well have been the climax to Jesus's activity, as he reported it to John the Baptist. The Messianic 'signs', the works of healing, exorcism and feeding, might well have done no more than open up a new life in the present age; but the good news that the kingdom of God had arrived, and that its doors were open, meant that a new life was opening up to a new age, a new world, endless in time, and universal in scope. No one had ever made such good news available before. No wonder that 'the common people heard him gladly' (Mark 12.38).

2

JESUS IN THE JUDAISM OF HIS TIME

Jesus grew up as one of at least nine members of the household of a significant citizen of Nazareth, Joseph, owner of the town's carpentry business. Besides Jesus there were the parents, Joseph and Mary; four other sons, with interesting names: James (=Jacob) and Joseph, after two of the great patriarchs of Israel, and Simon and Judas, after two heroes of the Maccabean revolt; and at least two sisters (Mat. 13.55f). The boys' names (that of Jesus included) indicate that it was an enthusiastically nationalist family, entirely appropriate to Galilee, where nationalist feelings were stronger and more militant than in Judea. There would have been much talk in the home about the resented Roman occupation, and the growing hopes of a speedy deliverance through the coming of a Messiah who would liberate Israel and establish the peace and plenty of the Messiah's kingdom. In 6 A.D. discussion would have focussed on the unsuccessful rebellion of Judas of Galilee, which would have left an indelible impression on the sensitive adolescent Jesus, who would have heard, and possibly seen, something of the crucifixion of the rebels. It is possible that Mary and her kinswoman Elizabeth kept up visiting each other; that would have meant Jesus knowing John for many years, and learning directly from him about his years in the desert (Luke 1.80), and about the life and teaching and hopes of the dissenting sects.

The home in which Jesus grew up was neither very rich nor very poor, but typical of much of the best of Judaism at the time. It was devout, but not excessively so; preserving the rhythms of personal prayer, attendance at the synagogue and an occasional journey to the Temple in Jerusalem, it kept alive the essential simplicities of Jewish religion. Jesus would have attended the local synagogue school, and there received an education meant to prepare him for a responsible life as a member of the nation which God had chosen for his special service in and for the world. He would have seen the scribes at their work, and doubtless developed an admiration and respect for them. On the Sabbath he would have gone with his family to share in the simple worship of the synagogue with its rhythm of psalms and prayers, scripture and sermons. He would surely have observed with a penetrating but understanding eye the behaviour of various sections of the congregation: the scribes in their place of authority, the Pharisees whose concern for the Law and zeal for God was exhibited in an observing – and observable – piety. In his movements about Nazareth and the surrounding countryside his keen eye and judgment would not only have noted the groupings already reviewed; but he would have sensed their tensions and hostilities, which constituted a real threat to the truly fruitful work of a people of God. He could not have avoided noticing the manifest ostracisms among his people – the rejection of the 'sinners', the tax-gatherers, the lepers and the demon-possessed. He would have heard talk of Zealots, and disciples of Qumran or the Essenes, seeking recruits for their movements. He would have known something of the cruel punishments meted out to rebels against Rome, Messianic or otherwise.

It is not too much to suppose that even by the time of his adolescence, coinciding as it did with the revolt of Judas of Galilee, Jesus would have realized that something needed to be done on God's behalf for God's people, and felt that he must have something to do with it. When his parents found him in the Temple at Jerusalem, and expressed their anxiety at having lost him, he responded to them with the words (according to one quite possible translation of the Greek) 'Did you not know that I have got to be busy with my Father's affairs?' (Luke 2.49). Luke could hardly have preserved the story for any lesser reason than to reveal an early indication of his sense of a divine call.

3

THE SHAPE OF A GOSPEL

Even the very brief review of gospel criticism which was made on pp.12-16 shows how courageously honest New Testament critics have been in pointing out the very considerable diversity of material and variety of judgment that the gospels contain. For they have been found to be composed from a number of written sources, incorporating in themselves many different individual items drawn from an obviously plentiful oral tradition. Even the work of the redaction (see above, p.15) critics, who have tried to understand and reveal the religious and theological motives which caused each evangelist to give his gospel the particular content, order and significance that it has, is unable to reduce their joint testimony to unity. The gospel tradition remains firmly varied.

Yet there is one thing that the four gospels share, different though they are from each other: all have a certain 'shape'. Each gospel tells of the ministry of Jesus from the time of his baptism in the Jordan by John the Baptist up to the time of his crucifixion and death outside Jerusalem. Each prepares his readers for that story with a prologue, and each supplements it with an epilogue.

Gospel prologues

The gospels differ considerably as to the content and length of the prologue provided. Mark's is the earliest and simplest. It includes a brief account of the ministry of John the Baptist (Mark 1.2-8), and a reference linking that ministry with the great tradition of Hebrew prophecy (Mark 1.2f.), thus anchoring John's ministry firmly to the history of Israel. Matthew and Luke add considerably to that, in an expanded narrative about John (Mat. 3.1-12; Luke 1.5-23, 57-80; 3.1-20), genealogical trees, and in nativity stories that have overtones of a legendary nature for the modern sophisticated ear, such as angelic communications, a virgin birth, tributes to the infant Jesus from significant personages, and so on. The fourth gospel also includes the story of John the Baptist (John 1.6-8, 19-37; 3.23-30; 4.1; 5.33; 10.41) but the prologue consists chiefly of a Hymn to the Divine Word, which not only links Jesus to the history of Israel, but plants him firmly among the divine work of creation and providence. The gospel prologues were clearly intended to prepare the reader to see the events recorded and the central figure portrayed as the focus of all historical occasions.

This reflects back to the doubts of modern scholars about the historicity of the gospel narratives, which were written, in their view, from the distorted and distorting perspective of the resurrection. After the resurrection the evangelists undoubtedly would have seen the events of Jesus's ministry as they had not generally been seen in his lifetime – but whether that constituted a change from accuracy to falsity or from falsity to accuracy is a matter for investigation and discussion. There are three main reasons why the critical assessment must be greatly modified if not wholly rejected. First, in such a review of already experienced events it is more than likely that the evangelists or disciples would have been in the position of the musical listener described on p.21, who hears a new piece of music for the second time: he hears it more accurately, and understands it far better, than on the first hearing. He knows more of what he heard on the first hearing. Second, the critic's complaint of distortion may well be no more than a reflection of the fact that what the evangelists have done is to indicate, with the limited means at their disposal (so different and so sparse compared with those available today), what was really going on in what took place. That is an indispensable part of being an historian rather than an annalist. Of course historians can err, and see things in a distorted way; in a world of relativities that would seem to some extent inevitable. But there is nothing inherently wrong in events having a very different 'look' at a date later than their historical occurrence. Indeed it would be better to recognize that 'events' do not have a 'momentary' occurrence, but are rather continuing occasions, so that one event flows into another, covering varying periods of time. In this way the 'event' of Magna Carta was not just the affixing of a royal signature to a piece of parchment on the island of Runnymede in 1215, but one critical focal point of an event that will continue for as long as men fight for their individual liberty. Third, these two reflections are supported by the way in which the evangelists describe events in the lifetime of Jesus which did not convey to those present at the time the real meaning (what was going on) which they came to see in the light of the resurrection. Such were, for example, Peter's insight at Caesarea Philippi (Jesus had immediately to begin to interpret Peter's insight to him and the Twelve), the experience of the 'inner three' on the Mount of Transfiguration a little later (Mark 9.2-8), and the cleansing of the Temple (John 2.22). The evangelists, it seems, do not 'distort' events in any way contrary to the veracity that integrity demands.

The gospels are certainly not professional historical works, but, like histories, they are concerned with much more than 'what took place'. Fundamentally they are attempts to indicate 'what was going on in what took place', and their prologues were designed to help their readers to understand from the start what was going on in the life of Jesus. Mark says, 'The prophetic understanding of Israel's history will find its promise completely fulfilled in the story I am about to tell.' Matthew states that in the story of Jesus there will be told the story of the creation of a new Israel, a new people of God, a new community of the children of Abraham. Luke asserts that in Jesus there has been started a new humanity, just as in Adam the old humanity had begun. John proclaims that in Jesus God has 'made all things new'; for there is in him a 'new creation', as there was a first creation 'in the beginning'.

The prologues imply two things: first, that the evangelists believed that when they or other believers witnessed the events of the life of Jesus they neither saw him as he really was, nor perceived what was really going on; and second, that this was a much greater and more dangerous distortion than any reorientation of their perspective in the light of their post-resurrection experiences and insights. It was the contemporaneous observation of Jesus that was the real distortion. The resurrection freed the evangelists from a false perspective on events and persons and brought them to a true one – the precise opposite of what many modern critics affirm.

The evangelists were concerned to spare their readers the

frustration of first learning about Jesus from a false perspective and then going on to learn all over again from the true one. And that was not simply the historian's desire to present his historical figure accurately. Jesus was more than a figure who had appeared in history, and in whose life – as in the lives, say, of David, Solomon and the Maccabean heroes – the history of Israel had been temporarily focussed. Jesus differed from these others in two ways: it was not only the history and destiny of Israel that focussed upon him, but the history and destiny of all mankind; and it focussed upon him not only up to the moment of his death, but focusses upon him still. Jesus was not someone who had 'ceased to be' and could therefore no longer be the focus of events. He had lived and died, like other men; but he had risen from the dead, and was, and still is, alive for ever more. All the history of man and his world, past, present and future, focusses on him. He is the one figure in human history whose life both embodies and conveys the meaning of it all. The gospel prologues were written to prepare their readers for such an incredible truth.

Gospel histories

The central section of each gospel sets out in its own fashion the story of Jesus's ministry so that its readers can not only learn for themselves what took place in it, but also perceive what went on. To achieve this end the evangelists used devices which are not easily regarded as valid by twentieth century readers. It is very important to 'decode' correctly the 'going on' indicators. If these are understood as 'taking place' affirmations, then the evangelists are reduced from historians, albeit biassed historians, to mere annalists. The gospels are not then understood at their proper intended depth. The story of the feeding of the five thousand is an excellent case in point. The narrative has sometimes been treated as no more than a bare statement of what took place. Modern sophisticated man then understandably says, 'Such things can't happen and don't happen: I can't believe a word of it!' But that is to miss the whole point of the story. For it is clear from its setting in each gospel, from the words and phrases used in its telling, from its exposition in the synoptic gospels, and particularly from its interpretation in the fourth gospel, that the incident was meant to convey the good news that in and through the words of Jesus God was bringing to final and historical fulfilment what he had begun when he first called Israel to be his people. He continued throughout their history to care for them in his providence. Now in Jesus he was providing 'food' for man in his society, for man who is more than a physical entity with a physical appetite that can be satisfied with bread. The bread which Jesus offered distinctively to men, and still offers, is not made of barley, which must either be eaten or become inedibly stale, but consists of his own self-sacrificing life which, given for men, can nourish them in and for the 'eternal' life for which they are created.

The reason for preserving the story of the miraculous feeding of five thousand people was not therefore to demonstrate that Jesus was an unquestioned and unparalleled miracle worker – and this conclusion accords with the general attitude of the evangelists, and of Jesus himself. The Hellenistic world had its itinerant 'divine men', whose miraculous powers were taken to be proof of supernatural nature or origin or both. But there is nothing like that in the gospels. On the contrary. In two of his earliest recorded temptations, in the desert, as in the last, experienced on the cross, Jesus declined to work miracles to evoke belief. And when the Jewish authorities asked him for a sign, he replied, 'Why does this generation seek after a sign? I tell you this: no sign shall be given to this generation' (Mark 8.12). Matthew and Luke add to that answer, but do not change its substance by promising that any miracle will be performed by Jesus. Both say that the only sign to be given will be that of Jonah, that is, of the good news being preached to the Gentiles. But both evangelists interpret it also as a sign of the coming resurrection of Jesus. (Mat. 12.39-41; Luke 11.29-32). Jesus's miracles should not be regarded as providing proof of his divinity. When Jesus invited the disciples of John the Baptist to observe what he was doing, and to report back to John, he cited to them that 'the blind recover their sight, the lame walk, the lepers are cleansed, the deaf hear, the dead are raised to life, the poor are hearing the good news'. He was not using miracles to establish a claim to divinity, but rather pointing to some anticipated features of the age and activity of the Messiah that were present in his own ministry (Mat. 11.4-6; Isa. 35.5f.; 61.1).

Miracle stories are thus primarily recounted as 'going on' indicators, rather than as 'taking place' narratives. This means that the problem of the miraculous is not so critically determinative as it otherwise would be, and as some critics and even apologists have supposed. The truth of the gospel histories does not stand or fall on the answer to the question whether what took place was the performance of a particular miracle or series or miracles by Jesus, but on whether what went on was a disclosure of Jesus as the person Christians came to believe he was, a universal saviour bringing true and eternal life to men (John 20.31). Such a disclosure can still be experienced and, if Paul is right, is the work of the Holy Spirit.

This does not mean that the whole idea of miracles must be given up. For some time it seemed to modern thinkers that rigid laws of cause and effect were universally operative and therefore miracles were impossible. But modern attitudes have abandoned that rigidity and are more inclined to think in terms of 'patterns of events', which could themselves seem to be interrupted in order to fit in with some wider patterning. Such an apparent interruption would yield the phenomena which have been called 'miracles'. Theologically such a pattern change could be seen as a divine 'miracle', an action 'against nature', i.e. against the apparent run of the 'pattern', whether it happened in the presence of some apparent intermediary, or appeared more like direct divine action. Belief in miracles is not necessarily excluded from the proper intellectual attitudes of the believer.

Gospel epilogues

The story of any normal human being must come to an end with the account of his death and burial. After that there can be no report of his presence and activity. Much may be said of his continuing influence years, decades, even centuries after his death, but not of his personal presence, for that has gone, never to return. But the story of Jesus does not end with his death and burial; each of the four gospels adds an epilogue to the story of Jesus telling of his personal living presence after his well-testified death and burial.

Two features demand notice: first, that the surviving eleven members of the Twelve became assured that the same Jesus of Nazareth who had been their leader for some years in Galilee and Judea had now returned to them in person, though in a somewhat different way. He had not died and ceased to be; he had died and risen from the dead, incredible as that seemed, and certainly had so seemed to them at first. Second, his return was a new beginning, a new birth. The pattern of the life of the new people of God had been disclosed in the life of Jesus himself; now it could be detected in the life of the community he had created, and to which he had returned. The Church was not a society for the memory and honouring of Jesus; it was the movement begun and continually stimulated by him, who was then and is now its author and life-giver, its perpetual guide. The Church remains the continuing 'epilogue' to the story of Jesus, who still challenges and redeems the world through its life.

4

JESUS IN HIS LIFETIME

In passing now to retell the story of Jesus in the three gospel sections of prologue, story and epilogue, it is important to underline the fact that this retelling is not, and does not purport to be, an exact reconstruction of what took place in the lifetime of Jesus. It does make some claim to help the ordinary reader of the gospels to understand what was going on in that life. It is certainly impossible for any author to recover 'just what took place'. It has been made quite plain that the incidents of the gospels are not given in their original chronological order, and that no certain chronological sequence can be reconstituted from them. Luke's claim to set his story out 'in order' (Luke 1.1) is unlikely to imply strict chronological accuracy. Further, no precise dates can be given for the birth and crucifixion of Jesus. The best that any author can do if he wants to give his narrative of Jesus a chronological shape is to make a choice, or series of choices, that he believes chronologically probable, both in regard to the actual span of Jesus's life, and to the order of happenings in it. Certainly the drama of his life is better depicted against a background of dates, and the present author has adopted certain possibilities as actual, without any dogmatic confidence that they are chronologically right – though he does believe that by their adoption what went on in Jesus's life will become clearer. To tell the story demands that certain presuppositions are made, e.g., that

John the Baptist had contacts with the desert sects. The author has felt free to cite the scriptures without quoting any particular English version. The whole story of Jesus will be preceded by a note on the virgin birth, and supplemented with a note on the resurrection.

The Virgin Birth

The idea that Jesus, or anyone else for that matter, came into human life by means of a virgin birth is totally inadmissible to a typically sophisticated modern man. That is why some defenders of the Christian faith have tried to show that the process of parthenogenesis (virgin birth) is neither impossible nor unknown in nature. Unfortunately the argument rebounds to the defender's disadvantage. On the one hand, if the process of parthenogenesis were shown to be a possible if infrequent natural process, then its occurrence in the birth of Jesus would give that birth only the quality of being 'unusual', and not the uniqueness that his alleged parthenogenesis has been taken to give it. On the other hand, if parthenogenesis is not a natural possibility, then the assertion in Matthew and Luke that it took place is the account of something impossible. That would remove Jesus so far from ordinary humanity as to leave him neither truly divine nor fully human, and certainly not the person to show to ordinary men what kind of life is proper to a man living responsibly in a world created, sustained and given a destiny by God.

But there are other, and more faithful, ways of dealing with the problem. This is important in an age when Christians themselves are divided on the factual truth and theological relevance of the doctrine. The debate is by no means ended, and will continue. A review of the problems involved is thus still timely.

First, proponents of both sides of the dispute should remember that the idea of the virgin birth of Jesus did not, according to what evidence is available to us, form part of the earliest preaching of the Christian Church. The preaching reported in the early chapters of Acts does not refer to it (Acts 2.22ff., 32-36; 3.13ff.; 5.30ff.) Paul makes no mention of it in his letters, even when he states Jesus's descent from David (Rom. 1.3); indeed he seems to have thought that Jesus came into the world like any other human being (Gal. 4.4), and shared ordinary human nature like any other man (Rom. 8.3f.; 2 Cor. 5.21; Gal. 3.13). Mark and John also wrote their gospels without any mention of it.

The phrase 'virgin birth' has entered Christian thinking because in his telling of the nativity story Matthew declares that the virgin birth took place to fulfil what the Lord had announced through the prophet, 'A virgin shall conceive and bear a son, and he shall be called "Emmanuel"' (Mat. 1.23). The Greek word *'parthenos'* is properly translated into English as 'virgin' but it does not, unfortunately, accurately translate the Hebrew word *'alma'* into Greek; the Hebrew word really means 'a young woman of marriageable age'. The use of the word *'parthenos'* has therefore introduced a new meaning into the prophecy of Isaiah. What Matthew had intended was a comparison of two historical situations. In the days of King Ahaz, Isaiah had found the king and his advisers and courtiers quite unwilling to think that anything could happen to constitute for them a sign that God had not deserted them and left them to the mercy of their enemies. Isaiah responded to their despair by saying that God would himself give them all a sign, which was this: 'A young woman will conceive and bear a son, and he shall be called "Emmanuel", which means "God is with us".' So the young mother showed by her naming of her child that she believed, what the 'establishment' of her day found it impossible to believe, that God could still aid and rescue his people. In the time of Jesus the religious and political establishment were in a like despair about their position as an occupied land. Mary, like the young woman in the days of Ahaz, saw the birth of her son as a sign that God would, through his birth, show himself as still working in and for his people and his great purpose for mankind.

But even if that is the way the term 'virgin birth' has come to be used in discussion about the birth of Jesus, it still leaves unexplained the care with which Matthew particularly, and Luke less emphatically, underlined the point that there was no normal participation by a human father in the begetting of Mary's son Jesus. If there was a parthenogenesis, and the Holy Spirit was the generator, the normal expectation would be that the fruit of such a birth would be some semi-human, semi-divine being, and not the fully human, fully divine being that Christians have believed Jesus to be. It is possible, indeed probable, that the report of a virgin birth taking place is basically meant to indicate 'what was going on' in the birth of Jesus.

There is some scriptural evidence that this may be so.

Jesus was on one occasion in discussion with some Jews who boasted that they were sons of Abraham; he told them that in seeking to kill him they were not behaving as Abraham their father did. They replied, with what could have been a sneer, that he was born out of wedlock, that 'We were not born of fornication', and then added, 'We have one Father, even God' (John 8.41). Those Jews were perfectly well aware that each of them had had a human father, but were here using language that, in another context, could well be taken to imply that they too had a supernatural conception. That idea of the Jews is reminiscent of the profound Word from the prologue to John's gospel. John tells of the Word, active in creation, coming as light into the world, coming to his own home, and not being received by his own people. 'But,' he went on, 'to all who received him, who believed in his name, he gave power to become children of God; who were born, not of blood, nor of the will of the flesh, nor of the will of man, but of God' (John 1.12f.). Thus John used language fitted to describe a virgin birth about every believer, but his intention was to say that belief in Jesus as the Son of God and saviour is not a human achievement, but the work of God alone. Paul made the same point in other terms when he declared that 'no one can say "Jesus is Lord" except by the Holy Spirit' (1 Cor. 12.3). God thus actually 'fathers' believers; from being children of this world they become his own offspring. What men become by their 'second birth' (John 3.3) is not the outcome of any human physical creativity, but of the saving work of God himself, through the gift of Jesus and the enlightenment of the Holy Spirit. The doctrine of the virgin birth is meant to safeguard the truth that nowhere, from conception to entombment – and beyond – did any human creativity endow Jesus with that relationship with the heavenly Father by which he lived and died and rose from the dead to become the saviour of the world. But that truth cannot be illuminated or proved on the grounds that parthenogenesis is biologically possible!

Mary's conception, however biologically occasioned, brought a new human child into the world. God's concomitant activity in that conception brought into the world a 'new man', a new sort of human being, one person who was God and man together in an indissoluble unity. That unity was at first present in one individual, and then in a community gathered by that one new being, by the activity of the same divine Father. The Church can also claim, 'We have one Father, even God.'

The Prologue:
Pointers and Portents

In the year 9 B.C. Palestine had been for a long time, and would continue for some years, to be a land of discontent, incipient rebellion and some actual uprisings. As so often in human history, religious and political enthusiasts were to be found sometimes in co-operation, sometimes planning and acting independently to liberate the land from its oppressors. The military-minded could make out a reasonable case for the success of an armed revolt in Palestine, if in no other part of Rome's vast empire. But Jewish leaders looked for discernible signs that would indicate God's imminent fulfilment of his promise to reinstate his chosen people Israel as the leaders of the nations in a world blessed with universal peace and prosperity. What the religious leaders looked for, the whole populace awaited expectantly – Sadducees, aristocrats, priests, 'desert fathers', the 'poor', the 'people of the land' (see p.87), and militarist Zealots. All were ready and eager for the arrival of the Messiah, the deliverer who would set them free. But it was not until some decades later that certain rather obscure events of 9 B.C. came to be seen as actually having started God's great act of final deliverance.

The first of these took place in the Judean home of an ageing Zadokite priest named Zechariah, who shared in the duty rota of the Jerusalem Temple. One day, in the course of his priestly duties, he was astonished to receive an angelic intimation that his wife Elizabeth, herself of a priestly but Aaronic family, though already past the normal age for child-bearing, would bear him a son, who would be a decisive figure in Israel's history. The sign that this would come about, he heard, would be his own loss of speech until the day his son was born and named. And, whatever explanation he offered to himself, that is what in fact happened: his speech left him, and returned only when he had written down that his son, newly born, must be called John (Luke 1.8-23, 57-64).

The second took place in Galilee, with another unusual pregnancy. Mary, a young townswoman of Nazareth, was engaged to the town's carpenter, Joseph. But her standing as an engaged maiden was imperilled when Joseph found that she was already pregnant. Mary had herself received an angelic communication that she would become pregnant, not by any human, but by a divine paternity. It took another such revelation to dissuade Joseph from divorcing Mary, which would have been the 'respectable' action for a Jewish bridegroom-to-be in such a situation. In due course Mary's child was born, and named 'Jesus'.

It is significant that both these boys were born 'against the normal laws of nature', and especially that the birth of Jesus was said to have been 'of a virgin', i.e. without dependence on the normal participation of a human father. Such unusual origins almost suggest that the two boys were marked out from birth (which some people believed) for an unusual destiny. Certainly, from the standpoint of their destinies, their origins look very much like portents of things to come, when each had his part to play in the drama of God's final act of deliverance for man.

Mary and Elizabeth were 'kinswomen' (Luke 1.36), and during her pregnancy Mary stayed with Elizabeth for three months. Both mothers thought it auspicious that when Mary met Elizabeth the young John made his first movement in the womb (Luke 1.39-56). Zechariah shared their intuition, as he showed vocally, once his speech had returned (Luke 1.67-79). The young John grew up in a priestly home that was deeply religious, in both public worship and private devotion. He learned there of the firm expectation that the God of Israel would, in the not very distant future, act decisively to implement his convenanted promise to restore Israel to its appointed leadership of the nations. So, in Luke's words, 'as the child grew, his spirit achieved strength, and he dwelt in the wilderness until the day when he was made manifest to Israel' (Luke 1.80).

John's resort to the life of the wilderness was both an expression and a development of a growing dissatisfaction with the religious and political attitudes of his home, where priestly and 'establishment' views held sway.

The wilderness was the resort of the prophet, not of the priest. It was also the refuge of many a guerilla band, as they fled from the Roman authorities. Even more significant, it was the place where the non-conformist sects of Judaism, such as the Essenes and the Qumran community, had their home, and lived their dedicated and ascetic lives. John shared that life, and learned much from it. Upon entry he had to surrender all his worldly possessions, and then serve a novitiate of two or three years before admission to full membership of the community. He was taught the high moral demands made on all members, with the accompanying emphasis on repentance for all wrong done, and the daily practice of baptisms of purification, by which the stains of sin were washed away. He came to appreciate the depth of the community fellowship as he shared in the common meal, open only to full members, at which bread and wine were blessed by the presiding priest. He learned that in this way it was possible, in what was acknowledged to be an imperfect world, even in an occupied 'promised land', to live the life of the kingdom of God on this earth. He came to share the community's eager and determined hope for the speedy advent of God's Messiah, and its readiness to spend and be spent in his service, in the inevitable war that would be necessary to establish his reign.

But just as his family's attitude proved inadequate for the ardent John, so did the attitude of the community. John was called to a mission on his own, for 'the word of God came to John in the wilderness; and he went into all the region about the Jordan, preaching a baptism of repentance for the forgiveness of sins' (Luke 3.2f.).

In the same year that John was born, Joseph was required by regulations promulgated for a census of the tetrarchies of Palestine to go to Bethlehem in Judea to be registered. It was David's city, and he was of Davidic descent. He took his betrothed bride with him. The nearer they got to Bethlehem, the more fellow 'census pilgrims' they met, and the more apparent it became that Mary's time of delivery was imminent. Arriving at Bethlehem Joseph went straight to the inn, but found that earlier arrivals had booked all the available accommodation. He had no need to protest Mary's condition, for it was plain to see; the kindly inn keeper offered what accommodation he could – the warmth and shelter of his stables. There the young couple settled down, and in the course of the next few hours Mary gave birth to her first-born child, a son.

Bethlehem, the 'capital' city for David's tribesmen, was agog with excitement at the return of so many expatriates for the census. Old friendships were renewed, and new ones made. And everywhere in the town the story was told of the young bride from Nazareth who had had to travel the many miles from Galilee in the very last days of her pregnancy, for no other reason than to satisfy Rome's cruel appetite for imperial statistics. The story was picked up by the local shepherds, and they talked about it, and about the iniquitous insensitivity of Roman political administration, as they left Bethlehem to take their flocks to pasture on the surrounding hills.

That night, as they sat round the fires that kept them warm and marauding animals away, they continued to express their resentful disapproval of Rome, and talked again about the Jewish hope for the promised deliverer of Israel. What if the arrival of the child to the young woman were to be a portent of the new deliverance, a sign that God had at last begun to act for their liberty? Things could not go on forever as they were. Then, almost as if their wishes had fathered it, a strange thing happened. Someone was on the lonely hillside with them. They had not seen him come, nor heard his approach; and though his dress certainly reflected the glow of their fire, it seemed as if he were giving a new glow to the fire, so bright and luminous he appeared. Was he someone 'out of this world'? Stunned to silence, they heard him say, 'You have no need to be afraid. For I have come with good news that will not only please you, but give joy to your whole nation. For this very day, in the Bethlehem you have just left, the great deliverer has been born, the one who is to be the Messiah and king of the world. And you can find out for yourselves that this is true. Just go to Bethlehem, and you will find there a baby wrapped in swaddling clothes, laid in a manger.' And as the strange visitor finished speaking, the whole area, hills and fields and sky, was filled with the sound of heavenly music, and the message of a song:

> Glory to God
> In the highest of heavens
> Peace to the good natured
> All through the earth.

Then the night seemed quite ordinary again – though it could never be that for them. The shepherds wondered what to do. What was going on? If what they had heard was true, this could well be the night of all nights for their people; and they said, 'We must go right away to Bethlehem, and see for ourselves that things are as we have heard.' So off they went, and found Joseph and Mary and her little son, just as the strange visitor had said. And they went back to their shepherding with hopes quickened and hearts thankful, for the new age had surely dawned. What else could explain such a night's doings as they had known?

When Jesus was eight days old, he was circumcized, and so

became a Jew in the full religious tradition of his people. He was then given his name 'Jesus', the new form of 'Joshua', the name of that great leader of Israel who, after the death of Moses, led his people into the land of promise. Yet this new 'Joshua' was to outdo by far the exploits of the former leader, for he was to take a new people of God into the final land of promise that has no physical boundaries to be printed on any geographical map.

Jewish law required a mother to observe a period of forty days of 'purification' of her blood after childbirth, and at the end of it to make a sacrificial offering (Lev. 12.4ff.). So Mary and Joseph remained in Bethlehem for a period, and attended the Temple in Jerusalem for the ceremony of purification. They elected to offer two pigeons (Lev. 12.8), which indicated that though they were presumably by no means poverty-stricken, they were not wealthy enough to offer a lamb for the sacrificial rite. Two portents occurred during their visit to the Temple. Simeon, an aged and devout Jew, who was quietly waiting for the deliverance of Israel, met the three from Nazareth. He took Jesus in his arms, and praised God in the words:

> Lord, you have kept your promise;
> So let your servant go now in peace.
> With my own eyes I have seen the deliverance;
> You have prepared it in full view of mankind,
> The light which will enlighten the Gentiles
> And be the true glory to your people Israel.

Then a very aged prophetess named Anna, a widow of eighty-four years, came up at that very moment, and spoke to her fellow worshippers in the Temple about the deliverance of Jerusalem. Her text was the sight of Jesus in Simeon's arms.

At a date now irrecoverable, the little family left Bethlehem in unusual circumstances that must have seemed portentous too. Some astrologers from an eastern country, possibly Babylon, had 'studied the stars' and concluded that a new king of the Jews was to be, or had already been, born. Their motives for crossing the desert to pay homage to so young a prince are not disclosed, but it would have been some prudential concern to ensure his friendship and co-operation once his reign had begun. That might have been the more so had the visitors known, as they in all probability did, of the hopes of the Jews that a Messiah-king would soon come to their deliverance. Unfortunately Herod had achieved an international reputation not only for his ambitious programme of public works, but also for a ruthless fear for his own safety and crown. The arrival in Jerusalem of astrologers asking for a new-born heir, when there was no such princeling in Herod's house, caused considerable anxiety to Herod. He inevitably suspected that some seditious movement was afoot. It would have to be nipped in the bud. Herod called his official doctors of theology together for consultation, and learned from them that according to the scriptures Bethlehem would be the birthplace of the new king. Herod directed the visitors to Bethlehem, with a request that they report back to him, so that he could follow and pay his homage too. The astrologers went to Bethlehem, found Jesus and his parents, paid their homage, left their gifts of gold, frankincense and myrrh, and, after a dream warning, went back home without further contact with Herod. Frustrated, and with not uncharacteristic cruelty, Herod ordered all male children under two years of age in Bethlehem to be killed.

But providence had a part to play. The young parents must have known how dangerous it was to have received, though unwittingly, such regal attentions, even for a tiny child. A dream warning fortified their natural apprehension, and Joseph and Mary with the young Jesus set out for Egypt, and escaped without harm. In the years that followed, Mary might well have reminded Jesus how, in his own life story, the pattern of the life of the Jews under Moses had been repeated.

Herod 'the Great' died in 4 B.C., and his kingdom was divided into three tetrarchies for his three sons, Archelaus, Antipas and Philip. When Joseph heard the news, he decided to return to his national home, though, because of the evil reputation of the new Tetrarch of Judea, Archelaus, he did not return to Bethlehem, but resettled in Nazareth, where he and Mary brought up a quite sizeable family. In the home were four boys, in addition to Jesus, and at least two girls. The boy's names reflect the intense nationalism of the parents: James (=Jacob), Joseph, Simon and Judas (cf. p.89). They attended the local synagogue school and learned to read the great story of their people. They heard in the streets of Nazareth, in its markets and by the well the rumours and reports of activities against Rome. Visits were exchanged between Mary's home and that of her kinswoman Elizabeth, and the two families had opportunity to meet each year when the Galilean families went up in caravan for the Passover in Jerusalem.

At the age of twelve a Jewish boy became a 'son of the Law', which meant that he took upon himself the responsibility for his own religious and social life as a loyal Jew. When Jesus was twelve there was a memorable happening as the family went to Jerusalem for the Passover. Jesus, breaking into adolescence, was excited at the thought of taking part in the great festival for the first time. There was also the fun of travelling 'in caravan', and the opportunity of spending much time, on both outward and homeward journeys, with other Jewish youths. The outward journey and Passover celebrations went off as happily as ever. It was on the way home that trouble came. Joseph and Mary became aware that Jesus had been away from them for much longer than could be regarded as properly safe. When their enquiries round the caravan produced no results, they went back to Jerusalem with anxious hearts to try to find the new 'son of the Law', the adolescent Jesus. It was three days before they found him, in the Temple, as if nothing had happened, listening to the learned doctors of the Law, and asking them questions with a discernment far beyond his years. Mary asked him why he had treated his parents so thoughtlessly, and his reply was revealing: 'Did you not know that I have to be concerned with my Father's affairs?' At the time this was sheer enigma to Joseph and Mary; what possible affairs of Joseph could be affected by the boy's lingering in the Temple?

Three years after this incident there was real trouble in Galilee, 'Galilee of the Gentiles' as it was called, not without reason. The presence of a large Gentile population in the tetrarchy made the Jews more nationally self-conscious and Rome more alert to rebellious tendencies. When Jesus and John were about fifteen years old, Judas of Galilee raised the standard of revolt (Acts 5.37) which, though speedily crushed, found continuance in the activity of the 'Zealots', guerilla bands who managed by their bold militancy to bring much suffering and final calamity to the nation at large (Jos. Ant. 18.1.6). Both John and Jesus would have known about the execution of the rebels. So the two children of destiny grew up in a time of anguish and anxiety for Judaism. No doubt that as they met from time to time, they would discuss the plight and future prospects of their people – and such discussions would have taken on a different aspect once John had become a member of one of the desert sects and imbibed their teaching and practices.

But for all their chronological contemporaneity, John belongs to the prologue to Jesus in his lifetime. When John left his priestly home, with its orthodox attitude to the Roman occupation, and joined himself to one of the desert communities, he was expressing his own dissatisfaction with the attitude of the Jewish establishment as represented in the priesthood, and his intention of finding some better alternative. Yet not even the ascetic life and the evangelistic zeal of the sects brought him satisfaction; it was thus that he was made ready to hear the word of the Lord that came to him (Luke 3.2).

It was the spring of 27 A.D. when John made his unheralded public début (Mark 1.4). He came with the classic Hebrew prophetic authority of the word of God (cp. Jer. 1.1f; 2.1, etc.). His appearing had three outstanding features: the clothes he wore, the message he preached, and the baptism he proclaimed and performed. His dress consisted of 'a rough coat of camel's hair, with a leather belt round his waist' (Mark 1, 6). Some might have thought this a likely costume for a desert ascetic, but the gospels record it because its description is in the very words that enabled Ahaziah of Samaria to identify a prophet who had displeased him as Elijah the Tishbite (2 Kings 1.8). In John's day Elijah was expected to return in person as the immediate forerunner and herald of the promised Messiah. John's message was that the final judgment of Israel as God's people had already begun; 'the axe is already laid to the roots of the trees' (Luke 3.9). He called for a new morality of righteousness and mercy: those comfortably off should share with the poor; tax-gatherers should act with honesty; professional soldiers should not misuse their power. All this he had learned from the sects, but his baptism, though derived from them, was essentially a very different rite. In the desert communities, the sins of each day had to be repented; this repentance was followed by a baptism, or lustration, which 'washed away' the stain of sin. But John's baptism was a once-in-a-lifetime ritual, and clearly meant something very different. It was a 'baptism of repentance for the forgiveness of sins'; the nearest equivalent to it was used in admitting a converted Gentile to the community of Israel. Each proselyte underwent a once-in-a-lifetime baptism, to indicate in that symbolic action that he had 'crossed the Red Sea' with Moses and all Israel, and had so been made one with the whole of God's people in all their history. This view of the crossing of the Red Sea finds an echo in Paul's writings (cf. above, p.32): 'all [our ancestors] passed through the Red Sea; and so they all received baptism into the fellowship of Moses in cloud and sea' (1 Cor. 10.1f.). John's baptism was therefore a call to Israel as a nation to repent of its failure to be truly God's people; the baptism signified that Israel would once more, and finally, be made God's people on earth. Each candidate for baptism was thus asked to do more than repent for his personal sins and failures; he had to join his fellows in repentance for not being a true and faithful people of God, as they were chosen and called to be.

The great prophets had specified the corporate offences of Israel: faithlessness towards God, and injustice towards the less fortunate. While such offences remained unrepented, Israel's religion could bring no true encounter with God, who could not compromise with either form of evil. He was a 'jealous' God, whose worship could not be shared with any other god or idol; he was a righteous God, and his people must manifest that quality in its social, political and personal life. But Israel had 'gone a-whoring' after other gods, and had not told other nations of God's gracious purposes for mankind. She had practised and permitted injustice: the poor man could not get justice in the courts, for he could not overbid the bribes that the rich gave to the judges; tradesmen, landowners, employers, priests and judges were all unscrupulous in pursuing wealth. The nation must repent, or cease to be God's people, even cease to be a people at all. John offered a way from divine rejection to a new life for Israel as God's people, and his baptism was its effective sign, the 'Red Sea' of the new and final people of God.

There is no record to say that the spring flowers of Palestine blossomed with special glory that spring. But something even more astounding is recorded: 'It happened at this time that Jesus came from Nazareth in Galilee and was baptized in the Jordan by John' (Mark 1.9). So the prologue was over. The central story begins – and what went on in that story was the great drama of God's final deliverance of man.

✠   ✠   ✠

The Gospel History

The baptism

The spring of 27 A.D. was an exciting one for the Jewish population of Palestine, and an anxious one for the Jewish authorities in Jerusalem, and a time of considerable apprehension for the Roman administration. All this was because 'John the Baptist' appeared in the wilderness proclaiming a baptism of repentance for the forgiveness of sins' (Mark 1.4). The response to his appearance was electric. Crowds went out from Jerusalem and from the whole of Judea to be baptized in response to John's preaching and his offer of a new Israel symbolized by the new 'Red Sea' crossing of his baptism in the Jordan. Not surprisingly the 'people were on the tiptoe of excitement, all wondering whether perhaps he was the Messiah' (Luke 3.15). It was in the midst of this kind of excitement that one day 'Jesus arrived at the Jordan from Galilee, and came to John to be baptized by him' (Mat. 3.13).

What sort of person was it that John saw coming towards him that spring? The evangelists recorded all that they believed to be necessary to know about him, taking care to prepare their readers for an encounter with a figure of divine destiny. Through him God had himself come to deliver his people, and to bring them to the new and better promised land of his eternal kingdom. But the television curiosity of twentieth-century man still asks, 'But what was he like? How would he have looked on our television screens?' The only honest answer is that nobody knows. There are some later traditions, which are not conspicuously reliable, to suggest that Jesus was under five feet high, somewhat ugly, and a bit crooked in figure. These traditions are not incompatible with what the gospels have to tell, even if they are not necessarily implied. When Zacchaeus, because of his lack of height, climbed a tree to catch sight of Jesus, this could have been as much due to Jesus's shortness of stature as to Zacchaeus himself being 'a little man' (Luke 19.1ff.). When Jesus spoke of man's inability 'by anxious thought to add a foot to his height', he might well have been thinking of his own height. As to his being 'ugly', this would not have troubled bible readers or scholars down the centuries, who have read Isaiah's description of God's suffering servant, and taken it to mean Jesus: 'he had no beauty, no majesty to draw our eyes, no grace to make us delight in him' (Isa. 53.2).

But whatever the truth about his physical appearance, and that is irrevocable now, there can be no doubt about the commanding presence that Jesus had. He spoke, and acted, as one who had authority (Mark 1.22, 27). When he preached in his home synagogue at Nazareth the congregation were so infuriated by what he said (Luke 4.28) that 'they leapt up, threw him out of the town, and took him to the brow of the hill on which it was built, meaning to hurl him over the edge. But he walked straight through them all, and went away' (Luke 4.29f.).

For John it seems to have been an unexpected meeting with his kinsman when Jesus arrived for baptism in the Jordan. The two men had often met and discussed the state of the nation, and there is little doubt that Jesus was already aware of the nature of John's message and mission, or that John had already surmised that Jesus would prove to be the Messiah to his Elijah (Mark 1.7; John 1.15, 26ff.). But then, why should Jesus have come for baptism? On any showing John had more reason to repent with and for his nation than had Jesus, for he was by birth part of the priestly tradition of his people, and the priests had in many ways hindered Israel in her evangelistic responsibility to God. So John met Jesus with a question natural enough to him: 'Are you coming to me for baptism? It is rather I who should be baptized by you.' In a searching answer Jesus replied, 'Let things go on as they are for now, and don't refuse me baptism. It is not our own righteousness, our own estimate of how much more or less we need to repent, that must govern our actions; rather it is God's righteousness which, as the great Isaiah taught, is his imminent deliverance' (Mat. 3.15 [paraphrased]; Isa. 56.1, etc.). John took the point. He had been preaching a baptism of repentance for the forgiveness of sins, and if God now forgave Israel, as the baptism symbolically stated, then the promised deliverance could not but be near.

So, as one among many candidates for baptism that day (Luke 3.21), Jesus went into the Jordan and was baptized by John. For Jesus this was an unmistakable assertion of his complete identification of himself with his people, wayward and unfaithful as they had proved to be. It was as a member of the old Israel that he came for John's baptism of repentance; he could not but repent of his nation's failures. But it was also as the first personal incorporation of the new Israel that he came and underwent the experiences that the gospels record.

Both men felt the solemnity of the occasion (Mark 1.10f.; John 1.32ff.), which came to them out of their common approach to the crisis of Judaism, and in a symbolism that objectified the direction that would be taken from Jesus's baptism onwards. Both saw the Spirit descend on Jesus, for whom it took the form of a dove, a 'Jonah', by which token Jesus knew that his mission was not to be to the Jewish people only, but to the Gentiles as well (Jonah 3.1-10). Jesus heard a voice which said, 'You are my son, my beloved; my favour rests on you' (Mark 1.11; cf. Ps. 2.7; Isa. 42.1), which could only mean that he was to be the embodiment of the new people of

God. God's old 'son' or people had long ago gone down to Egypt, and Hosea had told how God 'called his son out of Egypt' (Hos. 11.1) – and Jesus surely reflected how strangely that piece of history had been repeated in his own life. So the baptism of repentance for the forgiveness of sins had been effective. God had forgiven his people, for the new 'son' was now here. God was creating and calling his Israel anew. The son or people of God was born again. From Isaiah also came words of comfort, words that point also to great discomfort 'My favour rests on you.' The words were an assurance to God's servant: as he worked, suffered, even died for God, he could cling to the certainty that God's word would achieve its end. Though the path to be followed might entail difficulty, danger, suffering, even death, it would lead eventually to the full realization of God's promised favours. With such an inauguration, how would the new son of God respond to the call of the Father?

The temptation

Jesus could not immediately escape from the spiritual disturbance and exaltation of his baptism. The spirit that had descended on him drove him back into the wilderness, where he remained for forty days before returning to his Jewish community in the service of the Father. During these forty days he fasted – a spiritual technique used, for example, by the desert sects, as well as the conformist Judaism of the official authorities for brief periods each week. A long fast allows the periodicity and strength of bodily needs to recede for a while; the demands of the spirit can then be more clearly and continuously recognized. Jesus had just heard what he took for a divine voice say to him, 'You are my son.' But could that be true? If it was, then in him was incorporated the life of the new and true people of God. While in the wilderness could he find out if what the voice had said was really true?

It was in the wilderness under Moses that the old son or people of God had been fed day by day with manna, and that Moses had struck the hard rock to secure a miraculous supply of water. If he were the new 'son' could he not in his hunger convince himself by commanding the desert stones to become bread? His long fast made the temptation greater, but it had to be rejected. As the true son, his life must not be dominated by the demands of the body; he must first and foremost be responsive to whatever word God spoke to him. To ask for God's word to be verified, even for himself in the isolation of the wilderness, would be tantamount to not believing it in the first place. 'Man does not keep himself alive just by eating bread, for the real life of man is one that is kept alive only by the words that God has spoken' (Mat. 4.4 (paraphrased)). How could he ask other people to trust God's word and believe in his sonship if he demanded proof of it himself?

But if he went ahead trusting in God's word that he was God's son or people, how could he convince those he would invite to be incorporated into the new people of God? Would they accept him as the new son just on his own affirmation that God had said so? Would it not be necessary to have some irrefutable demonstration of his claim? Suppose that he climbed to the highest pinnacle of the Temple and threw himself down – scripture after all had promised that God's angel would protect him so that he would not so much as hurt his foot. Then everyone would really know that God's favour rested on him. But would they? They would certainly have to admit that something unusual had occurred; but they might just as well say, 'How lucky', or 'What sort of black magic was that?', or even 'How does he work a trick like that?' There was no certain and sure inference from an isolated if outstanding wonder to the conclusion that he was really the 'son'. Moreover, and more important, God had the right, as supreme creator and disposer of all, to put his children to the test; but God's creatures had no such right to put God to the test. As scripture reminded him, 'You are not to put the Lord your God to the test' (Mat. 4.7).

Supposing that the new son or people of God had come into existence, how would it reach the promised eminence in the world that divine prophecy assured it? How must it be related to and deal with other peoples and societies in the world? History of course provided the answer: world empires had always used persuasion and diplomacy in their expansion, but they had always reinforced, and sometimes replaced them, by force of arms. No universal kingdom, even the kingdom of the people or son of God, could hope to achieve or sustain world dominion without the use of force. If dominion is desired, it can always be secured by sufficent power and might. Such arguments were tempting and strong, not least to Jesus, who knew he had a mission for all mankind. But, attractive and right as they sounded, they were really a call to the profanest idolatry. To prize securing dominion for God above the service of God himself is basically to give more worth (=worship or worth-ship) to something other than God himself – which is precisely opposite to the divine guidance already given. So Jesus put the temptation away. 'Go away, Satan!' he said, 'Scripture puts it rightly in saying "Worship God, and serve him alone"' (Mat. 4.10).

The word 'satan' is revealing. It makes plain that Jesus experienced temptation just as other men do, as the attempt by some adversary ('satan' means 'the adversary') to undermine his goodness and integrity. Temptation takes place 'inside' a man; but it reflects each man's vulnerable situation in a war that is going on all the time, with a 'front line' passing through every man's consciousness, a war of cosmic dimensions, in which the contestants are God and 'the adversary'. For a time Jesus's temptation was over – though it recurred at intervals during his life, not least in his last few hours. Now Jesus could return to his fellow Israelites knowing that he had faced and dealt victoriously with the evil forces that corrupt human life by corrupting the human person. He left the isolation of his forty days still trusting the word he had heard at his baptism, that he was the new son or people of God, the human point at which God was about to reconstitute his people. The future may not have been clear to him in any sort of detail, but it could not have been hidden from him that he was a man of destiny.

Jesus and John the Baptist: side by side

Some six weeks after Jesus was baptized the authorities in Jerusalem sent a delegation to the Jordan to investigate John the Baptist and report on what was going on (John 1.19-28). The interrogation was terse and pointed:

'Are you the Messiah?'
'I am not the Messiah.'
'What then, are you Elijah?' (Mal. 4.5)
'No.'
'Are you the prophet we are waiting for?' (Deut. 18.15, 18)
'No.'
'Then who are you? We must give an answer to those who sent us.'
'I am a voice crying aloud in the wilderness, "Make the Lord's highway straight."' (Isa. 40.3)

The investigation was undertaken because of the popular speculation that John might be the Messiah. When the Messiah appeared he would lead his people to freedom, which would involve war against Rome; but if a false Messiah were to come, the war would still come, but there would be no divine assurance of its success. But John did not share this politico-military conception of Messiahship, and so declined to be taken as an Elijah to that sort of Messiah. What he claimed to be doing for contemporary Judaism was the same task that Isaiah had performed for the exiles in Babylon when he asked them to prepare God's highway across the desert to Palestine – though John was now asking for a way to be constructed across the even more arid desert of disobedience to God to the land of no geographical boundaries, the life of the true people of God, which Jesus announced to be the kingdom of God.

The final question put to John was this: 'Then why are you baptizing people, and so reconstituting the people of God, if you are not the Messiah or Elijah or the expected prophet?' John, remembering what had happened when he baptized his kinsman Jesus, replied that his water baptism was only symbolic and provisional, and would give way to something and someone else, who was literally on his way. The very next day John saw Jesus coming towards him, and he exclaimed, 'Look, there is the lamb of God; it is he who takes away the sin of the world.' He spoke further of Jesus as the one on whom he had seen the spirit of God alight, and remain, by which token he knew that Jesus was the son of God (John 1.29-34).

The following day John was with two of his disciples, one of whom was Andrew. Jesus went by. John repeated his affirmation about Jesus, 'Look, there is the lamb of God.' The two disciples left John and spent the day with Jesus. They talked about Messiahship and what it might mean. As disciples of John they would not have been looking for, or been contented with, the sort of Messiah that popular imagination expected, or the Messiah awaited by offical Judaism. But they learned enough from Jesus for Andrew to tell his brother Peter, 'We have found the Messiah!' (John 1.41). The next day, Jesus decided to return to Galilee. He met Philip, who came from the same Galilean town as Andrew and Peter, and said to him, 'Follow me' – which seems to imply that Jesus had learned a good deal about him from Andrew and Peter, and that it was not 'unprofessional conduct' for him to invite one of John's disciples to join his own circle. Philip had evidently been prepared for this encounter, for he went at once to find Nathanael, and told him that they had met the one spoken of in the Law and the Prophets, who was Jesus of Nazareth. Nathanael replied somewhat cynically by citing the proverb, 'Can anything good come from Nazareth?' Jesus met Nathanael, and greeted him with the words 'Here is an Israelite worthy of the name; there is nothing false in him' (There had been something false in the original Israel, Jacob, whose name meant 'deceiver', until it was changed to Israel – Gen. 32.28.) Nathanael asked how Jesus knew about him, and Jesus said, 'I saw you under the fig-tree before Philip spoke to you.' Nathanael caught the allusion from the man he had been told was the Messiah, for he knew that in the peace of the Messianic age each man would 'dwell under his own vine, under his own fig-tree, undisturbed' (Mic. 4.4). Jesus had used a 'chance' circumstance to suggest to Nathanael, at least in symbol, that the Messianic age was already here; and Nathanael accepted the suggestion. So, as Jesus gathered his community about him, the new 'son' of God was already passing from being embodied in one single individual, and had begun to assume his corporate form. Jesus set out for Galilee; John the Baptist remained in Judea.

Jesus at Cana: Replenishing Israel

Jesus went to Galilee to accompany his mother to a wedding at Cana. It seems that by this time Joseph was dead. Jesus's disciples accompanied them. A Jewish bridegroom was about to claim his bride, and, by begetting children, to ensure the continuation of Israel. Similarly Jesus, who could be thought of as the divine bridegroom (Mark 2.19) who had now come to claim his bride, the chosen people of Israel (cf. Isa. 54.5; 62.5, etc.) to ensure the continuation of a true Israel of God.

It so happened that what took place surprisingly, indeed miraculously, indicated what was going on. The ceremony went according to the provisions of Jewish law and piety. There was wine for celebration, and water aplenty for the special washings or 'baptisms' by which the old Israelites achieved, at least for a time, a ritual purity adequate for the wedding solemnities. But misfortune struck. The supply of wine ran out, a sign that the reality which it symbolized, Israel's communion with God, would not last forever. Mary told her son of the social crisis. He replied that it was not for him to deal with such a situation, whether at the request of his mother or to ease the embarrassment of the bride's family. He had not come to 'react' to human difficulties in human situations but to act creatively to restore human beings to their proper relationship with God. The time for that creative action had not yet arrived. Nevertheless, in eloquent symbolism of what his final creative act would be, he acted now.

Six large water vessels, each holding some twenty or thirty gallons, had been provided by the host so that each guest could perform for himself the required lustrations or 'baptisms' to make him ritually pure, and so eligible to share in the marriage ceremony which would replenish Israel. Wine had been provided so that each guest, ritually cleansed, could share in the celebration of the divine provision for that replenishment. But now the supply of the required elements for a proper ceremony had failed. What could be done? Jesus ordered the six water vessels to be filled with water, a symbol of the need for purification. Then he told the servants to draw some off and take it to the steward, who found that the water was now wine of a quality better than that originally provided for the ceremony. And the symbolism? Writing from the impressive and meaningful perspective of the Christian eucharist, John is affirming that in what Jesus has given – himself in self-sacrificing death – he has turned the purificatory waters of Judaism into the celebratory wine of the Christian eucharist, the feast at which the true Israel of God is replenished in both rite and reality.

John adds that this was the first sign by which Jesus revealed his 'glory'. It is important, to avoid serious misunderstanding, that for John the glory of Jesus was not as that of earthly monarchs in their splendour, like Solomon (Mat. 6.29), but was displayed in its fulness as he was crucified. He adds that the sign led his disciples to believe in him. But if here the disciples came to see an action as symbolizing Jesus's true glory, it could only be because the 'miraculous' element was of secondary importance. For that miraculous act told of his glory only as it foretold the cross. The wine which replaced the purificatory waters of Judaism was the symbol for the sacrfice of Jesus. It foreshadowed his death as it manifested his glory. To realize this was to enter the new creation, to become part of the new people of God which God was fashioning in the life and death of Jesus. Small wonder that Jesus could say of such men, 'Happy are the eyes which see what you are seeing! Many kings and prophets have wanted to see what you now see, but never saw it; and to hear what you are hearing, but never heard it' (Luke 10.23f.).

It is clearly not difficult to recover, in this way, what it was that

John believed was going on at the wedding in Cana of Galilee. But it is not so easy to recover what actually took place on that occasion. If the same story had come from a twentieth-century wedding the changing of water into wine would need to be very fully documented or it would be rejected out of hand by every reasonable person. But John's narrative cannot be so summarily dismissed. He wrote for an age in which miracles were no less miraculous, but in which they were much more readily given credence. The disciples and the early Church certainly believed that the miracle of Cana was possible if Jesus was the one in whom and by whom the new Israel of God, the new creation itself, was being brought into the world. The present author has no means, and certainly no right, to make up his readers' minds; he can only observe that to give credence to the miracle of Cana can still be reconciled with the general scientific attitude of the twentieth century (see above, p.96). But he must point out that whatever may be deemed to have taken place at Cana, John and the Christian Church have been, and still are, persuaded that the story primarily bears adequate and fruitful witness to what was going on at Cana and at the cross. Jesus's glory first glowed in Cana: at the cross it shone to conquer the darkness of the world.

Passover I: Nicodemus, statesman and disciple

Jesus returned to Jerusalem for the Passover of 28 A.D. He performed some signs, and had some response, but not sufficient to establish the new people of God. But one significant encounter took place: the important Pharisee Nicodemus, a member of the Sanhedrin or Great Council of the nation, came to Jesus by night, genuinely wanting to discover the meaning of what he had seen. As he said, 'No one could perform these signs of yours unless God were with him' (John 3.2). Jesus replied that to see beyond the signs to the reality they represented (the arrival of the kingdom of God) a man needed to be born all over again. This echoes John's statement in the prologue to his gospel about becoming 'children of God' (see above, p.101). Jesus then went on to affirm that as one who had 'come from heaven' he had authority to speak of heavenly things, of the kingdom of God (or heaven). Moreover, his coming into the world was not like that of an invading king bent on the destruction of his enemies, but like that of a king intent on saving his people, for 'God so loved the world that he gave his only begotten son, that whoever believes in him should not perish but have eternal life'

(John 3.16). Men fear the coming of God because of the judgment they believe they must undergo; but Jesus declared that the judgment and condemnation connected with his coming would not be a separate action of God, but the reaction of men to his arrival. The light had come into the world in him, and men could live in the light. Some already did. But some prefer the dark life of sin to that of the light, and it is that choice which is the exercize of the judgment, and the condemnation inflicted by sinful men upon themselves. But the deeds of the men who come to the light are clearly visible as having God's activity in them, which is also God's 'judgment'.

Jesus and John the Baptist: Jordan baptisms

From Jerusalem and the Passover Jesus went further into Judea to the Jordan, not far from where John was continuing his mission and baptizing. Understandably Jesus's disciples, some, if not all, of whom had been disciples of John, began to baptize as they had done under John. The fourth evangelist reports that the new arrivals were baptizing more converts than John and his disciples. John's disciples reported this to him, and he replied that it did not surprise him. With a clear reference to what had happened at Cana, he said, 'It is the bridegroom to whom the bride belongs. The bridegroom's friend who . . . listens to him, is overjoyed at hearing his voice . . . As he grows greater, I must grow less' (John 3.29f.). The evangelists may not agree as to whether the ministry of Jesus overlapped with that of John, but they are very clear that there was no overlapping in the actual significance of what the two men achieved.

The outcome of such activity was that the authorities in Jerusalem heard that Jesus was being even more successful than John had been. Learning that this report had reached them, and knowing full well the dangers of being suspected of being a self-constituted Messiah or a collaborator of John, Jesus decided to retire from the area and return to Galilee. As he had already said at Cana, his 'time had not yet come'.

Jesus, Jews and Samaritans

To go from Judea to Galilee Jesus and his disciples went through Samaria, contrary to the custom of many Jews. About noon one day they arrived at a town called Sychar, near which was a well linked by tradition with the great patriarch Jacob. Jesus sent his disciples into the town to do some shopping, while he rested by the well. The well was a deep one, giving good quality water, though well water was never as good as 'living' water taken from a running stream. While Jesus sat there a Samaritan* woman came to draw water. Jesus, breaking the racial and sexual conventions of his day, spoke to her and asked her to give him a drink. The woman, surprised and possibly startled by the apparent audacity of Jesus, temporized with the response, 'What, you, a Jew, ask me, a Samaritan woman, for a drink?' So the new 'son' or people of God was faced with the question of the rival claims of Jews and Samaritans to be the real people of God in succession to the patriarchs of old. Jesus's reply shows that he wanted the woman to know something new was being done for both Jews and Samaritans in what he had come to do: 'If you knew what God gives, and who is asking you for a drink, you would have asked him and he would have given you living water' (John 4.10). The Samaritan woman protested that Jesus could not draw water from the well, because he had no vessel for doing so, and that he could not in any case have drawn her 'living water'; surely Jesus could not pretend to be better than the patriarch Jacob, who drank the well water himself, and used it for all his needs. Jesus then explained that the water he gave was such that it left the drinker without thirst in the future, for it would become in him a constant spring, 'welling up to eternal life' (John 4.14). The woman, still not discerning the depth of what was being said, replied, 'Give me some

---

*Jewish-Samaritan discord was bitter and of long standing. It went back as far as the ninth century B.C. when the Israelite king Omri decided to clinch his kingdom's independence from Judea and its capital Jerusalem by building a new capital for himself, which he named Samaria. The small kingdom suffered attack from Assyria, and in 721 Samaria was destroyed by Shalmaneser, the people were taken into captivity, and foreigners settled alongside the survivors. In 586 B.C. Jerusalem suffered destruction, its temple was ruined, and the Jews were taken captive to Babylon. When the Jews were allowed to return from exile (538 B.C.) and rebuild their temple and city, they were much hindered by the renewal of rivalry with the Samaritan people. It was in 350 B.C. that a final break came, when the Samaritans built a temple of their own on Mount Gerizim, and instituted their own priesthood. The Jews resented this deeply; in 128 B.C. the temple on Mount Gerizim was destroyed, and in 108 B.C., when Pompey captured Jerusalem, independence was again granted to Samaria. In Jesus's day both countries were 'occupied territories', though that did not prevent their own rivalries from finding bitter expression. Against this background the relationships of Jesus with Samaritans as described in the gospels are an eloquent testimony to his 'way of peace'.

of that water, and then I shall neither get thirsty nor have to come here to draw water again.'

Jesus then caused the woman some embarrassment, by asking her to return home and fetch her husband. The woman had to confess that she had no husband, upon which confession Jesus displayed a very full knowledge of her marital history: she had had five husbands, and her present 'partner' was not her real husband at all. As something that 'took place' this acquaintance of Jesus with her history demands no supernatural intuition: Jesus could easily have learned about a woman with so unusual a story for her time, either on a previous visit to the well, or in Sychar, on his way to or from Jerusalem. But beyond taking the woman's story at face value, it is possible to see in it an example of John's eye for the symbolic in ordinary life, for the Samaritan people had had 'five husbands' in the five books of the Law, the only authority that they acknowledged. But living as they did outside the community of Israel, they really had no 'husband', no community with the God of Israel.

It may have been her embarrassment that caused the woman to 'change the subject'; or it may well have been that the woman saw the force of what Jesus had said about five husbands and none. In any case she now raised the issue between Jews and Samaritans, whether God should be worshipped in Jerusalem, or in Samaria on Mount Gerizim. Jesus then, in the confidence that he was the new embodiment of the people of God, replied that the time was coming, had indeed already arrived, when true worship of God would not be tied to a physical temple, but would be 'in spirit and in truth', befitting the true nature of God as spirit. The woman answered in terms of the current ideas about the Messiah, and said, 'I know that the Messiah is coming. When he comes, he will tell us everything.' Jesus then made a unique admission of his Messiahship, heard only by the Samaritan woman. 'I am he, who am speaking with you now,' he said (John 4.25f.).

The disciples returned with the food that they had bought – but Jesus had found it his food to be doing the thing that God had sent him to do. He looked around the countryside and observed that the harvest was much earlier than usual that year. He used that to show his disciples that their harvest would also be early, and one that they had not sown (see p.144). The episode ended with Jesus spending two unforeseen days in Sychar, finding there a number who came to believe in him as he talked with them.

A Galilean welcome

Jesus set out again for Galilee. On his arrival he was met by a group of 'Galileans' (see above, p.84f.), political nationalists, who had seen what he had done during the Passover in Jerusalem. But if they had hoped to recruit Jesus for their own movement, their efforts were in vain. He did not link up with them, but went on to Cana. While he was there an army officer of Herod's guard asked him to go to Capernaum where his son was ill, and to heal him. Jesus did not go to the house, but told the officer, 'Return home; your son will live' (John 4.50). The officer returned to Capernaum, and found that his son had revived at the very time that Jesus had made his promise. The officer and his household became 'believers': they began to understand what was going on as Jesus spoke and acted.

Passover II: Jerusalem, from paralysis to mobility

In the following spring of 29 A.D. Jesus went once more to Jerusalem for the Passover. While he was there he performed a healing which, in the very way it took place, enabled John's alert eye to detect some features that seemed almost to disclose what was going on.

It happened at the Pool of Bethesda, which had a reputation for healing qualities during certain irregularly intermittent disturbances of the water, popularly ascribed to angelic visitations. Jesus visited the pool, as he had doubtless done on a number of occasions in the past. He saw once again the lines of the disabled, lying on their mats waiting for the decisive movements to make themselves plain. One man, whom Jesus almost certainly recognized, had been waiting for thirty-eight years to reach the water early enough to benefit from the angelic activity – that was the precise period which the old people of God had spent wandering in the wilderness before reaching the land of promise (Deut. 2.14). The disabled were gathered under the shelter of a five-arched colonnade, symbolic, to the sensitive eye of John, of the five books of the Law that sheltered Israel. Into that symbolically charged situation now stepped the new Israel, the new son of God. What took place itself suggests what was going on.

Jesus went to the man who had been waiting thirty-eight years and asked him 'Do you want to be healed?' – a very searching question for the officials of the old Israel to answer. The man explained that he had no one to help him reach the water early enough to be cured. Jesus told him, 'Take up your mat, and walk!' At once the man did so.

The healing was performed on a Sabbath, the day when God had 'rested' from his creative work (Gen. 2.3; Exod. 20.11), so giving a rhythm to the life of the people who were called to belong to him and be like him. That Jesus had infringed the very important Sabbath law at once caused controversy, and became the reason why the authorities pursued a policy of active opposition to him (John 5.16). Jesus clarified the issue: God had indeed spent six days at his work of creation and then 'rested'. But he had not therefore ceased forever from his creative activity; rather had he continued it up to the present; and now, in the person and community of the new 'son', he was continuing it in Israel's history. 'My Father has never yet ceased his work, and I am now working too' (John 5.17).

As he developed this theme Jesus pointed out that what he had done was far more than simply restoring mobility to paralysed limbs; he had done something which was the intention of God when he brought Israel from thirty-eight years of desert wandering to the borders of the promised land. Jesus had brought the paralysed Israelite not to the geographical border of an earthly territory, but to the point of transition to the real 'promised land', where men live and are sustained by the living power and love of God. He, the new 'son' of God, had thus performed not just a human remedial action, but the very thing that God had wished to do for his 'paralysed' Israel as the Israelites waited under Moses to enter the promised land. The healing that had taken place was indubitably a human event, but what had gone on in that human event was something more: God's purpose in creating his world, and in calling his people Israel, had begun at last to be implemented in the work of Jesus. Paralysed and dying Israel was being offered a new and eternal life in God.

This was not easy teaching for the authorities to take, but Jesus reminded them that two years previously they had been to the Jordan to 'investigate' John, and had accepted his disclaimer that he was the Messiah; why should they not equally now accept John the Baptist's testimony about Jesus? John had asserted that there was already present in Judaism a figure of much greater significance than John himself, and very shortly afterwards he had identified that person as Jesus, on whom the Spirit had alighted, and who would be the one to baptize God's people with the Holy Spirit (John 1.31f., 33f.). If the authorities could not themselves accept John's testimony, then they had ready to hand an even more important witness to Jesus: what Moses had recorded in the written and inspired scriptures of the Law. If that divine authority were rejected, nothing more could be said. The disagreement and the antagonism would have to continue. And it did.

John the Baptist: arrest, imprisonment and execution

Jesus's kinsman John was still continuing his mission of national repentance and his offer of a baptism of repentance for the forgiveness of sins. He had survived the 'investigation' from Jerusalem, and in all probability the immediate excitement his advent had caused was by now much abated. He was certainly free from serious suspicion by the Jerusalem bureaucracy. But his perils were not confined to Messianic questions, or to the realms of religion and theology. Like the great prophets of the Old Testament he could lay himself open to danger by fearless comment on wrong-doing in high places. In an exposition of his very 'puritan' morality and his respect for scripture, he had taken it upon himself publicly to rebuke Herod Antipas, son of Herod the Great, for marrying the wife of his brother Philip while Philip was still alive. He said, on the basis of Leviticus 18.16: 'You have no right to your brother's wife' (Mark 6.18). Such public criticism did not go unreported, and Antipas himself, and even more Herodias his wife, were very displeased – though Antipas seemed to have some lingering respect for the outspoken John (Mark 6.20). But the danger of such a critic at large could not be ignored in troubled times by an unpopular ruler, and action had to be taken. John was arrested and placed in an isolated prison where he could do no more damage.

But Herodias was more resentful than her husband. She eventually contrived to get Antipas to promise her daughter any reward she requested for giving an exhibition dance at a royal banquet. Prompted by her mother Salome asked as her payment 'the head of John the Baptist on a dish' (Mark 6.25). Antipas was helpless, and had to redeem his promise. John was beheaded and his head given to Salome, who passed it on to her mother (Mark 6.28).

How long John was in prison before his execution is not known, but it was some considerable time, during which he was free to be visited by his disciples (Mat. 11.2).

126   JESUS IN HIS LIFETIME

Jesus: the Galilean ministry

'When he heard that John had been arrested, Jesus returned to
Galilee; and leaving Nazareth he went and settled in Capernaum. . . .
From that day Jesus began to proclaim the message: "Repent; for
the kingdom of Heaven is upon you."' (Mat. 4.12f., 17). The first
public activity of Jesus had been alongside John in Judea. Why had
he now decided to begin his solo activity in Galilee? Judea and
Perea across the Jordan had proved uncomfortably near Jerusalem,
and John had been 'investigated'. Moreover, Judea was in the
tetrarchy of Antipas, who might as easily suspect Jesus as he had
resented John. The southern wilderness seemed an unpropitious
place for the announcement either of a strict moral code, or of the
inauguration of a new people of God. But Galilee might well be
different. The Galileans, like all Jews of the time, were awaiting the
arrival of the Messiah, and even if, as the presence of the 'Galilean'
party showed, some of the hopes they entertained would need
considerable modification, that was something that would have
been true of any area of Palestine. Furthermore, Galilee was more
distant from Jerusalem, and would give a very different political
climate to work in. Galilee was also a place with a considerable
Gentile community, which might offer Jesus some real hope of
becoming the 'Jonah' of his generation.

'After John had been arrested, Jesus came into Galilee, proclaiming the gospel of God: "The time has come. The kingdom of
God is upon you; repent and believe the good news"' (Mark 1.14f.).
That is very concise shorthand. 'The time has come.' Ever since
their bondage in Egypt the Hebrews had looked forward to the day
when God would finally vindicate them and give them their rightful
place under him and for him as the leaders of the nations. They
thought that day had dawned when they crossed the Jordan and
began the conquest of Palestine (Josh. 3.14-17). They thought that
their future had really taken shape when they were allowed to
become a political entity like their neighbours, and be governed
(under God, of course) by a king, the Lord's anointed. But calamity
followed calamity: a divided empire collapsed, the south following
the north in defeat and exile. The brave experiment in monarchy
was over, and hope seemed lost. When the exiles of Babylon were
able to return and rebuild Jerusalem and its Temple, the great day
seemed once more to have dawned. But Israel, demurely placed
between the 'super-states' of the time, had her dreams shattered

again, and in the time of Jesus the promised land was itself a
territory occupied and governed by Rome. Would the time of
liberation never come? The message of Jesus must have electrified
his hearers. 'The time has come' – What excitement. Especially in
Galilee, where actual rebellion was not unknown. Perhaps Jesus
would stage another and successful rebellion. At least some of those
who heard him thought so (John 6.15). Jesus proved not to be that
sort of rebel. He proclaimed the arrival of a kingdom, but he was
not himself the usual 'political' king. What remains clear today is
that his announcement that the time had come meant for him and
his hearers of various political and religious views that the day had
now dawned when at last God's full purpose for Israel would be
fulfilled.

'The kingdom of God is upon you.' *The final ordering of human
society for which Judaism had so long been waiting had now arrived
as an historical reality. To become a citizen of that kingdom, to
enter it, had nothing to do with making an advantageous concordat
with Rome, as the Sadducees had done; nothing to do with ensuring
that every Israelite kept the Law completely, down to the tiniest
detail, as the Pharisees taught; nothing to do with a two- or three-
year 'apprenticeship', as the communities in the desert insisted. It
had to do with recognizing that the people of God already called to

---

*It is gratifying that the N.E.B. translates thus these basic and seminal sayings of
Jesus. Other translators say that the kingdom is 'near'. The Greek word used can
certainly mean 'near'; it can as surely mean 'arrive'. Luke reports that on Easter
Day two disciples walked to Emmaus and were met by Jesus, who walked along
with them. When they arrived at (or drew near) the village to which they were
going, Jesus made as if he intended to go on further; but they persuaded him to
stay with them. He stayed, and broke bread with them. It is surely right to suppose
that it was when the trio had reached Emmaus that Jesus showed that he meant to
walk further, and not as they were getting near. That does not decide the whole
issue – but it is relevant to note how difficult it was for the Twelve to understand all
that Jesus meant by the arrival of the kingdom. A 'present' kingdom of God has
also proved difficult for modern disciples, who suppose that if it did exist, then evil
would not have the obvious power that it still has. But surely the presence of the
kingdom is the great restraint on evil? It seems to the present writer clear that the
gospels, almost in spite of themselves, imply in very many ways that the kingdom
did come in and with Jesus. Certainly the question cannot be decided on the way
one word is translated in one passage (or in a number of passages); it can only be
answered by comparing the important differences of outlook on the world
produced by the different viewpoints, and asking, first, how each really accords
with the teaching actions of Jesus, and, second, how far each one can yield a
coherent and satisfying religious understanding of the world and an ability to live
responsibly in it.

serve him had failed lamentably to be his faithful servants, repenting for that failure as a people, and being ready to accept the forgiveness of God and begin, with his promised aid, a new life as citizens of the newly arrived community of the final people of God in history.

So Jesus began his 'solo' ministry. The 'son' began to announce the arrival of his Father's kingdom. But as the son he was not to be a solitary figure, a solitary 'Messiah'. On the contrary, before he ever performed any act or spoke any word in his mission as son or Messiah, he began to gather a living community, the nucleus of the true and final people of God, citizens of the kingdom that had now arrived. One day, as he walked along the shore of the Sea of Galilee, he saw Peter and Andrew working at their nets. They had left the group of John the Baptist's disciples previously in Judea, in order to become part of his community. He called them again now: 'Come with me, and I will make you fishers of men' (Mark 1.17). They at once left their work and went with him. Farther on he saw James and John; he called them in the same terms, and they responded in the same way. (This similarity of the call to Peter and Andrew and James and John may be an indication that the two latter disciples had also at one time been disciples of John.)

That Jesus began his solo ministry with recruits from the disciples of John the Baptist suggests that John's message was in substance very much the same as that of Jesus himself. This receives some support from Matthew, who alone among the evangelists reports that John's message was couched in the same language as that of Jesus: 'Repent; for the kingdom of Heaven is upon you.' That is not supported by the other evangelists, though all four agree that John 'baptized' people with a once-in-a-lifetime rite which was the sign that the new and final kingdom of God was being formed. His baptism symbolized the transition from the life of the old, disobedient, unrepentant and therefore unforgiven Israel, to that of a new, obedient, repentant and therefore forgiven and liberated people of God. So the new 'son' of God began to gather his community about him. That was the substance of the good news to be proclaimed. To a discerning 'old Israelite' it meant that the great 'day of the Lord', the hope of all Israel, had at last dawned. The news spread quickly over all Galilee.

The 'day of the Lord'

In their long anticipation of what God would do for them when he finally fulfilled their destiny, the Jews spoke of the 'day of the Lord'. They first imagined it as nothing but a joyful entry upon a new and wholly prosperous way of life; history and nature would be so ordered that they would enjoy all that a good and loving God could possibly give his people. The great prophets, while keeping that image of ultimate dealing between God and his people, emphasized a more sombre truth: that if God were to visit them in their unjust idolatrous society they could expect nothing but disaster. God was much more against evil, wherever it might be found, than he was for Jewish blood. The God of Israel, a God of righteousness, could only come in wrath and judgment to deal with Israel's sins, imposing due penalties for wrongs done and justice left undone. But now the news of the arrival of God's kingdom came in the person of one who had been divinely named 'God's beloved son'. That was unambiguously good news. The door into the kingdom of God was open, the lowly door of humble repentance for the nation's corporate failure to be a faithful people of God.

Such a message heartened the Jewish man in the street, who had neither time nor inclination to achieve the detailed legal obedience which the Pharisees proclaimed as the necessary preliminary to God's coming finally to deliver his people. So Jesus found a ready response from people seeing in him, what they had previously seen in John the Baptist, the arrival or the heralding of the promised Messiah. In his story of Jesus in his lifetime Mark sets out as the first day of the full public ministry what the 'day of the Lord' was actually like when it came. There was no immediate entry upon days of peace and plenty, nor the prophets' anticipated doom of judgment and disaster, but a day when God drew near to those who were ready to receive him.

Significantly it was a Sabbath, and Jesus went, as was his custom, to the synagogue. As a new teacher in the neighbourhood he was invited to expound the scriptures. It proved to be a new experience for the congregation, for he did not make his points by citing authority, but simply and straightforwardly with a manifest authority of his own. On that particular Saturday one member of the congregation was 'possessed'. With the heighened sensitivity that such a person often has for a presence other and greater than himself, he cried out during the service, 'What do you want with us,

Jesus of Nazareth? Have you come to destroy us? I know who you are – the Holy One of God' (Mark 1.24). Mark does not relate what Jesus said in his exposition that day; it is therefore impossible to be certain how the man's outburst related to it. Yet it seems safe to assume that Jesus would have announced in the synagogue his new message that the kingdom of God had come (Mark 1.15). If that were so, the man's question might have been politically based, asking why Jesus (a man of Nazareth and not of Capernaum) should come to teach the men of another town than his own. He might have been expressing his fears that to talk of a new kingdom would only bring destruction upon the tetrarchy of Galilee. He let the whole synagogue know that Jesus was making exalted claims for himself as a divine personage. But the man could equally have been voicing the fears of the possessed about what might happen to him were his 'demon' to be cast out. Certainly one feature of the expected Messianic age was that demons would be conquered and destroyed. Whatever the man meant, Jesus spoke to him with the words: 'Be quiet! Come out of him.' The afflicted man was shaken by convulsions, and the possessing spirit left him. The story quickly spread through Galilee.

Jesus now went to share in the family life of an Israelite home, where God was still honoured. He joined in the family Sabbath with Peter and Andrew. Peter's mother-in-law was in bed with a fever. Jesus was told of her condition, went to her side, took her hand and helped her to her feet. She had received the strength to wait upon the little community of the new people of God, and found a new life in that service.

After sunset, when the Sabbath was over, and 'work' could be resumed, the townsfolk brought to the door of the house all the sick and possessed that they knew. Jesus healed them all. But he forbad the spirits to speak, as that would have meant the spreading abroad of the news that he was some divine or Messianic personage, a matter that would be so liable to misunderstanding and misrepresentation, and so little likely to reflect Jesus's own convictions, that it would be positively dangerous to let it be so reported.

Very early the next day (Sunday) Jesus got up very early and went away to a lonely place to pray. Peter and his friends missed him, and searched for him. When they found him they said, 'Everybody's looking for you' – an invitation to return to Capernaum and enjoy the advantages of an enviable reputation for success. But for Jesus the good news could only be served by making it known, and he answered Peter and his friends, 'Let us go on to the towns in the neighbourhood; for I have started my ministry with that very objective in mind.' So he went through Galilee, preaching in the synagogues and exorcizing demons.

This one-day epitome of the 'day of the Lord' is enlarged upon in the rest of Mark's gospel. But just as Mark has provided an account of the 'day' of the Lord, so has Matthew given his readers an account of the 'Law of the Lord', which was as different from what contemporary Jews expected as was Jesus's manifestation of what the 'day of the Lord' was like.

The 'law of the Lord': the Sermon on the Mount

To call Matthew 5-7 a 'sermon' is strictly a misnomer; for it was not a single address delivered on one occasion. Luke puts some of its contents in quite different places in his gospel. The 'sermon' has sometimes been called the 'law' of Christ, or the 'law' of love – and in the sense that it is a guide to Christian living in the way that the Law of Moses was meant to be the guide to Jewish living, it may be called 'law'. Yet it was not meant to be used as the Pharisees used the Mosaic law (see above, p.74); nor was it like civil or criminal law, determining what actions and persons may be legally judged to be reprehensible. Nor was it offered to men as any insurance of heavenly bliss. Indeed, if the sermon is read as positive legal enactment, it is nothing but a mixture of the unattainable (5.48) and the out-of-date (5.40). The sermon is basically descriptive rather than imperative, putting into words what it means to be a citizen of the kingdom of Heaven. Perhaps the most potent imperatives are always in the indicative, whether in the form of words or a person's exemplary activity.

This sermon was in fact actualized in a human life. In Jesus's life was exhibited what 'obedience' to God's will really involved. The Jews were familiar with the idea that God and themselves were, like husband and wife, partners in a 'covenant'. The evangelists portray the life and death of Jesus as the historical enactment of a new covenant, which passes beyond the impersonal realm of 'keeping commandments' and 'being punished' for infringements into a world of personal relationships. There the 'good' life is lived and sustained not by enforcement of the Law, but by repentance and forgiveness, by spiritual death and resurrection to eternal life.

The sermon begins with eight Beatitudes. The heavenly citizens are said to be 'happy' or 'blest', or 'how blest' or 'to be congratulated'. The important point is that Matthew is not thinking of what subjective feelings they may have; neither is he making an objective assessment of their situation. Heavenly citizens may appear to be unfortunate when, for example, they suffer exploitation or bereavement or persecution. They will feel as 'unhappy' as any other human being in such a situation, but because they know of God and his utterly trustworthy purposes, they will know that their sufferings will be used by him for his own good ends. That is a good fortune that others do not share. 'How fortunate' would indeed be a better translation of the word '*makarios*' than 'happy' or 'blessed'.

How fortunate, first, are the 'poor in spirit', those heavenly citizens who realize that they cannot secure all they need for life by themselves, but know that God will provide them with all that is really necessary. How fortunate, too, are these who mourn their loved ones, in the knowledge that God is utterly trustworthy, and that his good purposes cannot be finally frustrated by misfortune, willing or unwilling opposition, or even death itself. Their mourning is but the pain of parting, not the agony of final loss. How fortunate are the meek. Aggressive people seem to get what they want by their aggression; but they only generate opposition. But the gentle-spirited cannot lose their greatest possession, their trust in God at all times. How fortunate, too, are those who long to see right prevail everywhere. Righteousness cannot be attained by individuals or societies 'on their own', but God's grace is available to all, and he can be trusted to vindicate justice in the end. So whatever the present lot of the heavenly citizen in the world, he will not lapse into cynicism or despair, but will be sustained in godly hope. How fortunate also are those who can enter with sympathy and understanding into the actions and motives of others; in so doing they share in a real attribute of God himself. So it is not futile to be merciful in a merciless world, but a goodly and godly piece of fortune. How fortunate are those who serve God with single-minded devotion, without any ulterior motive. In all the ambiguities of worldly life they will see divine providence, see God at work. Fortunate also are all peacemakers; God sees them as his sons, doing his work in the world, working for peace between God and man, and between man and man. They are sons because, like Jesus, they gather men into a community where strife will be replaced by reconciliation. Finally, how fortunate are those who suffer persecution for the sake of righteousness; they really belong to the community of Jesus, who also suffered in this way, yet emerged triumphant from it (Heb. 12.2). The Christian can find joy in his suffering for Christ (1 Pet. 4.13).

The community of the beatitudinously fortunate is one where suffering is transmuted into joy, not as an assurance of heavenly bliss, but as a present possession in this world. Heavenly citizens are the true heirs of the joyous suffering of the Old Testament prophets, as they are of Jesus himself. Such a community in the world is like salt, whose quality cannot be lost, or like a lamp whose own visibility makes everything else visible too.

A section now follows in which Jesus clarifies his own attitude to the Law. The new order, the kingdom of Heaven, has certainly arrived; but the old order continues alongside. Heavenly citizens, though in the new order, are yet still subject to the divinely given Law of the old order, though the whole concept of 'goodness' as obedience to the Law has to be revised. The heavenly citizen cannot immediately dispense with the guide to conduct contained in the moral and legal traditions already in existence; but he must understand them differently, and in particular 'fulfil' them. He will thus not respond to the prohibition of murder by saying that he is innocent of murder because he has never taken a human life, but will see that the purpose of the law is to secure the rejection of all attitudes that lead to murder – hatred, enmity and any 'inhuman' treatment of another human being. Statutes cannot give a fully detailed guide to the whole will of God, but they do constitute a reliable guide to its general direction. Heavenly citizens must have a goodness more complete than that of the scribes and Pharisees. 'Commandment obedience', as Luther saw, is not enough. The 'good news' of the kingdom is news, not law; it leads to a new way of life, not to the piecemeal observance of an ever-expanding and unattainable statutory code.

Heavenly citizens must therefore find some springs of conduct in their secular society; but they must also have others. These are to be found in the demands and promises of Jesus: 'You have heard it said . . . but I say to you' – a formulation which sets his advice to men on the same level of authority as the commandments given to the old Israel through Moses. The new people of God would receive its own 'guide to conduct' from the same high authority as the old.

Jesus joins to his more-than-legal insight into the sixth commandment a positive duty of reconciliation. Heavenly citizens will not go through life without personal relationships going awry, sometimes through their own fault. But the heavenly citizen will always work for reconciliation, else he will be unable with integrity to worship God the reconciler. Sometimes distorted relationships will lead men to seek remedies from the civil law. Even then, on the very way to court, reconciliation must retain an absolute priority. For once the legal process starts, it will grind its way relentlessly forwards to its legal and impersonal end, and the disputants will be as unreconciled as ever – perhaps even further apart. So the heavenly citizen abandons revenge and the Law, and seeks to live with other men as God has shown he lives with all men, in constant readiness to forgive and be reconciled.

Adultery is treated in much the same way, taking self-examination much farther than a question about the adulterous act itself. Jesus does not try to establish another series of rules to be viewed as prohibitions about which a plea of 'not guilty' could be made, for example on the grounds that 'I cast no lustful look'. Rather does he turn the mind away from the legal concept of conforming to a rule, to the religious reality of acting in a way compatible with the will of God embodied, though not exhaustively stated, in the seventh commandment.

The 'old' law on divorce enabled a man to give his wife a 'bill of divorcement' were she to find no favour in his eyes because of some indecency. There were two conflicting Rabbinic expositions of that law in Jesus's day. The stricter Shammai school held that 'indecency' must mean adultery, while the liberal school of Hillel thought that any displeasure a man suffered, even burnt food, could be an adequate ground for divorce. One thing is known for certain about Jesus's attitude to divorce: he did not share the liberal views of Hillel. But did he in any way countenance divorce? By itself the passage in the Sermon on the Mount suggests that he did in the sole case of 'unchastity'. There are those who believe that the 'act of indecency' referred to in Deuteronomy 24.1 in fact meant an act of pre-marital adultery (a betrothed couple had the same legal status and rights as a married pair), which would make the 'bill of divorcement' allowed equivalent to a modern 'decree of nullity'. If that were so, the Christian Church would be able to say that Jesus did not countenance divorce.

But this passage does not exhaust the gospel records of Jesus's teaching on adultery and divorce. The theme recurs in a later passage in Matthew (19.3-9), in a parallel passage in Mark (10.2-12) and in a very terse repetition in Luke (16.18). In the later section of

Matthew and in Mark Jesus uses the same method as in the Sermon on the Mount, going behind law as commandment to the fundamental purposes of God that the Law is meant to serve. God's creative purpose in marriage, Jesus affirmed, was that man and wife should become 'one flesh', and on that basis he affirmed the essential indissolubility of the marriage bond. But he admitted to his questioners that 'for man's hardness of heart' (unwillingness and inability to listen to God) he had been allowed to practise divorce. This raises an important point: Jesus's whole concern in the Sermon on the Mount so far has been to show how those live who have become citizens of the kingdom of Heaven; he has not enunciated a 'law' for the whole of mankind! Presumably those outside the kingdom will still be given the concessions that citizens of the kingdom neither desire nor need. A modern parallel could mean that the Church should uphold standards of marital behaviour that she cannot and ought not to ask of those outside. In any event the Church member must always remember that Jesus did not enunciate laws for legal enactment; he exposed and expounded the basic principles on which a truly human life may be lived in accordance with the purpose of its creator.

But even within the legal framework of the Judaism Jesus knew, what he said about adultery and divorce had astonishing consequences. In that society a woman could commit adultery against her husband, but he could not commit adultery against her, but only against another married man. So Jesus was being quite revolutionary when he stated, 'Whoever divorces his wife and marries another commits adultery against her . . . ' He broke new ground in asserting the reciprocal relationships of man and woman in marriage.

Jesus next dealt with oaths. Heavenly citizens need not bolster up their affirmations with any oath. He then turned to the problem of retaliation. Jewish Law had already made a basic advance from the unfettered exercize of revenge to the lawful exaction of an equivalent for the injury sustained. Neither Jesus nor the best of contemporary Judaism was content with that, but for Jesus evil activities were not to be resisted. The practice of 'tit for tat', even on a legal basis, could only imperfectly embody the will of a God who loves, forgives and saves. The heavenly citizen will therefore seek to overcome evil with good (cp. Rom. 12.21), confident that he will thus serve God's purposes, who himself opposes and overcomes sin by vicarious suffering and forgiveness. This was illustrated in practical examples: personal affront and insult; being sued at law; and having compulsory service required by the occupying forces of Rome.

Finally Jesus contrasted the attitude of the old law of love with his own. 'Love your neighbour and hate your enemy' was the 'old' way of putting things. And though that is not found so stated in any written code, it certainly described the different attitudes to fellow-Jews and to Romans. But the heavenly citizen will not restrict his love to his fellow-countrymen; even those who oppose the kingdom of Heaven, individually or in groups, are to be loved. To be a 'son' of the heavenly Father means to become like him, and he sends the good rain and the blessed sunshine to good and bad alike. The heavenly citizen must therefore make his love 'perfect', that is, unrestricted and universal, as the heavenly Father makes his.

In all this it is perfectly clear that Jesus had no intention whatever of adding new 'laws' to those already written; rather he wanted to show how those already written were intended to lead men to understand and co-operate with the purpose of God for the world.

Jesus went on to speak of the practice of heavenly citizenship in the world. His first injunction was not to parade that citizenship, lest religion become something practised for human observation and personal reputation. A reputation for charitable giving, prayerful piety and ascetic practice is easily enough gained. But the heavenly citizen will practise all three unobtrusively: his prayers will not be loud and long, his charity will not be paraded or his asceticism noticeable. All will be done quietly and in secret. Prayer will be simple and direct, on the model:

> Our Father in heaven,
> Your name be hallowed;
> Your kingdom come,
> Your will be done,
> On earth as in heaven.
> Give us today our daily bread.
> Forgive us the wrongs we have done,
> As we forgive those who have wronged us.
> And lead us not into temptation,
> But save us from the evil one.
> For yours is the kingdom,
> The power and the glory
> For ever and ever.

For Jesus forgiveness was central to the life of the heavenly citizen, for in the new order in which he lives forgiveness is the power that binds sinful men to a holy God – and if sinful men do not forgive one another, in that very failure they put themselves beyond the reach of the heavenly Father's forgiving love.

There is a 'life style' that befits the kingdom of Heaven, whose citizens should in certain matters appear different from other men. Wealth, for example, should not be of fundamental importance for him, for while 'possessions' can be stolen, the inward treasures of the heavenly citizen cannot be taken away. The heavenly citizen knows that he cannot be a true servant of God and a slave to any sort of cupidity. No man can serve two such masters.

In a world where God's gifts are immensely bountiful, the heavenly citizen must live differently from other men. Others may try to 'corner' certain necessities for their own advantage or commercial profit, but the heavenly citizen trusts God's rule and his universal providence. The political, economic and social policies open to the heavenly citizen are not those which corner markets for self or class or nation, but those that facilitate a universal sharing of God's bounty. The heavenly citizen can do his work for God in complete confidence and trust. Nothing can be wasted or lost in that service (cp. 1 Cor. 15.58). Tomorrow is mercifully largely hidden from men, but the heavenly citizen knows that, like today, it will be under God's sovereign care. So he can live very happily, 'a day at a time'.

Jesus then considered the heavenly citizen in his human relation-ships. He knew how easy it was even for such a one to detect another's faults more easily than his own. But the man who, in his zeal for universal goodness, becomes more aware of others' faults than his own has fallen into the worst sort of hypocrisy. The greatest misfortune of that condition is that it puts the critic outside the operation of divine forgiveness. The mark of the true citizen of Heaven is an awareness of his own faults, and repentance for them; he then enters into the community of the forgiven and forgiving citizens of the kingdom of Heaven. These can meet one another without the hypocrisy of a pretended self-righteousness. But a harsh world is apt to exploit the 'softness' of forgiving and being forgiven. In living his forgiving life, the heavenly citizen must therefore take care not to provoke even more ruthlessness and cruelty.

Nevertheless the central facts of life in the kingdom of Heaven are all positive. The would-be entrant asks for entry into it; God grants it. He seeks the way into the kingdom; God shows it. He knocks at the door of the kingdom; God opens it. And if that statement of God's generosity seems too good to be true, it is worth reflecting on the generosity of a good earthly father. The heavenly citizen can live by two principles: he may treat men as he wants them to treat him, and he can place unremitting confidence in such action, however costly, because he knows it accords with the nature, will and purpose of God. Judaism had already formulated the former maxim in negative form – don't do to others what you don't want them to do to you – but the positive form comes from Jesus, who is the embodiment of the rule in a human life. He suffered and died as the servant of God who completely trusted his Father. In this demanding maxim the real purpose of the Law and the prophets finds its ultimate expression.

God quickly responds to those who seek him, yet the opened door is not so open that anyone may enter. Repentance is one condition of admission. Life without repentance may be easy and untroublesome, but it is destructive of true humanity in the end. To find life, and avoid the destruction of humanity, means to live sensitively and repentantly, which is neither easy nor popular.

Jesus closed his 'sermon' with two warnings: first, against false prophets, who claim proper authority but cannot exhibit the fruits of the true life of the kingdom of Heaven, where beatitude and repentance go hand in hand. Second, against mistaking form for substance. It is easy enough to 'go through the motions' of heavenly citizenship, and say 'Lord, Lord'. But again, it is in the fruit of the true life of the kingdom of Heaven that the reality begets its only adequate evidence.

To hear Jesus's words and act on them is to be like the man who builds a house on solid rock. When the storms and floods come, his house stands firm. But to hear Jesus's words and not act on them is to be like the man who builds his house upon sand – very near the solid rock, maybe, but on the sand. When the storms and floods come his house is swept away. Only the city of God remaineth!

The Galilean ministry

First phase

Jesus's mission in Galilee was as swiftly successful as that of John the Baptist had been in Judea two years before. Could he avoid the disturbing consequences that John had experienced – an 'investigation' by the Jerusalem authorities, leaving them with a permanent suspicion that he might well prove to be a difficult Messianic claimant, and a preventive arrest by the political authorities for some alleged 'indiscretion' about permissive morality in high places? John had survived for two years. Could Jesus do better? The ready response he had evoked was followed by some quick, decisive and revealing action. Jesus began to 'show his hand', both in the things he did, and in the kind of person he invited to join his missionary band.

His actual message was clear enough. 'The time has come. The kingdom of God has come upon you. Repent, and believe the good news.' But his actions spoke louder than his words – in particular with regard to the sort of person who would become citizens of the newly arrived kingdom of God, who would be ready to place themselves under God's sovereignty and live in loving communion with him.

Jesus healed a leper, thereby showing that the new community would not tolerate the cruel exclusion of lepers from the life of the community. He invited one of the hated tax collectors to join the small band travelling round with him, thereby showing that loyalty to the new kingdom and its king was stronger than even the bitter political prejudice that made all Quisling workers for Rome outcasts. He healed many possessed by demons, thereby showing that the love and understanding given to them inside the kingdom could bring peace and unity to the disturbed and disunited mind. He sat at table with some who were known to sit loose to the law, even with some whose morally irresponsible life was a public scandal, thus showing that the forgiveness of God was something that went out towards men as the initiative to their repentance and entry into the kingdom of Heaven. As Paul put it in one of his letters, 'It is God's kindness that leads men to repentance' (Rom. 2.4). He healed the servant, or 'boy', of a Roman centurion, thus showing that the benefits of the new community were not for Jews alone, but available to Gentiles as well. (see below, p.153f.).

To those who could see and hear, Jesus's actions were often eloquent about himself as the person in whom the new community was being formed. One day in Capernaum he was talking about his mission to some people gathered in his own home there. It may have been a wet or showery day. But as he spoke the numbers grew until quite a crowd crushed round the door outside, trying to hear what he was saying. He was already known in the town as a healer of considerable power, and some of his fellow citizens decided to bring a friend to him to see whether a paralysis could be cured. The 'Capernaum cripple' was probably a well-known figure in the community, and Jesus may well have known him by sight and by reputation. Four friends of his went to fetch the cripple, and they brought him to Jesus's home on a make-do stretcher. When they arrived it became clear that they would never get the man to see Jesus because of the numbers round the door. They then conceived the ingenious plan of taking their friend to the roof, where they removed part of the roofing and lowered him into the room where Jesus was talking. Whether Jesus knew the man or not, whether he knew him as a 'sinner' or not, remains unknown; what is quite certain is that everyone else in the room knew well enough that the popular explanation in Jewish terms for such an affliction was that it was a consequence of sin committed. What is also known is that Jesus at once said to the man, 'Son, your sins are forgiven.' That simple phrase compressed into one short promise the necessary psychological basis for any cure. But it was a theological, not a psychological question that disturbed the minds of some of Capernaum's professional theological teachers. They fastened on this assurance of forgiveness and thought, 'But it is only God who can forgive sins. How can this man, without being blasphemous, pronounce that a man's sins are forgiven?' Jesus easily discerned their bewilderment, and said to them, 'Why are you bothered? Is it easier to say to this paralysed man, "Your sins are forgiven", or to tell him, "Take up your stretcher and walk"? But so that you may know that the Son of Man has the right on earth to forgive sins . . . ' He turned to the man on the stretcher and said to him, 'I tell you now to take up your stretcher and go home.' And that is precisely what the cripple did. Everyone there was utterly amazed.

One Sabbath day Jesus and his disciples went for a walk. Their path took them through a cornfield. His disciples plucked a few ears of corn as they went through, and rubbed off the husks and ate the grain. This was, in strict legal terms, 'work', which was forbidden on the Sabbath. Some of the local Pharisees saw what had happened, and asked Jesus why his disciples should be allowed to break the Sabbath law. In reply Jesus said to them, 'But surely you have read the story of David. After he had been anointed king by Samuel, he had to go into hiding with his band of followers, and they found life very hard at times. On one occasion they entered the house of God and ate some of the consecrated bread which the law reserved for consumption by the priests alone.' The Pharisees knew very well from this response that Jesus saw himself as the already consecrated new 'king' of Israel, even though, as with David of old, there was in actual possession of leadership at the moment an already constituted authority in Judaism.

One day Jairus, one of the rulers of the synagogue in Capernaum, came to Jesus as he was talking to a large crowd by the lake. He came to him (an interesting incident showing that relations between Jesus and local Judaism were not always hostile), prostrated himself before him, and begged him, 'My little daughter is dying. Please come and lay your hands on her, so that she will be healed and live.' Jesus went with him, followed by a large crowd. On the way to the house, Jesus was held up by the action of a woman who had suffered for over a decade from a haemorrhage condition which seemed medically incurable. She went quietly and touched the 'fringe' of Jesus's cloak (on a Jew's clothing the 'fringe' was the visible symbol of the Law), and as soon as she did so was healed. That was surprising enough, but even more so was the fact that Jesus stopped, with the crowd all about him, and asked, 'Who touched me?' The crowd was puzzled, as were the disciples, who asked him, 'With such a crowd about you, how can you ask, "Who touched me?" ' Jesus looked around to detect who it was that had touched him, and the woman, fearful perhaps of what might happen to her, came and prostrated herself before Jesus and told him her story. To her joy, Jesus said, 'My daughter, your trust has saved you. Go in peace, free from your affliction.'

At that very moment men came from the home of Jairus with the news, 'Your daughter is dead: why trouble the Teacher any more?' But Jesus said to him, 'Don't be fearful; just have trust.' From that point he would not allow anyone to go on with him, except the parents of the girl and three disciples, Peter, James and John. When they came to the house, they saw the crowd, and heard the professional weepers at their task. Jesus said, 'Why all this mourning? The child is not dead, but simply asleep.' They all laughed at him. But with that strange authority that belonged to him, Jesus dismissed them all. Then, taking the parents and the three disciples into the room where the girl was, he went to her, took her by the hand, and said to her, '*Talitha cumi*' – 'Little girl, get up'. And she got up, and walked about normally.

Any story that tells of the restoration of someone well attested as dead is bound to present great if not insuperable difficulties for modern men. What then can be said of this, and other stories of Jesus's power to raise the dead to life? The evangelists tell also of his raising of a widow's son at Nain (Luke 7.11ff.), and of Lazarus of Bethany (John 11.1-44). The evangelists were certainly not concerned just to present Jesus as the world's most amazing wonder worker. In any event, Jairus's daughter, the widow's son at Nain and Lazarus all returned to a mortal life which brought them to death later on; such a return to human existence is not obviously the best gift for a mortal man to receive. The point of all three stories was to show that the life which Jesus brought and bestowed was one whose bounds were not limited to human historical existence. All three subjects returned from death to a life that was still mortal, but which, from the fact of their return from the dead at Jesus's bidding, was seen not to be bounded by death, for it had been made clear by their return from death that the word of Jesus could be heard and answered beyond death. As each returned to mortal temporal existence testimony was given that to respond to Jesus was to be already living, even in time, by the power of a life over which death had no power. No doubt the three stories could not have been so told save from the perspective of the resurrection. But that perspective is the only one that can express the reality of the stories, and point out what was really going on.

Jesus said that Jairus's daughter was 'asleep'. He was laughed at for his pains. But Jairus's daughter was asleep in the sense that it required only a word from Jesus to wake her. It is that hearing of Christ's word and responding to it that marks the passage from death to life. As Jesus told the Jews at the Pool of Bethesda, 'Anyone who gives heed to what I say and puts his trust in him who sent me has hold of eternal life, and does not come up for judgement, but *has already passed from death to life.*'

Did Jesus really have the power to raise dead people to life? The answer to that question must be decided by each hearer of the gospel stories for himself. The answer need not be negative. A positive answer does not necessarily gainsay all modern science and philosophy (see above, p.96). To accept that Jesus had such powers implies that the gospel records can stand all the tests of historical integrity that may rightly be posed. Some readers will find them adequate on this score. But there are some critics who think that in any such traditions there is a 'legendary' element which inevitably detracts from precise historicity. If the gospel reader accepts that judgment, he needs to remember the question posed was by no means the most important one in the minds of the evangelists. For them the real issue was whether their testimony, either by recounting historical facts (what took place) or by the use of legendary material ('going on' indicators in narrative form), would enable their readers to hear Jesus's quickening word. If it does, such readers have already, by trusting Jesus, begun to live in continuing community with him, and to share in its fellowship a life that his resurrection has shown to be beyond the destructive power of death.

John the Baptist, who though in prison was allowed visits from his disciples (Luke 7.18), heard about Jesus, and wondered whether the great hopes he had entertained of the emergence of a new people of God were now being fulfilled. He sent some of his followers to ask Jesus, 'Are you the one who is to come, or have we still to wait for him?' Jesus replied, 'Go and tell John what you have seen and heard: that the blind see, the lame walk, the lepers are clean, the deaf hear, the dead live, and the poor are hearing the good news of the kingdom.' This was in effect a clear claim by Jesus to be 'the one who is to come', for his reply borrowed its chief contents from two passages in Isaiah, (35.5f. and 61.1) both of which are Messianic in tone and content.

Second phase, AD.30

John had been concerned to proclaim the institution of a new people of God, symbolized in the 'Red Sea' baptism in the Jordan. Jesus was also concerned to announce the arrival of the new people of God, inaugurated at his own baptism. John's mission had ended abruptly with his arrest and imprisonment, and this posed questions for Jesus's ministry. Could it be made publicly and unequivocally clear that a new people of God had been born, without occasioning an official move by religious or political authorities which would end it prematurely?

After his early and successful tour of Galilee Jesus went into the hill country of Galilee and called to his side some specially chosen men. From them he chose twelve for posts and duties of special responsibility in his new movement. The number twelve itself was a skilled if silent statement that in him a new Israel had been formed, for the Twelve symbolized in the new people of God the patriarchs of the twelve tribes of old Israel. The twelve Jesus called were: Simon, Peter, Andrew and Philip, from among John the Baptist's disciples; John and James who, like Peter and Andrew, were Bethsaida fishermen; Matthew, a tax collector, whose office was in Capernaum; Thomas, Bartholomew, James the son of Alphaeus, Thaddeus, Simon, a recruit from the guerilla Zealot movement, and Judas Iscariot. The list is not universally agreed, for Luke replaces Thaddeus in his list of names by another Judas, the son of James; and the fourth evangelist also wrote of a 'Judas, not Iscariot' (John 14.22). But the variations only emphasize that the number Twelve is more important than any particular list of names.

So Jesus 'made' the Twelve, to use the word Mark employed in his account, a word which he sometimes used to tell of the performance of a miracle (Mark 6.5). The special duties to which they were to be assigned were three: 1. To 'be with' Jesus, which meant not just spatial proximity, but much more a growing like him through sharing the life of the new people of God with him. 2. To go out to proclaim the good news that the kingdom of God had now arrived; that the total legal obedience demanded by the Pharisees as a prerequisite to its coming was not therefore a divine requirement; that the two-or three-year 'apprenticeship' for life in the kingdom that the desert communities insisted upon was a superfluity; that there was no need to rely on armed conflict to inaugurate the kingdom. 3. To expel from the hearts and minds of men those demonic powers that could dominate and enslave mankind. So they were to share the authority and power that belonged to Jesus himself. It would become theirs through community with him.

Jesus sent them on their first mission. From their own expectations and from instructions reported to have been given them by Jesus (though these have been affected by the resurrection perspective), the Twelve were apprehensive about their undertaking. Since some of them had previously been disciples of John the Baptist, this is not wholly surprising. Jesus heartened them by pointing out that they were not like farm labourers going out to sow, who would have to wait for months before gathering any crops; they were more like men going into the harvest itself to gather what had already ripened as a result of work already done. Their labour would be God's means of separating the good grain from useless and alien weed.

Harvesting needs to be done at the right time – and the early response to the good news of the kingdom made it clear that the time was indeed ripe. Harvesting must also be done speedily, and speed was a tactical necessity for the Twelve, particularly in view of the abbreviated career of the Baptist. So Jesus counselled that no time should be spent in Gentile settlements, for they would be without the preparatory 'sowing' of the word of scripture; nor should Samaritan towns be visited, for no Samaritan would normally listen to a Jew talking about the arrival of a new Israel of God. The mission should therefore confine itself to the towns and villages of Israel, and the Twelve might find even that too large a task for the time available. And in the exercize of their authority to exorcize demons and to heal the sick they would be saying things in action that would speak even more loudly than their words.

Jesus warned the Twelve of the difficulties they might encounter on their journey. In some towns they might be met with hostility and inhospitality; that would be a self-condemnation of the community concerned. They might meet with downright opposition, and find themselves liable to arrest as likely disturbers of the peace. Disappointed parents might resent their children accepting the message, and conservative young people react bitterly to parents who accepted the good news. But there was no need to fear. God's universal providence controls even the life and death of a sparrow, and can be trusted to care for those who labour for him. Two final things: half-heartedness, whether in the missionary or the listener, would be self-defeating; but, equally, any service done for the new 'son', however small, would receive its due and rich reward.

There is no unequivocal evidence about how the mission of the Twelve was organized and conducted, though it appears to have been very successful. It also seems that the Twelve were not yet left entirely on their own, for Jesus went round with them. The procedure seems to have been for the Twelve to visit a number of neighbouring villages, secure enough interested people to make a public open-air meeting useful, and then bring Jesus to address it (Luke 8.1, 4). It was certainly sufficiently successful for the authorities in Jerusalem to send down a deputation to investigate and report. The deputation made contact with Jesus in Capernaum, where they found that even his own family were infected with the tendentious rumour that Jesus was, or was going, 'out of his mind' (Mark 3.21). The deputation agreed. They stated that in fact Jesus was 'possessed' by the very prince of demons, Beelzebub, for in what other way, they argued, could he command lesser demons to leave their victims, and be obeyed? The sanity of Jesus showed in his response, that Satan could not oust Satan without actually destroying himself. Moreover, to see the work of the Spirit as the work of the devil is to place oneself beyond help, for any true help that could come from the Spirit would be rejected as diabolic!

The mother and brothers of Jesus had come to take him back to the peaceful and protected anonymity of Nazareth. But Jesus, speaking in terms of the divine sonship revealed to him at his baptism, asked, 'But who are my mother and my brothers? My real mother, and my real brothers are those around me who learn and do the will of God' (Mark 3.31-35).

In spite of all this Jesus found himself well received in Galilee generally, and in Capernaum in particular. Even the Pharisees of that town felt able to invite him to their homes, though not always with entirely agreeable social (or religious) consequences. One Pharisee, named Simon, put on a dinner party for Jesus, who went happily enough. He noticed that his reception was a little cool for the guest of the evening, indeed for any guest at all, for he was given no foot bath, no kiss of welcome and no perfume to wear at the feast. Yet he went in and reclined with the other guests on low divans, with feet away from the table. As quite often on such occasions, the doors of the house were left open, and anyone could enter to watch, hear and enjoy what was taking place. On this occasion a Capernaum woman came in from the street who was a well known, and probably attractive 'bad lot', with no respect for religion or the morals and puritan respectabilities of her Jewish society. She had probably heard Jesus preach, and she certainly arrived a changed woman to offer Jesus her tribute of gratitude. She produced a flask of perfume, and as she went to use it she burst into tears, and some fell on Jesus's feet. She wiped them off with her hair. She kissed his feet, and anointed them with the perfume.

Simon watched all this with horrified amazement. As a Pharisee he knew the shocking uncleanness of having such a sinner make bodily contact; and he recognized that if Jesus were really a prophet concerned with morality, public and private, he would have done something to keep the woman away from himself. Jesus divined what Simon was thinking, and told him a story of two debtors. One owed £500 and the other, to the same creditor, £50. Neither could pay, so the creditor forgave both debts. 'Which of them,' asked Jesus, 'would love the creditor most?' Simon answered, 'The one who had been remitted the greater debt.' 'Quite right,' said Jesus, and went on to point out how this 'sinful' woman had done for him what the 'righteous' Pharisee had failed to do: she had given him a foot bath, kissed him, and provided him with perfume for the feast. 'And that is why,' he added, 'her many sins are forgiven, because she loved much.' But the love, of course, was the consequence of the forgiveness, and the forgiveness had came because the woman had heard Jesus speak of the kingdom whose doors were open to the penitent wrong-doer. 'Your trust has saved you,' he finally said to the woman.

On another occasion, a Sabbath day, Jesus accepted an invitation to dinner from a leading Pharisee, and it turned out to be far more than a social evening to meet a distinguished Galilean. One of the 'gate-crashers' to the dinner was a man afflicted by dropsy. He placed himself with his noticeable symptoms right in front of Jesus in what seemed to be a silent plea for help. The assembled company reclined fascinated, wondering whether Jesus would heal the man on the Sabbath day. Jesus broke the tense silence by putting their question into words, 'Is it legally permissible to do a work of healing on the Sabbath, or not?' The silence persisted. Jesus then healed the man, and sent him home. He then put another question to the company, 'Which of you, with an ass or an ox falling into a well on the Sabbath day, will not nevertheless pull it out right away?' They knew that each of them would, though to say so would put them technically in the wrong. Jesus had made the point that if mercy could override Sabbath legalities in the case of an animal, how much more should it do so in the case of a human being.

Jesus, a somewhat unpredictable guest to entertain, then went on to comment on human behaviour at the sort of party they were having. He was the chief guest, and had noticed how the others had used every sort of social trick to get a seat at the top of the table near him. He observed that to do so is only to court disaster (perhaps some unfortunate guest had!) as the host comes to you and says, 'I'm very sorry, but that place has been reserved for this other guest of mine.' The only thing to do is to leave the 'top place' and go to the bottom of the table, scarlet with blushes. But if you take the opposite line and sit yourself at the bottom of the table, your host may come and say, 'My dear friend, you must not sit there. Come up here' – and your blushes will be spared. This is exactly the order of things in the kingdom of God where 'everyone who exalts himself will be humbled, and whoever humbles himself will be exalted'. God alone really determines and knows a man's real place in the order of things. And that very truth was spoken in action in Jesus's own 'humbling of himself' and the subsequent glory that was his (Phil. 2.8f.).

Jesus then commended the behaviour of the kingdom of God

even for normal social engagements. Don't invite friends, relations and rich neighbours to your social occasions, for they will only invite you back again, and the endless rote will go on. Instead, invite the poor, the crippled, the lame and the blind; they won't, because they can't, ask you back, but you will be relieved of the anxiety that normal social life imposes. Again this picture of a new sort of social life is a parable of what life in the kingdom of God is like now. For no man can invite God to a divine feast. God's guests can only accept his invitation and be grateful for it.

Finally, at that memorable Sabbath dinner, Jesus told a story of how God sends out his invitations, and how men respond. What prompted the story was a face-saving exclamation by one of the guests at what Jesus had already said. 'How fortunate is the man who will sit down in the kingdom of God!' he piously ejaculated. Jesus then told the story of the man who planned a great feast, and sent word out to his guests about the day and time of the feast. On the day itself, at the appropriate hour, he sent out again and let his guests know that everything was ready, and that they should now come. One after another they excused themselves: one had bought a piece of land, and the host would know that unless certain formalities were complied with right away the land might well be sold to another buyer. A second had just purchased a couple of oxen, and unless he went forthwith to ensure that the right beasts were delivered he could be severely out of pocket. A third had just begun his marriage ceremonies, and, as the host knew well, they took a whole week, so clearly he could not come. So, implied Jesus, men can, for reasons to do with what they believe to be their own prosperity, or for social, even religious reasons, fail to accept the invitation that God had now extended to all men in his new 'son'. So God would do what the healing at that meal had demonstrated: send out for the poor, the crippled, the blind and the lame, and take them into the heavenly feast of the kingdom of God.

At this stage of his mission in Galilee it was not only Jewish leaders who turned to Jesus and acknowledged to some degree the authority he possessed. Stationed in Capernaum was a Roman centurion who had proved himself an understanding friend to the Jews. He had built them a new synagogue, a very distinguished and exceptional piece of generosity. His servant had fallen ill, and was dying. Being attached to him, he asked some of his Jewish friends to go to Jesus and ask his help. They did so, and pleaded strongly for the centurion on the grounds that he had done so much for the

Jews. Jesus went with them, but had not reached the centurion's quarters when some of his friends met Jesus with the message that the officer did not deem himself worthy to receive Jesus into his home, or even to approach Jesus himself and ask his help. Jesus had, he realized, just to speak the word, and his servant would be cured. After all, a centurion knew all there was to know about orders and obedience! Jesus was himself astounded, and turned to the Jewish crowd that was following him and said, 'I've not found faith like that, not even in the Israel that ought to manifest it.' The centurion's friends returned to find that the servant had recovered.

Jesus's 'acted' word found a richer and deeper statement one day as he journeyed with his disciples. They were on their way to Nain, followed by a large crowd, and as they came to the town gates they met the funeral procession of a young man who was the only son of an already widowed mother. She was much distressed, and Jesus, moved with compassion, went to her and said, 'Don't cry.' He then went to the hearse, laid his hand on it, and said, 'Young man, get up' (or, to give the word used in a post-Easter translation, 'be resurrected'). The young man sat up, and began to talk, and Jesus gave him back to his mother. The crowd offered two significant comments: 'A great prophet has come amongst us', and, 'God has shown his care for his people'. The real message was beginning to get through: Jesus was no 'ordinary man', but one specially inspired by God, and in his ministry God was showing his care for his people. But there was still more for the crowds to learn.

The end of the season of 30 A.D. saw Jesus pay a visit to his home, family and friends in Nazareth. Reports survive of one incident only. On Saturday he went, as he always did, to the synagogue. As a now distinguished visitor he was asked by the ruler of the synagogue to read the scriptures and expound them. He stood up to read them, found the appointed passage, and read:

> The spirit of God is upon me
> because he has anointed me;
> he has sent me to announce
> good news to the poor,
> to proclaim release for prisoners
> and recovery of sight for the blind;
> to let the broken victims go free,
> to proclaim the year when God will show his favour.

It was a heady text for a preacher who claimed to incorporate in himself the arrival of the new Israel of God, speaking in the most nationalist province of Palestine, where revolt was always a possibility for the adventurous patriot. Had the day of *the* revolution arrived? The congregation was even more excited when Jesus sat down for his exposition, and began with the words: 'This very day, while you have been listening, this scriptural saying has become an historical reality.' He went on to expound the text in the way that Galileans had heard all through the summer, and he carried the congregation with him for some time. They naturally expected a strong nationalist interpretation of Isaiah, but as Jesus went on they began to realize that nothing like that was going to come. 'How can the son of Joseph, father of a nationalist household, talk as he is now talking to us?' they asked. Jesus sensed the latent hostility becoming open, and he naturally remembered the scene at Capernaum when his own family had thought that he was going out of his mind (see above, p.145). He answered the challenge by saying, 'I can assure you that what is happening here today is the actualization of the old proverb which says, "No prophet is ever honoured in his own country." ' 'And don't you recall,' he went on, 'that during the great historic drought the prophet Elijah was not sent to an Israelite home or town, but to a Gentile one; and that Elisha was not told to cure an Israelite, but a Syrian, Naaman, of leprosy.' This 'Jonah-like' saying infuriated the congregation, who rushed him out of the synagogue, took him to the crest of the hill on which Nazareth was built, and were about to throw him down and have done with him then and there when, with the strange and irresistible authority he had, he calmly walked right through them and returned to Capernaum.

Third phase, AD.31

The year 31 A.D. was fateful. Some time before Jesus thought it wise to renew his campaign news came through of the tragic death of John the Baptist. That news served but to underline the urgency for Jesus to press forward with his mission. But how did the campaign appear after two years' work in Galilee, the last intensely active after the arrest of John? There had certainly been a most encouraging popular response. Wherever they went, Jesus and his disciples drew large crowds, who listened eagerly to the message that the kingdom of God had arrived, and that Jesus and his company were the actual nucleus of the new and universal people of

God. But for all that, popular acclaim was not necessarily popular understanding – and a great deal needed to be done to achieve that.

The Galileans, more than most Jews, were eager to hear that the days of their subjugation were over, and that Israel would once more become a great and independent nation; but they realized, as perhaps no other Jews could, that independence could never be achieved without armed conflict with Rome, with all its attendant dangers and severities. The Galileans also knew that their own authorities recognized this. The Pharisees and Sadducees knew that conflict was eventually unavoidable. The Zealots believed it to be the only way of banishing Rome, and inaugurating the Messiah's rule, and in the meantime used violence and robbery to support their guerilla existence. The desert sectaries held it as part of their doctrine that a holy war was an inescapable element in the great upheaval which would come on God's appointed day. Yet Jesus never mentioned armed rebellion. Rather he spoke of 'loving your enemies' and 'praying for them that despitefully use you', and doing a double quota of forced labour for the Roman occupiers. He evidently had no plans at all for an armed campaign. Certainly he performed healings, and though these were far from military activity, yet did they not represent the health and happiness that were the promised accompaniments of the Messianic age? Perhaps after all Jesus was just quietly biding his time before launching the final attack on the might of Rome?

When Jesus heard the news of John's execution he took urgent steps to get his mission swiftly under way once more. He called the Twelve together, reminded them of their task, and sent them out two by two. They went out, and had the same sort of success as they had had the previous year. News of the campaign reached Herod, and he was disturbed. He gathered various opinions from friendly Jews (the 'Herodians'), and was told that Jesus was possibly John the Baptist risen from the dead, or the expected and promised Elijah to herald the coming of the Messiah, or even the great prophet expected to signalize the final beginning of the final Messianic age. But Herod himself, perhaps of his own guilty conscience, was sure that the figure leading the new campaign was none other than John the Baptist whom he had executed.*

---

*It is interesting to discover in this indirect way that popular belief of the time had room for the notion of 'rising from the dead'. The dead person rose to new life in some other person, as Herod thought John had risen in Jesus. This forms an interesting background to the good news that the disciples announced on Easter

The Twelve completed their mission, and returned to Capernaum to report to Jesus. He decided that what was needed was a quiet retreat to some lonely place where they could think and pray together about the mission and its future. But their plans were thwarted, for news got around that they were about to leave Capernaum, and a considerable crowd eventually followed them. Instead of trying to get rid of them Jesus turned to meet them, and spent time talking to them about his work and his message. The day wore on, and as evening drew near the Twelve suggested to Jesus that the crowd be sent away so that they could to go nearby villages and farms and get 'bed and breakfast' for the night. As they pointed out, they had come into very rural and sparsely inhabited country-side. But Jesus said to them, 'Why not give them something to eat yourselves?' Their ready answer was, 'But all we've got is a mere five barley loaves and two dried fish! What use are they for the five thousand people here?' Jesus told them to get everyone to sit down; and they did. So now, in a 'desert' place, the new people of Israel were about to be fed, as the old Israel had been fed long ago (Exod. 16.35; Deut. 8.3). Jesus took the five loaves and the two fish, looked up to heaven, thanked God for them, and gave them to the disciples to distribute to the crowd. They did so, and afterwards gathered up twelve basketfuls of leftover scraps.

The modern mind must wrestle for itself with the problems that the story raises. Suffice it to say that whatever was or was not done in miraculous action that day, the significance of what took place, what was really going on, was that the new people of God had been provided with their food in a desert place, just as the old people of God had been under Moses. What Jesus had rightly been unwilling to ask for as a private proof of his 'sonship' in his earlier temptation (see p.113) was now eloquent confirmation of his message. It confirmed his conviction that the life of the new people of God had begun in him, and that it was enjoying, as he had heard at his baptism and read in the synagogue at Nazareth, the 'Lord's favour'.

But there were other interpretations of the events of that memorable day. Numbers in the crowds were convinced that at last the Messiah had come, and they therefore decided to proclaim him king, raise the standard of revolt, and fight for independence. Jesus saw the move coming, and forestalled it by going away to a quiet

day, that Jesus had risen from the dead, which clearly meant more than Herod would have deemed possible.

place some distance off, leaving the crowd to disperse.

The Twelve were also somewhat apprehensive as to what might transpire, and they took to the lake. They got into a boat, and set out for some other lonely place along the shore. It was already dark when they embarked, and as they rowed the boat a strong head wind blew up, and the struggle with it brought them near to exhaustion. They were almost finished when, of a sudden, they saw Jesus walking, they were sure, on the lake itself. They thought they must be seeing a ghost, but the calm voice of Jesus came across to them, 'I am here. Don't be frightened.' And, as if he had spoken directly to it, the wind died down. He got into the boat, and they rowed on contentedly, and eventually landed back in Capernaum.

On the morrow, the previous day's crowd sought them out, and Jesus began teaching them about what had really been going on the day before. They had been fed with barley loaves, he said, but life was not just a matter of earning enough money to buy bread to feed oneself and one's family. That was the real meaning of yesterday. For they all had an appetite for a food far more basic and important than bread made from cereal. To be really human meant to have a hunger for God, and it was that which yesterday's meal had really satisfied. It was able to do so because God had included them in his new people or 'son' of God, which had been born into the world by Jesus's coming. It was now a functioning reality. The real miracle of yesterday was not the sheer multiplication of loaves, but the astounding gift of God in sending Jesus to be the life of the new people of Israel, which would only come to full self-awareness by his own self-giving on its behalf. If they reflected on it, that was the real meaning of what had happened long ago to the old Israel in the wilderness under Moses, when they had eaten manna through forty years of God's providing.

After this, Jesus renewed his search for a place of quiet. He went away to the Gentile territory of Sidon, where there would be less likelihood of being disturbed by crowds. He was alone, and wanted to be alone. He found a house where he could get lodging for the night, and thought himself well settled. But he could not even remain there undetected. In the same town there was a Greek woman who had a daughter who was 'possessed'. She had heard of Jesus, found out where he was lodged, and begged him to heal her daughter. Jesus, feeling bound by what he had told the disciples about concentrating on the 'lost sheep' of the house of Israel' and unwilling to start up a Gentile mission in so Gentile an area, said that it was not right to give the children's food to 'dogs'. The woman caught the allusion, for Jews often referred to Gentiles as 'dogs'. She answered that even dogs were allowed to eat crumbs dropped by the children under the table. Jesus was delighted with the discerning reply, and healed her daughter forthwith. In spite of his useful strategy of concentrating on the Jews, he remained a true 'Jonah' in his generation.

That further showed itself on the way back from Sidon. Jesus seemed still uncertain about the revolutionary tendencies of the Galilean crowds, and so took the longer route back through the territory of Philip, Herod's son, to the north-east of the Sea of Galilee. He came in due course to the new residential area of 'Decapolis' (the ten cities), where there was a large Gentile element. But as in Sidon he was recognized, and a large crowd gathered. Jesus realized how wrongly a 'strategy' might lead one, and summoned the Twelve to assist him. For three days he talked to them of his message and mission. At the end of that time history repeated itself: the crowd was hungry. Jesus asked about provisions. Seven loaves and a few dried fish were available. Jesus took the bread into his hands, looked up to heaven, thanked God for providing food, and had the Twelve distribute the loaves to the people. When the meal was over, seven basketfuls of scraps were gathered up. So just as the lost sheep of the house of Israel had been gathered and fed, so now the scattered sheep of 'other flocks and other folds' were assembled and fed. In these two symbolic feedings Jesus stated in action what he put into words in the fourth gospel: 'I have other sheep, that are not of this [Jewish] fold; I must bring them also, and they will heed my voice. So shall there be one flock, one shepherd' (John 10.16).

Wisely avoiding any chance of a repetition of the earlier attempt to make him king, Jesus quickly left by boat with the Twelve and returned to the western Galilean shore of the lake.

The two feedings are by no means unconnected. In them Jesus simply continued a practice of which the authorities had already expressed disapproval, of having 'table fellowship' with people who were religiously or morally 'undesirable'. In terms of the celebratory meals that John the Baptist would have learned from the Essene or Qumran communities, this was tantamount to affirming that those who sat to eat with Jesus were already full members of his community, which, in his own terms, was the kingdom of Heaven (cp. Mark 2.15; Luke 5.30; 15.2). At each of the two great feedings there would have been present many of whom the Pharisees would have thoroughly disapproved. But Jesus was making plain in action what he had stated in words, that the doors of the kingdom were open to all those who responded to his call.

The two great feedings were linked in another highly significant way. At the earlier feeding it had been stated in the action of a real historical occasion that the new Israel was both the heir and the replacement of the old, open to all Jews willing to repent and accept the sustenance that God alone could give, and was in fact giving in Jesus the 'son'. In the second feeding it was equally and dramatically affirmed that even Gentile 'dogs' were part of the family of God, part of the divine household, and therefore entitled to much more than the privilege of 'picking up the crumbs under the master's table', even to the privilege of sharing in the family feast itself.

But great public acclaim was still a problem for Jesus, who had been seeking a quiet retreat. He decided once more to seek an opportunity for leisured reflection on his mission in the company of the Twelve. So they set off for the northern uplands of Philip's territory again. On the way, leaving the Sea of Galilee, they had to pass through Bethsaida. There Jesus was asked to heal a blind man. He did so, but with more difficulty than usual – symbolic, perhaps, of the difficulty he would have in 'opening the eyes' of the Twelve to the reality of what was going on.

Jesus and the Twelve went on, and eventually came to the villages near the rebuilt town of Caesarea Philippi, which Philip had erected in honour of the Roman emperor. It was thereabouts that Jesus asked his first question, easy enough to answer, since it asked simply for a factual report. 'What are the crowds saying about me?' he asked, and received the same answer that Herod Antipas had received when he asked his advisers about the person and activity of Jesus. 'Some say you are John the Baptist risen from the dead; some say you are Elijah, the great forerunner of Messiah; while still others say that you are one or other of the great prophets returned to work for our people.' Then Jesus put a searching question to those he had selected to be the inner nucleus of the new 'son' or people of God. 'But what have you to say yourselves?' he asked. There was a moment's pregnant silence. Then Peter burst out with a conviction that, though none of the crowd had voiced it, was already his own, and probably the Twelve shared belief, 'You are the Messiah.'

The answer was one which Jesus had really wanted, even expected, but also dreaded! Although he believed himself to be

Israel's true Messiah, he had quite distinctive ideas about the office and destiny of that crucial figure. How far would Peter or any or the Twelve have come towards sharing his own conception of the Messianic office? Would they mean what some of the crowds meant when they hailed him as 'Son of David'? Would they mean what those meant who after the first feeding came to try to make him king? So very much depended on the answer to that question.

To Peter it was no new thing to think that Jesus was the Messiah. It was in fact this very title which Andrew his brother had used in those seemingly far-off days when they were both disciples of John the Baptist (John 1.37, 41). Yet Peter knew that John the Baptist had some uncertainty about Jesus's Messiahship, for he had sent from prison to enquire whether Jesus really was 'the one who was to come' (Mat. 11.1-5). Jesus on that occasion had sent back to John an answer that could only be construed as a clear affirmative (see p.143) And now, in his answer to Jesus's question, Peter reaffirmed that Jesus was the Messiah.

'You are the Messiah.' The truth, hidden until now, was exposed; the closely kept secret was now revealed. Jesus accepted Peter's reply as if it coincided with his own conception of what Messiahship meant. He told Peter that to see him, Jesus, as the promised Messiah was to have been given an insight from above, and that such a heavenly based conviction would be the very stuff out of which the new community of the 'son' would be fashioned. But everything really depended on what was meant by 'Messiah'. If his mission were linked, as it was in popular Judaism, with a political kingdom and the inevitable war with Rome, no honourable claimant to Messiahship ought to shrink from public acknowledgment of his status. The Jews believed that in any conflict in which the Messiah was involved, victory was assured him, for God would be with them and fight on their side. But that was not the way that Jesus envisaged his Messiahship. The 'kingdom' linked with his Messiahship was not one to be established in the future, near or distant, by military encounter; it was a kingdom already present, and faithful, repentant Jews – and Gentiles! – could enter it now.

It was therefore important to clarify and determine the issues right away. Were the contents of Peter's confession made public, Jesus would naturally be popularly acclaimed as the military Messiah of Jewish expectation. He and his followers would be regarded by Rome as revolutionaries, and end up, as the followers of Judas of Galilee in his adolescent days, hanging on a cross! Yet to make plain and have accepted by the Twelve his own conception of Messiahship would also create difficulties. The Jewish authorities were already more than suspicious of him, and had shown their opposition and hostility. He had been accused of 'blasphemy', and he might end up, if he followed his own convictions, on the capital charge of being a Messianic rebel, and suffer crucifixion just the same. It was not the cross that he rejected in itself, but the kind of comment that crucifixion might pass on himself and his work. He did not want to die as a defeated rebel against Rome, or as a self-proven false claimant to be the Messiah of Judaism; rather he must die as the one who, as the king of a realm that had neither geographical nor temporal boundaries, exhibited the truth that his kingdom had come, and needed no war to bring it to pass. There could be no easy way for any Messiah. But for Jesus the way forward from now on would have to be chosen with great care, so that whatever might happen to him, or whatever fate lay in store for him, his message, both spoken and acted, that the kingdom of God was a reality in the present, would not be invalidated but endorsed.

So, though the Messiahship of Jesus was now openly stated and accepted within the circle of the Twelve, Jesus at once charged them to keep all talk about it to themselves. He began to alert them as to what lay ahead for him as he went forward to fulfil the Messiahship he accepted for himself. He must go to Jerusalem (where else could the Messiah go?). But he would not announce himself there as the Messiah, for the authorities and the populace would both misunderstand the term. He would go as the self-acclaimed 'Son of Man', a title he had begun to use already, drawn from the scriptural source of the prophet Daniel, and the contemporary fashionable theological writing of Enoch. Yet, however much he thus tried to avoid a confrontation arising from differing conceptions of Messiahship, the Jerusalem authorities would be bound to reject him on what were for them quite basic religious and theological grounds. They would hand him over to the Roman authorities as a potential Messianic rebel, to receive the usual penalty of crucifixion. But that, Jesus affirmed, would not be the end of the story. Already the Twelve had seen one mission, that of John the Baptist, continue after his own imprisonment and death. If he was the sort of Messiah he believed himself to be, then not even death could frustrate his mission, for with the coming of the 'son' into the historical order God had come himself, and no temporal act of crucifixion could destroy the eternal life so made manifest in him.

But for Peter all such foreboding was totally unacceptable. No true Messiah could ever suffer the fate that Jesus was evidently envisaging. 'That is impossible,' he exclaimed, 'That sort of thing will never happen to you!' This reminded Jesus of his forty days in the desert, when he had had to face the same sort of issue, and in what Peter said he heard once again the voice of the tempter. Once again he replied with the words, 'Go away, Satan.' And he said to Peter, 'What you have just said is the way Satan thinks, and not the way in which God plans.'

Peter's confession at Caesarea Philippi marked a change in the way Jesus talked to the crowds. When, as inevitably happened, a crowd came together at this time, he spoke to them in new and sombre terms: 'If anyone, any of you, wants to become my follower, let it be quite clear what is at stake. For the issue is literally one of life and death. If you want your present earthly life to be safe, don't follow me. But if you are willing to put your life at risk for the sake of the good news about the kingdom and myself, then you will save the only life worth having, life in the eternal kingdom of God. For it is not really worthwhile to gain control of the world, not to mention Jewish independence, at the cost of losing the only life that really lasts and satisfies. Whether you have that life or not turns on the response you make to me. How you respond determines your presence in or absence from, the kingdom, and that settles your ultimate destiny: either to be in the kingdom of eternal life with me, or to stay in the dying world that rejects me and my good news, and be lost to really true and lasting life. And you must not suppose that in talking about "ultimate things" I am just speculating about some distant "end of the world". On the contrary, many of you listening to me today will see for yourselves before you die that the kingdom which I proclaim will have made its presence known in convincing demonstration of its power and authority.'

For almost another week Jesus and the Twelve journeyed on, and Jesus found much to say to them in the light of the new situation that Peter's confession had created and exposed. The Twelve were excusably apprehensive at the ominous tone of some of Jesus's remarks. 'There is no need to be afraid,' he told them, 'Your heavenly Father has chosen to give you the kingdom. What more can you have than that? That is why you can afford to be generous with your possessions, for your real treasures are not in purses or property, but in those things that cannot be stolen, worn out or destroyed. But be very much on the alert for the time when the decisions will be called for which will determine your ultimate destiny, for when it comes you will be surprised. But your duty remains constant – as my stewards you are to see that my followers are properly supplied with the real food that will keep them spiritually and healthily alive. If you fail in that task because you suppose that everyday life lacks the depth and meaning that I find it to have, then you cannot complain if you suffer the proper penalties appropriate to untrustworthy stewards.'

On another occasion, he was asked, 'Will only a few find their way into the kingdom?' He answered, 'Try to get in through the narrow gate; many people will try to do so, but find themselves unable to get in. And once the door into the kingdom has been closed, it will be no good standing outside and crying out, "Please let us in"; for you will be told, "I have no idea who you are, or where you come from." You will then declare, "We sat at table with you [cf. above, p.139], and that was a real act establishing fellowship with us; and you taught in our streets; so surely you were intending us to have the benefits of your message." But I shall say to you at that time, "Get out of my sight, all of you, with your wicked ways!" You will be full of remorse as you see the great forefathers of your people, Abraham, Isaac and Jacob together with the prophets who have spoken to you, all sitting down in the kingdom of God, while you yourselves are kept outside. And you will see all sorts of people, from north and south, from east and west, coming in great numbers to share in the feast of the kingdom of God; but yourselves will not be participating. You will discover how the precedences of the kingdom are very different from those of the world. For many who are eminent people now, will then be taking a very back seat, while some who are practically outcasts now will be seated at the top table in the feast of the kingdom.' In other words the mission to the lost sheep of the house of Israel would not lead to the national repentance which he and John had called for at the beginning. Israel would largely reject him, but many Gentiles would join repentant Jews to share the life of the true people of God.

Six days after the 'confession' at Caesarea Philippi Jesus took Peter, James and John away to a high hill in Galilee. What exactly took place on that occasion is impossible now to determine, though it has certainly had its basis in normal human experience as it certainly transcended it. That basis is twofold. First, in the well-attested experience of a change of countenance. The young man who has just proposed to his beloved will often be surprised at the astonishing radiance that lights up, even transforms, her face as she promises herself to him in acceptance. The Christian pastor, who was one day disturbed while lost in meditation as he was saying his prayers, seemed to his unwitting intruder to have not only his face aglow, but his whole person surrounded with a clearly unnatural radiance; he was scarcely recognizable as the person he normally was. Second, in the equally well-attested fact that many of the apparently 'random' thoughts that come into the mind or the scenes that compose dreams, are not 'chance' invaders, but elements from past experience that have been dropped into the subconscious and not fully integrated into the conscious personality.

Jesus and the special three climbed the steep hill, and spent some time meditating and praying together. As they continued their devotions the three men saw an unbelievable change come over Jesus. His features lit up with a glow of quite unearthly radiance, and his whole appearance seemed to them more heavenly than earthly. Surely this must be some verification of their belief that he was the Messiah, that he was what he had come to call himself, the Son of Man. And as they gazed at him – for they could not take their eyes away – they became aware that two other figures were emerging into their heightened vision as though coming into sight in a mist. They recognized the two at once: Moses and Elijah. Moses had been much in their minds for months now. For Jesus had talked like a new Moses as he gave a new 'law' to Israel in his Sermon on the Mount. He had acted like Moses when he fed the new people of God with a new 'manna' in a new 'desert place' in the Galilee of an occupied territory. They often recalled the promise God had made to Moses that a new prophet would come to speak God's word anew to Israel. Moses, they rememberd, had spoken of dying before his life's mission had been accomplished. Elijah had also been much in their minds and discussions. They had heard others wondering whether Jesus were John the Baptist or Elijah come back to herald the expected Messiah. They recalled how Elijah had not completed his life's work in the world, but had been transported to heaven in a chariot of fire before his human days were ended. They were awestruck and silent, watching and listening to what was transpiring before their eyes. They saw the three figures conversing together, and clearly understood what the talk was about: Jesus's own 'exodus' from his life, which would come to pass in Jerusalem. By a kind of divinely extra-sensory perception they were learning how Jesus himself was facing the unavoidable issue of how his message and mission would end.

But as it took place, it was all too much for the three to absorb. As so often, the abnormal proved unbearable. Peter just had to 'normalize' the experience, and he blurted out, 'Its a good thing we are here, sir. For we can make three shelters, one for you, one for Moses and one for Elijah.' But before the words were out of his mouth, another voice intervened, and said, 'This is my son, my well beloved one; listen to him.' So, hearing the same supernatural voice that Jesus had heard at his baptism, the three disciples were now also brought to the conviction that he had been given: here in the person of Jesus was the new 'son' or people or Israel of God. What Jesus had been saying about the kingdom of God having already come into human history was true. Furthermore, the three had been told to 'listen' to Jesus. They were not to discount what he had told them after Caesarea Philippi about his future suffering and death, but rather to accept it as part of the good news about the 'last things' that had begun to take place in the story of which they were now a part.

When the voice had finished, the tension dropped. Everything returned to normal. But Jesus and the three on the hillside had an understanding of his mission and their respective parts in it that was deeper, stronger and, because they were now ready to absorb the coming tragedy, more profoundly satisfying than ever before. In that frame of mind they returned to the valley and the other nine.

On the way down Jesus told them to keep the whole story of the hilltop experience to themselves until, as he put it, 'the Son of Man had risen from the dead'. They tried to imagine what he meant by 'risen from the dead', but made no real progress. So they approached the question at something of a tangent. They asked him about Elijah: 'Why,' they asked, 'do our religious authorities teach that the coming of Elijah must precede the coming of the Messiah? If that is really to be so, how can you properly claim to be the Messiah, or, in your own new words, the "Son of Man"? Jesus replied that the authorities were quite right. Elijah had to come and set things right for the advent of the Messiah. But, Jesus claimed, Elijah had already come, and had been treated shamefully by his opponents. The same fate awaited the Son of Man. The three realized that Jesus was talking about John the Baptist, and that he believed that John had played the role of Elijah to his own Messiah. That gave the three a further revealing insight into the way Jesus's mind was moving. John had symbolized God's formation of a new Israel by his Red

Sea baptism of many Israelites. At his own baptism Jesus had
identified the historical nucleus of that new people of God in
himself as the 'son' divinely appointed. But now it was clear that
Jesus believed that the new son could only come to his full birth in
human history through a suffering and death that might appear to
be fatal, but which, Jesus believed, would be an indestructible
beginning. So the four went down the hill and came to the others.

The next day found them once again surrounded by all the
problems of being citizens and heralds of the newly announced
kingdom of God. The three came to the town where the others had
been staying, and found quite a large crowd gathered round them;
some authorized teachers of the Law were arguing with them about
something that seemed important. He asked, 'Whatever are you
doing with my men?' One of the crowd replied, 'Teacher, sir, it's
about my son. I brought him along to see you, because he is
troubled by an unclean spirit. This gets into him every now and
again, and he foams at the mouth, grinds his teeth, and goes quite
stiff. You were not here, so I asked your followers if they could cure
him. They tried, but failed.' Jesus answered by saying, 'You people
of little faith and trust! How much longer have I got to be with you?
How much longer must I bear with you? Bring the boy here to me.'
They brought the boy, but when he reached Jesus the demon took
possession of him, as if claiming his right, and the boy fell on the
ground, foaming and rigid. Jesus asked the father how long he had
been subject to this sort of trouble, and had the answer, 'From
childhood.' Jesus then charged the demonic power to leave the boy,
and after a final convulsion the spirit left him, and he was healed.

When the crowd had gone away, the disciples asked Jesus, 'Why
couldn't we cure him?' Jesus answered, 'Because you don't believe
and trust. Don't you realize that if you had the tiniest bit of belief
and trust, you could say to that mountain yonder, where some of us
have just been, "Come down here to where we need the healing
power of the kingdom", and it would come. Nothing would be
impossible to you; nothing at all!'

So they went on their way through Galilee, and Jesus reminded
them of what he had said after Caesarea Philippi, that the good news
about the presence of the kingdom in his coming, and in their life
together, would demand much from him. He would be given up to
the 'proper' authorities, who would put him to death; but that
would not be the end of his story, for he would 'rise again'. They had
little clue as to his meaning, and what little they thought they

understood made them hesitate to probe further. If after the death of John the Baptist Jesus could be thought of as the Baptist risen from the dead, the question arose, which of the Twelve would prove to be 'Jesus risen from the dead'!

Eventually they arrived home at Capernaum. When they were settled down, Jesus asked them what they had been discussing among themselves on the homeward journey. They did not answer, for they were ashamed to confess that they had been arguing as to who was the greatest among them. So he called the Twelve together and said to them, 'Anyone who wants to be first in the kingdom of God must be content to be the last of all, and the slave of all.' Then he took one of the children of the house and said 'Anyone who receives a child like this as a piece of service to me, receives me too. And anyone who receives me, receives also the Father who sent me.'

On that searching note the third year of Jesus's ministry the second after John's arrest, came to its end. It would begin again the following spring, when it would move swiftly to its climax.

The parables of Jesus

During the years of campaigning in Galilee, particularly after the arrest of John, Jesus had exercized a pedagogical gift which he possessed in superb measure, the use of the parable as a means of effectively publicizing the arrival and nature of the kingdom of God. To recover the precise situation in which each parable was first told is now impossible. But it is not only possible, but necessary, to give some illustrations of what Jesus said and taught in his use of parables.

Each parable contains some information about the kingdom of God that had 'come upon' Israel in the person and ministry of Jesus, and about its impact on the society of his own day. There are, for example, two parables with parallel meanings, those of the Lost Sheep and the Lost Coin. In all probability the incidents portrayed come from the domestic life of Jesus and his friends in and around Nazareth. There is a shepherd who owns a hundred sheep. One gets lost. The shepherd leaves the ninety-nine on the hillside pasture and goes to look for the one lost ewe. That would be a familiar picture to any audience in rural Galilee. But the commendable conduct of the shepherd is quite different from that of the official authorities in Jerusalem, who were, in Ezekiel's phrase, the 'shepherds' of God's flock Israel. They greatly resented the fact that

Jesus 'goes after the lost sheep of the house of Israel', the 'sinner' and 'tax-gatherers' and 'people of the land', who sit loosely both to the written law and to the tradition by which the Pharisees tried to up-date the Law and make it comprehensively applicable. To them, Jesus was wholly wrong to be so concerned with such worthless 'law-breakers'. The same point is also made by the story of the Lost Coin, a coin which is perhaps 'worthless' to the wealthy man, but of real importance to the poor housewife.

Jesus also likened the kingdom of God to yeast, which is put into a lump of dough; though at first it seems to make no difference at all, it is not long before the whole lump is changed into a new substance with quite new qualities. So, Jesus implied, with the situation of his own day. His work was to put the yeast into the dough of the old Israel; at first there would be no apparent change, but within a short time it would effect that radical change which would be apparent to all.

One of Jesus's best remembered parables is that of the Sower, who sowed seed by casting it all over his field. Some fell on the pathway crossing the field; but the birds at once spotted it and ate it up. Other seed fell on the stony ground, only to grow up quickly and die for lack of water and food. Still other seed fell in the thorns at the edge, only to be choked out of existence while still very small. But the greatest part fell on good ground, and produced a large and profitable crop. So Jesus pointed out that however many setbacks his work received the final success of his labours was never in any peril or doubt.

Other parables were in longer narrative form, for example, the parable of the Prodigal Son, full of material for the preacher of every age. But in Jesus's day it was a penetrating analysis of the relationship of the old Israel to the new. Of two sons one prematurely claimed the part of the patrimony due to him, and with it went off to a life of luxury and self-indulgence in foreign parts. The elder son stayed at home on the farm. In time the younger son's fortune vanished, and he was left destitute. He then thought of the home he had left, and resolved to return; he did not expect to be received and honoured as a son, but was willing to become a hired hand on his father's estate. So he went home. Little did he guess what lay ahead. His father had long kept watch for his return, and when he saw him, still a long way off, he went out to greet him. The son said, 'Father, I've done wrong against you and against God. I'm utterly unworthy to be called your son. Let me join the ranks of your hired men.' His father embraced him, and told his servants to bring out the best robe and shoes for him, and a ring for his finger; to kill the fatted calf, and prepare a feast worthy to celebrate the homecoming of the prodigal, for, he said, 'this my son was dead and is alive again; he was lost, and is found.'

The household began to make merry. The elder brother returned from the farm, and asked what was going on. He was told of his brother's return and the feast that his delighted father had prepared for him. But he angrily refused to join the merry-making. His father came out and pleaded with him, but he remained resentful, pointing out how unswervingly loyal he had always been, with never so much as a goat to have a party with. To which his father replied that all that he had belonged to the elder boy; but it was fitting to have the feast, 'for this your brother was dead, and is alive; he was lost, and is found'.

So Jesus again tried to make plain why he sought the 'lost sheep', the law-breakers, the despised 'people of the land', the poor and even the Gentiles, and how wrong it was of the old Israel, the 'elder brother', not to rejoice that those who had wandered far off had now returned home.

Jesus told another parable of two brothers which makes the same point. A certain vineyard owner had two sons. One day he went to the first and said to him, 'Son, please go and work in the vineyard today.' 'No, I won't,' replied the son, but afterwards he regretted doing so, and went and worked as his father had asked. Meanwhile the father went on in his disappointment to the second son, and said to him too, 'Son, please go and work in the vineyard today.' 'Of course I will,' said the son, but he did not go. So Jesus asked his hearers, 'Which of the two sons really did the will of his father?' The answer rightly came, 'The former.' 'That is why,' said Jesus, 'some of the "lost ones" will find entrance to the kingdom of God long before those of you are much more meticulous about the law!'

Another oft-repeated parable of Jesus is that of the Good Samaritan, which again offers the preacher a perpetual text on good neighbourliness. But in Jesus's day it made a very pointed reference to Jewish-Roman relationships, in which the typically 'haughty' Roman despised the Jew, and the typically nationalist Jew despised the Gentile conqueror. The 'good' Jew would certainly decline aid to a Roman in any personal emergency, for contact with him as a Gentile would result in ritual uncleanness (cp. John 18.28f.). Jesus was asked who was the neighbour referred to in the summary of the law he had given, which bad the member of Israel to 'love the Lord his God with all his heart and soul and strength and mind, and to love his neighbour as himself'.

Jesus responded with the parable. A certain man, evidently a Jew, was on the road from Jerusalem to Jericho, which passes through some wild country. On the way he was set on by a band of guerillas, who stripped him of all that he had, beat him badly, and left him half dead. That, too, would have been a not unfamiliar story for the time. As it happened a priest came along not long afterwards. He saw what had happened and, presumably from fear of falling to any lurking guerillas, went on his way. Precisely the same thing happened soon after when a Levite came down the road. The third traveller to reach the injured man was a Samaritan; though the victim was a Jew, he did not hesitate to go to his aid. He bound up his wounds and dressed them, put him on his own ass, and took him to the next inn along the road. There he paid the debts the now penniless Jew might incur, and promised to return to ensure that the innkeeper did not lose by his hospitality.

Jesus then asked, 'Which of these three, do you think, was a neighbour to that unlucky Jew?' The answer had to be, 'The man who helped him.' 'Go and do likewise,' said Jesus. Likewise? As the Jew to the Samaritan so the Roman to the Jew. Jesus's very 'homely' parable was a story-paraphrase of the injunction 'Love your enemies, do good to those who hate you, bless those who curse you, and pray for those who despitefully use you'. This is much more than the world asks of a 'neighbour', but precisely this is the mark of citizenry of the kingdom of God. So Jesus combined a quite specific comment on a first-century situation in Palestine with the enunciation of an eternal standard of God's kingdom.

On another occasion he told a story about a rich man, 'Dives', and a poor beggar named Lazarus who used to sit at his gate. The rich man, well clothed and sumptuously fed day after day, made a great contrast with the beggar, who could not even get a scrap of the food he so needed and desired. Lazarus died, and was taken to Abraham's side in heaven. Dives also died, and was removed to Hades, the underworld, where he was tormented. From there he saw Abraham, with Lazarus at his side, and he cried out, 'Father Abraham, have pity on me! Send Lazarus down just to dip his finger into some water and cool my tongue, for it is agony here with the heat.' But Abraham answered, 'Remember all the good fortune you had in the world, and the misfortunes Lazarus suffered. Things are reversed now. He has some compensation, and you are in agony. And nothing can be done about it, for the gap between Hades and heaven is absolutely uncrossable.' 'Then please, father Abraham,' said Dives, 'send Lazarus to my five brothers to warn them, so that they can avoid this place of torment.' To which Abraham answered, 'Your brothers have all the warning necessary in Moses and the prophets; they can listen to them.' 'No,' Dives retorted, 'if someone were to go to them from the dead, then they would listen and repent.' This brought the final answer from Abraham, 'If they won't heed Moses and the prophets, they won't take notice, even if someone were to rise from the dead.'

This is both a parable of the kingdom, and an indication of the proper basis and authentification of belief. For Dives is the old Israel, sumptuously fed by God with spiritual food which she is content to devour with no thought for the unfed people outside, who both need and desire a share in the divine bounty. The penalty for such callous misappropriation of God's goodness is certain and severe. This is a parable of the same type as that of the Prodigal Son or the Two Brothers; its message finds other expressions in Jesus's teaching about the entry of tax-gatherers and sinners into the kingdom before the scribes and Pharisees, and in Paul's exposition of the place of Jews and Gentiles in the universal purpose of God (Rom. 9-11). The parable makes it clear also that the truth of the kingdom is not based on some extraneous miraculous act, nor authenticated by it. Jesus had wrestled with that in the desert temptation. Luke, who alone preserves this parable, seems to be claiming the authority of Jesus himself for the view that belief in him does not rest on the fact that he has risen from the dead; rather, belief in his rising from the dead rests on believing in him and what he was and what he did.

A final example of the art of the parable in making unpalatable truth plain and palatable concerns the 'grace-centred' operation of the kingdom of Heaven in contrast with the 'reward-centred' operation of the kingdoms of the earth.

The owner of a certain vineyard was set to gather his grapes. He went out at six in the morning to the market and hired a good number of men, agreeing to pay them the current rate for that particular job. They agreed, and set to work. Later on, at 9 a.m. and at noon, he went out again, hired some more labourers, and agreed to pay them 'a fair wage'. Then, quite late in the day, under pressure to get all his grapes gathered – the weather seemed to be threatening to break – he went down once more to the market and found a few men there still unemployed. He asked them why they were still without work, and they said that no one had offered them any work that day. So he sent them to work for what still remained of the day in his own vineyard.

When the working day ended, and the men lined up for their wages, the owner told his foreman to pay all the men precisely the same wage, starting with those last employed, and finishing with those who had been taken on at 6 a.m. When it came to the turn of the men who had been 'signed on' first, there was considerable grumbling. 'These men who started work only an hour ago have been given the same wage as us,' they complained, 'who have worked all through the hot and sultry day! That's not fair.' But the owner said, 'I'm not being unfair to you. I've kept my promise and given you the agreed current rate for your day's labour. If I choose to give the men who've been working for only an hour the same wage as yourself, it is coming out of my pocket, not yours! Surely it's my right to do what I like with my own money? Or does my generosity fill you with envy?' This is yet another story that lights up the grace which admits Gentiles and retains Jews in the kingdom of God –though men may misunderstand God's kindness.

Jerusalem interlude: the Feast of Tabernacles

Though it seems a reasonable assumption that Jesus kept his evangelistic campaigns to the dry months of the Palestinian summer, it is clear that he did not spend all his remaining time in Nazareth, Capernaum, or anywhere else in Galilee. John records one visit to Jerusalem in October, when Jesus went up for the Feast of Tabernacles. There were some notable features about the visit.

It was late summer in 31 A.D. Jesus was in Galilee and proposing to stay there, for he knew that the authorities in Jerusalem were set on having him silenced. He paid a visit to Nazareth and his home, not forgetting but forgiving the hostility that some of them had shown some time before in Capernaum (see above, p.145). His brothers were still sceptical, and somewhat jealous about the career of the eldest of the household. They were planning to go themselves to Jerusalem for the Feast of Tabernacles, a very popular festival, and they taunted Jesus for his intention of remaining in Galilee. 'Why don't you go to Jerusalem?' they asked him. 'If you want to put your case to the nation at large, that's the place to do it, not here in provincial Galilee! You'll never catch the real eye of Jewry up here!' Jesus answered them calmly, 'There's not only a place, but a time to catch the public eye. It makes no difference to you when you go to Jerusalem. But it matters supremely to me, for when I go will greatly affect the issues that I can put to the nation. I shall have to wait until I am sure that it's the right time for me to go. So you be off to Tabernacles; and I shall stay in Galilee. It's not my time to go to Jerusalem yet.' So the brothers went to Jerusalem, and Jesus stayed in Galilee.

But after his brothers had left for Jerusalem, Jesus decided, for reasons not disclosed, to go up himself, incognito. He avoided joining any party from Galilee for the journey, and arrived in Jerusalem unrecognized. He had not been there for some time, and discovered that many people were speculating about him. Would he be coming to the feast? Was he really a good man? Or was he but another of those misguided false Messiahs who misled the Jews into revolt against Rome, and brought penalties not only on themselves and their followers but on the whole nation. But all this was whispered in quiet places, lest the authorities should think that the gossipers were his followers.

In the middle of the celebrations Jesus decided to go openly into the Temple and teach. The authorities had their agents out to listen and report. They were astounded at what they heard, for Jesus's discourse was such as they would never have expected any uncouth and untrained Galilean to be able to give. Jesus gave them the answer, 'It isn't my teaching that I am giving, but the teaching of the one who sent me. If anyone wants to do God's will he can quickly discover if my teaching is from God or just my own fabrication. And what is there wrong in proclaiming God's will? That is only doing what the law of Moses does! So why do you people in authority want to eliminate me?' The crowd replied to Jesus, in an ugly echo of Capernaum, 'You are possessed! Who wants to kill you?' At this some Jerusalem citizens asked whether this really was the man the authorities wanted to kill, and wondered whether they had decided that Jesus really was the Messiah, and were leaving him alone to carry through his Messianic rebellion and victory. Jesus pointed out that he could not be the Messiah they expected, for it was said of the Messiah that no one would know where he came from, and everybody knew that he came from Nazareth in Galilee. This was a superb escape from any possible report that he had actually claimed to be the Messiah, the one popularly expected. Yet even then some asserted that he must be the Messiah, for, they argued, no one could talk and act more like a Messiah than Jesus was doing. How differently different people can view precisely the same circumstances.

The authorities were naturally disturbed at so much explosive, not to say seditious, talk during a popular festival, when the Roman Procurator would be in residence to ensure the preservation of peace. They sent officers from their own guard to arrest Jesus in order to forestall any major disturbance. But when they reached Jesus he addressed the crowd and said, 'I shall only be with you a little longer, and then I'll be going back to him who sent me to you. You will look for me then, though you won't find me as you've done at this feast; and where I am going you won't be able to come' (John 7.33f.). The crowd speculated as to what he really meant. Would he go to Greece, where there were a number of expatriate Jews, and launch a mission to the Greeks? Evidently Jesus had not given them the impression that his work was of necessity to be confined to the Jews.

Two customs repeated daily at the Feast of Tabernacle joined to make it the most popular of the Jewish year. It served as a Harvest Festival, as a celebration of God's caring for the Jews in their journey across the desert, when they lived in 'booths' or 'tabernacles', and also as a time for intercession for rain, that the next sowing of grain might be fruitful. The first custom was connected with this. Each day in the Temple there was poured out a libation of water brought from the Pool of Siloam. The other custom was the daily lighting of candles in the Court of the Women, so many that the saying went that there was not a courtyard in all the city that was not in part illuminated by the light in the Temple. These two popular rites provided Jesus with a non-verbal text for two of his audiences in the Temple.

On the last day of the feast, Jesus stood up and declared, 'If anyone is thirsty, he should come to me and drink. For if anyone believes in me and so drinks in what I can give him, he will find that out of his heart there will be flowing a stream of living water.' He thus made to the Jerusalem crowd much the same point as he had put to the Samaritan woman at Sychar (see p.121). Some of the crowd were impressed, and said, 'This must be the prophet Moses promised to us' (cf. Mark 6.15), while others said, 'He must be the Messiah himself.' Thus was immediately countered by others who pointed out that scripture taught that the Messiah would come from Bethlehem in Judea, and not from any place in Galilee. Some in the crowd wanted him arrested forthwith, before there was any serious disturbance of the peace. In the event, no one laid a hand on him.

On another occasion in the feast, very probably as the candles were being lit in the Court of the Women, Jesus expounded on the other 'real life' text. He said, 'I am the light of the world. The man who follows me won't be stumbling about in the dark, but will walk in the light of high day, with the strength and standards of the true and eternal life to help him.' The Pharisees were at a loss for a telling reply, and had to be content with a purely legal argument. They said to Jesus, 'You're just giving testimony about yourself. Don't you realize that before any testimony can be accepted it has to be given in substantially identical terms by at least two witnesses. So what worth has your self-testimony got?' Jesus replied by pointing out that the Father who sent him had borne witness to him, so his testimony could stand.

After considerable and intensive debate the authorities angrily said to Jesus, 'Isn't the rumour true that you are really a Samaritan, and that you are possessed by a demon?' Jesus responded, 'I am not demon-possessed! As for my parentage, I am content simply to honour my Father, whereas you are set on dishonouring me. But I am not concerned with my own reputation, though there is One above who is concerned with it, and he will decide the issue. I can only add, with utter sincerity, that if anyone holds to what I say, he will enter the kingdom of God, where life is eternal and no one sees death' (John 8.49ff.). This served but to heighten the exasperation of the authorities, who burst out with, 'Now we know you're possessed! Abraham, the father of all of us, died; all the great prophets of God have died, and you talk of your followers never dying! Who do you think you are?' Jesus quietly answered, 'If this were just a matter of my own self-glorification, there would be nothing to say in reply. But it is really a matter of my Father glorifying me. You say that he is your God too; but it's quite clear that you don't really know him, though I do; and I keep his word. Our great father Abraham rejoiced that he was to see my day; and he saw it and was glad.' That brought out the sharp response, 'You're not yet fifty years old, and you talk of seeing Abraham? What nonsense!' Jesus said quite calmly, 'Before Abraham was born, I am.' Speechless with anger the authorities present took up stones to throw at Jesus. But with that disarming authority that he possessed, he passed through them and left the Temple.*

But the surprises of the feast were not yet over. As Jesus left the Temple with the Twelve, he saw a familiar figure begging near the entrance. He was a man known to have been born blind. Such a misfortune was then, as now one of the inexplicable mysteries of life. Why should it happen so? Jewish theology, both professional and popular, had an answer that, if not wholly satisfying, at least made it bearable to heart and mind. Such blindness was, like any affliction, a consequence of sin. Those who thought, as some did, that a child could sin in the womb, held this to be a normal instance of individual sin and its reward. Those who believed that an unborn child was incapable of sinning had to accept that in such cases God was 'visiting the sins of the fathers upon the children' (Exod. 20.5). Here were two explanations, but no insight into the justice of God that could really satisfy.

Perhaps the Twelve wanted to take Jesus's mind away from the menacing conclusion of the debate in the Temple. They put the question to him: 'Teacher, was it this man himself, or was it his parents who sinned, that caused him to be born blind?' (John 9.2). In answering Jesus certainly intended to direct their minds away from the past when trying to understand such an affliction. He pointed them instead to the future, when God's action would have so demonstrated his goodness that there would be great cause for thanksgiving. He said, 'It is not something lying in the past that can

---

*The Johannine language in which this episode is related makes it less comprehensible to the modern reader. But when adequate translation is made into and from synoptic language, an underlying unity is revealed. According to the synoptist the kingdom of God entered history at the moment when Jesus was born, and in his person and mission that eternal order was historically incorporated. But the kingdom or reign of God did not begin with Jesus's birth nor end with his death. God had always reigned, and always will. When Jesus was born, into a world where there had been many attempted usurpations of the divine rule, God himself came in human form in the person of a new 'son' to gather round that divine nucleus the new people of God. They would live as obedient citizens of his kingdom, and recall other men to their proper human destiny, citizenship of God's kingdom. Whatever the actual terms of the debate between Jesus and the authorities, at the Feast of Tabernacles or at some other time, it could hardly have avoided raising the question whether what was taking place was simply a matter of human initiation of events, or whether in Jesus, the new 'son' of God, the eternal Father had himself entered into time. If that were so, there was meaning to be given to Jesus's claim that 'before Abraham was born, I am'. Only if the Jesus of the historical order is thought of as being as independent of God as all other creatures must the difficult and enigmatic saying about Abraham be rejected as absurd and impossible.

ease the weight of this tragedy; it is what lies in the future, when God has done his work on it.' He went on to say, in recalling his words in the Temple, that while the light of his day lasted in the world, he must do God's work. So saying, he spat on the ground, made a paste with his spittle, put the paste on the blind man's eyes, and told him to go and wash in the Pool of Siloam; its water had been used ritually every day during the feast, but Jesus would now put it to more fruitful use. The man left his begging station, went to the Pool of Siloam, washed there, and came back to Jesus – seeing. He was quite literally 'transfigured', his joy making him look an entirely different man (see above, p.160). He had changed so much that the crowd at the Temple entrance argued about whether he were the blind beggar or not. But he told them, 'I am the man.' 'Then how have you come to see?' they asked him. 'It was the man Jesus, who made some paste with his spittle, anointed my eyes, and sent me away to Siloam to wash. I went there and washed, and here I am, with my sight.' They then asked him where Jesus was. He had to say that he did not know.

It was the Sabbath day. The man healed would have known well enough that Jesus had broken the Sabbath law in healing him and he may well have been anxious to protect both himself and his healer by his negative reply about the whereabouts of Jesus.

But he did not escape trouble for himself. He was taken to some Pharisaic members of the Sanhedrin, and questioned by them. They first asked for an account of what had taken place. 'He made paste, put it on my eyes, and I washed and now can see,' was his terse summary. Some of his questioners warned him, 'This man Jesus cannot be from God, for he is a Sabbath breaker.' But even some of them wondered aloud whether a sinner could really do such things as this. They then joined in asking the man, 'What do you say about Jesus, now that he has opened your eyes?' The reply came quickly: 'He is a prophet.' His questioners found it hard to believe that a man born blind could have been given his sight, so they called for his parents. They asked them, 'Is this your son, who you say was born blind? How is it that he can now see?' They answered that he was indeed their son, and had been born blind; but they could say nothing more about how he had been made to see. 'Ask him yourselves,' they said, 'He's old enough to speak for himself!' So the authorities questioned the man again. They told him, 'Give credit for your sight to God. This fellow Jesus is a known sinner.' The man replied, somewhat pertly, 'About his being a sinner I can't say. But what I do know is that all my life so far I've been unable to see, but now I can.' He was then asked, 'How did he do it?' The man, still unabashed, said, 'I've told you that already. Why do you want to hear it all again? Do you want to become his disciples?' To this came the quick retort, 'You are his disciple! We are proper disciples of Moses, real Israelites. We know that God spoke to Moses, but we don't even know where this fellow comes from.' 'This is a real miracle,' said the man. 'You don't know where this man comes from, and yet he has given me my sight! Of course I know God doesn't listen to sinners, but if anyone worships God and does his will, God listens to him. Never before in any place has anyone born blind been given his sight. If this man were not from God, he would not have been able to do anything for me.' This only provoked the sharp retort, 'You sin-begotten creature!' And they excommunicated him from the community of Israel, depriving him of the normal religious and social privileges of being an Israelite.

Jesus heard about his excommunication, and went looking for the now outcast man. He found him, and asked him, 'Do you believe in the Son of Man?' The answer came, 'I don't know who he is, sir, so I can't tell you.' Jesus then said to him, 'You've seen him already with your own eyes, and he is talking with you now.' The man looked at his questioner again, with the new sight that Jesus had given him, and a new miracle happened. For human eyes, which often, as in the case of the Jewish authorities, could not see in Jesus anything more than a difficult and dangerous Messianic claimant, saw in the figure before him one who was more than the 'man' he had first called him, more even than the 'prophet' he had described to the authorities; this was surely the Son of Man, who at the last day would come as God's representative to men. He said to Jesus, 'Lord, I believe', and bowed himself before him in adoration.

Jesus said, 'I came into the world so that in the end everything may be done in terms of a true and godly evaluation. That means that those who are blind to it will be able to see, and those who now think they see things aright will recognize that they are blind.' Some of those in authority heard him say this, and asked him, 'Are we among the blind?' Jesus replied, 'If you were blind, you would not be at fault, for you just wouldn't see; but since you claim to be able to see things aright, your guilt is clear, and it continues.'

The healing of the man born blind is the only healing of a blind person recorded in John. This accords with his normal practice. He tells of seven signs, none repeating another, and is knowingly selective (John 20.30). The synoptists tell of several healings of blind persons. In doing so they seem more ready to describe 'what took place whereas John seems eager to add more than a hint of 'what was going on'. In telling this story John is making clear that official Israel, which claimed to 'see' what God required of men, was really blind, while those whom Israel thought to be blind from their birth – the various undesirables, sinners, tax-gatherers, 'people of the land', lepers and the like – were really able to hear what Jesus said, and to see what God was doing in him.

It is therefore the more significant that the story of the man born blind should, like the story of blind Bartimaeus in the synoptic gospels, precede the opening of the Passion story. For in the arrest, trial and crucifixion of Jesus, those who had heard and believed his words would be able to see what God was doing in him, even through his death; while those who claimed to know independently what God was doing in the world would only reveal their blindness as they rejected the 'son' of God.

Later in that same year Jesus went again to Jerusalem for the festival of the Dedication of the Temple. As he was walking in Solomon's porch the Jews again confronted him, and demanded that he should end all uncertainties about himself and his claims. 'If you are the Messiah, say so plainly,' they said. Jesus answered them that he had already told them what he had to say. He said that the things he had done spoke his claim, but that, because his questioners were not members of his community, they did not understand what was going on. As the 'shepherd' of his flock, as opposed to the authorities who were the 'shepherds' of the flock of the old Israel, he brought his sheep the gift of eternal life, because he was acting with the authority of his Father God. The Jews once more made as if to stone him; Jesus reasoned with them again, but to no useful purpose. The Jews then tried to seize him, but he escaped from them and their designs.

The Galilean ministry: termination and transfer

Jesus returned from Jerusalem once more to Galilee. As the new year of 32 A.D. opened, he realized that his mission had reached crisis point. It was not difficult to get a large following in Galilee, but even there most of those who followed him did not do so because they understood his message and mission. Many came to him because he was a 'wonder worker', able to cure the sick and the distressed, or because he was ready to offer friendship and hospitality, even to the outcast and disreputable of society. Many also came because they believed him to be, what they addressed him as, the Son of David, the militant Messiah who would speedily free the Jewish people from the resented yoke of Rome. Jesus knew that his kingdom was neither territorial nor political, but so far it had proved impossible to persuade even the well-instructed Twelve of the truth of his own conception of the Messiah – or, as he preferred to call himself, of the Son of Man. Moreover, as his last two visits to Jerusalem had shown, he had incurred the suspicion, if not the downright opposition, of the Jerusalem authorities. He had been watched and questioned in Galilee; his own town and synagogue had rejected him; he had been declared 'beside himself'; deputations had come to Galilee from Jerusalem to 'investigate' him (as they had investigated John the Baptist) and had gone away clearly disapproving. So how should this new year be planned?

Another season spent predominantly pursuing the Galilean mission would at best leave things as they were, with crowds still gathering for inadequate reasons, and the Twelve still unable to share his vision of Messiahship. But things could, and almost certainly would, get worse. His experiences in the Temple during the autumn and winter had showed how wide was the gap between himself and the authorities, and how strong their opposition was. Herod might well arrest him and imprison him, as he had done John the Baptist, and that would prevent him from stating his claim publicly in the only truly national forum available – Jerusalem. He had therefore to make this year the one in which he took his message and his works to Jerusalem, and made them properly eloquent before the authorities and the great public alike. His brothers had been quite right in what they had said about Jerusalem, the city in which God had chosen to dwell with his people. To the religious centre of old Israel he had to take the life and promise of the new Israel in his person as the new 'son' of God.

If his visit to Jerusalem was to make the greatest possible impact, it would have to be at Passover time, when Jews gathered from all parts of Palestine, and from foreign lands as well. Further, Passover was linked with the Exodus, which was the prelude for the old Israel starting out on the journey to the promised land. As the conversation on the Mount of Transfiguration had indicated, there was to be another 'exodus' for God's son or people, from Jerusalem itself this time. Surely Peter, James and John would understand that, whenever it came, and whatever form it might take.

It is clear from the gospel narratives that Jesus made very careful and detailed plans for his visit to Jerusalem. He did so in a way that would suggest to the scripturally discerning what was going on in what was about to take place. He acted in terms that the prophet Malachi had once used: 'Behold, I send my messenger to prepare the way for me. The Lord you are looking for will suddenly come to his temple; the messenger of the covenant you delight in is already with you.' So, instead of setting off with the Twelve, he sent them on ahead 'to prepare his way' (Luke 9.51f.).

Jesus himself set out a little later, and made his way through the villages toward the border with Samaria. News of his departure spread quickly. Some Pharisees of the Herodian party heard of it, and came to Jesus with the message, 'You are right to leave Galilee. We happen to know that Herod means to kill you.' Jesus answered, 'Go and tell that old fox that I shall go on my way in my own time, whatever his plans may be. I shall continue my healings and exorcisms for another couple of days, and then I shall go to Jerusalem, for that is the only proper place for a modern prophet to appeal to the nation.'

So what proved to be Jesus's last journey to Jerusalem began. The Twelve started out on the shorter route from Galilee through Samaria. It was not a popular route, either with Jewish pilgrims going to religious festivals in Jerusalem, or with their Samaritan neighbours, who resented Jews using their territory to bypass what they held to be the true Temple of God on Mount Gerizim. The Twelve tried to arrange for Jesus to stay one night in a certain village, but were refused hospitality. (Could it have been Sychar, disappointed that the Jesus who had expressed doubts about both Mount Gerizim and Mount Zion was now showing an apparent preference for the latter (see p.122)?) When Jesus caught up with them, and was told about the refusal of a lodging, the suggestion was put to him that they might 'do an Elijah' on the village, and call down fire from heaven on it for its xenophobian parsimony. Jesus refused, and the group went on to another village.

When they set out again, Jesus took another step to indicate, particularly to his disciples, the true significance of what was to take place. In a re-enactment of what Moses had done much earlier in the story of old Israel, he appointed seventy more 'messengers' (Luke 10.1) to precede him and prepare the way for him eventually to reach Jerusalem for the Passover. They were clearly not sent on a mission to arrange hospitality en route, nor were they simply to preach and enact the good news of the kingdom – though that was clearly part of their mission (see below, p.179). They were, by the intention of their 'Mosaic' appointment (Num. 11.16ff.), a group that, in days of stress and danger ahead, might bear with Moses 'the burden of the people, so that he did not have to bear it all by himself'. So what it really meant to be a 'follower' of Jesus was becoming clearer, and would become clearer still. As Jesus had already told them after Peter's 'confession' at Caesarea Philippi, any man who decided to follow him must deny himself, and take up his cross day after day (Luke 9.23ff.). When the critical time came, as it surely would during the coming Passover, it would mean much to know that there was a band of supporters giving their moral and spiritual support and understanding. The seventy went off on their mission, leaving Jesus and the Twelve to continue at their own chosen pace.

Jesus realized on the way that he was being left alone, and that the Twelve were lagging behind, worried and anxious. So he let them catch up with him, and told them once more what he thought lay ahead: he would be handed over to the chief priests and scribes (i.e. the Sanhedrin), who would find him guilty of a capital offence, and in turn therefore hand him over to the Roman authorities for sentence and execution. But that would not end the story, for, as he believed, there would be a speedy resurrection. At first what he said saddened the Twelve. That is where the matter lay for a while.

But not for long. James and John reflected on what had been said, and, as two of his most trusted lieutenants, came to Jesus and said that they had a favour to ask. 'What is it?' Jesus enquired. They replied, 'When you are finally enthroned in all your splendour, give us the privilege of sitting, one on either side of you, sharing the splendour with you.' Jesus said to them, 'You don't realize what you're asking. Do you think you can drink the cup I have to drink, or undergo the baptism that I shall be given?' They said, 'Yes, we can.' Jesus answered them, 'Very well. So you shall. But it is not even for me to say who shall sit on either side of me in the seats of honour; that is something kept strictly within the prerogative of the Father himself.' Inevitably the other ten came to hear about this request, and understandably they were angry. So Jesus called them all together, and said to them, 'You all know how in the power-dominated world the great rulers of the nations lord it over their subjects, and that a nation's great men are seen in those who exercise authority. But that's the very opposite of the new order of the kingdom of God, which is now beginning with ourselves.

Among you, then, a great man is one who serve, not one who gives orders; and if anyone has ambitions to be the greatest in our new kingdom, he must be ready to be everybody's slave. Don't forget that the Son of Man himself, for all his true greatness, has not come to be served, but to be a servant, and to give his own life as the ransom that will set men really free' (Mark 10.42ff.).

Very soon the seventy returned from their mission, and quite elated by their success. They told how, in Jesus's name, they had found that they could make demons surrender to them and leave the possessed – a strangely paradoxical combination of complete dependence on Jesus with a really unjustified self-congratulation. Jesus put it all in its proper perspective. They had certainly witnessed wonders taking place, but they were nothing compared with what was going on in them. The exorcism of one demon was of course a marvel, but what that symbolized was the real wonder, which was nothing less that the fall of Satan's empire. 'I watched how Satan fell, like lightning out of the sky' (Luke 10.18). This was confirmation of the good news that the kingdom of God had come in Jesus, and that his dominion was secure. There was no room for self-congratulation at the surrender of particular demons. Rather must their contentment be rooted in their being already citizens of the great kingdom that had come, in their being alive as the old order passed away and the new one was born.

Jesus at Bethany: the resurrection and the life

Jesus and the Twelve continued their journey southwards. On the way they were met by a messenger from a family Jesus knew very well, and loved very much, Lazarus and his sisters Martha and Mary. They lived in Bethany. When Jesus learned that Lazarus was ill he said, 'This illness will not prove fatal, but events will combine to demonstrate the true glory of God.' For Jesus divine glory was something which submits to situations of frustration and difficulty, and overcomes them in and through submitting to them.

For reasons not disclosed or readily discernible, Jesus stayed two more days where he was before saying to the Twelve, 'Let's go back now to Judea' (John 11.7). The Twelve were apprehensive, as their reaction indicated. 'Teacher,' they said, 'Don't you remember that the last time you were there they wanted to stone you? Do you really intend to go back there?' Jesus seemed to give a very tangential answer; 'As long as we walk in the light of the day we shall not come to harm, for we shall be walking in the light of the world. It's only men who walk in the dark that get harmed, because the true light of the day is not shining.' What he meant was that no real harm could come to Jesus and his community, for he had told them, as he had declared to all Jerusalem, that he was the 'light of the world' (John 8.12).

Jesus went on to tell the Twelve that 'Lazarus has fallen asleep', using an expression that in the Old Testament refers to death. 'But,' he added, 'I shall be going there to wake him up' (John 11.11, cp. above, p.141). The Twelve found it difficult to suppose that Jesus could have been using 'sleep' in that Old Testament meaning, and said to him, 'But if Lazarus has only fallen asleep, he will be able to recover from his sickness.' Then Jesus made the situation absolutely clear, and said, 'Lazarus died. And I'm glad for your sakes that I was not there at the time, because now your faith will be deepened. So let us be off to Bethany.' Thomas said to the other disciples, 'Yes, let us go with him, so that we may share death with him if and when it comes.' And in that desperate and brave self-commitment they followed Jesus.

When Jesus eventually reached Bethany he found that Lazarus had been buried for four days; the home he was to visit was full of family and other friendly mourners from Jerusalem. The sisters had made arrangements to be informed when Jesus arrived, and as soon as they knew he had come Martha went out to meet him. As she came up to him, she burst out with, 'Oh, if only you had been here, my brother need never have died; and even now I am convinced that whatever you may ask of God, he will grant it to you.' Jesus made no direct response to what Martha had said, but replied, 'Martha, your brother will rise again.' To this Martha responded, 'Yes, I know he will, but on the last day, when the general resurrection will take place.' Jesus then made her impeccably orthodox statement seem archaic and anachronistic as he said to her, 'I am the resurrection, and I am the life. Anyone who believes in me will never really die.' 'Do you believe that?' he concluded. Martha struggled for her reply, in which she used all the terms she knew to tell Jesus that she believed in him. She said, 'Lord, I do believe that you are the Messiah, the son of God, and the prophet who was to come into the world, as our great Moses promised.'

That said, she went to fetch her sister, more suited, she may well have thought, to such profound conversations (cf. Luke 10.38-42). She told her quietly that Jesus had come and was asking for her.

Mary quickly got up and left the house; her friends and family thought that she would be on her way to the tomb to mourn there; so they followed her. But instead she went to where Jesus was, and when she came up to him she fell at his feet, crying, and repeated Martha's very words: 'Oh if only you had been here, my brother need never have died.' The sight of Mary crying and her friends weeping with her deeply moved Jesus, and he was greatly disturbed in spirit. 'Where have you laid him?' he asked. 'Come and see,' they answered. Jesus went, and as he went he wept. 'How he must have loved Lazarus,' some of the mourners said, while others, like the sisters, declared that a man who could cure a man born blind, as Jesus had done, would surely have been able to prevent Lazarus from dying.

That again deeply disturbed Jesus – probably because it indicated that still no on had any inkling that his authority and power were not primarily or exclusively over a man's physical body, but extended beyond it. So he went to the cave-tomb, and asked that the stone covering the entrance be removed. Martha protested, fearing the effects of releasing the odours of a body after four days of interment. But Jesus reminded her of what he had also told the disciples, that by trust in him they would see the glory of God in action. When the stone was removed, Jesus looked upwards, and prayed in the words, 'Father, I give thanks that you have listened to me, as you always have listened to me; and this prayer is the means by which the mourners here may come to believe that you have sent me.' Having said that, he cried out with a loud voice, 'Lazarus, come out!' And out Lazarus came, to the astonishment of all, with hands and feet still bandaged, and face still covered with the facial cloth. Jesus simply said, 'Take off his bandages, and let him go home.'

What can be said of this tremendous story of bringing a man dead and buried back to life? The author would remind the reader of what has already been said about raising the dead in commenting on the story of the raising of Jairus's daughter (see above, p.141). But John the evangelist has his own way of indicating what was going on. It may be called recording the miracle within the miracle. When he related the story of sight being given to the man born blind, he gave clear details as to 'what took place': Jesus made clay with his spittle, applied that to the man's eyes, and told him to wash in the Pool of Siloam; when all that had been done, the man born blind could see. The sight that Jesus gave to the man was one that brought him the ability to 'see' natural things. He could 'see' Jesus,

as he could 'see' his Jewish questioners. That was one clear
miracle – but the much less wonderful one. For the other 'seeing'
which Jesus gives is one which many possessed of natural vision
totally lack. When the man born blind was told that he was talking
with the Son of Man, he was able to take another look at Jesus and
see that it was so, as many 'seeing' Jews could not. And the gift of
that sight was more wonderful and more truly miraculous than the
physical gift of natural vision.

So with the story of Lazarus. There is one miracle apparent to the
reader: a man dead and buried for four days was raised to life to
rejoin his family, his tribe, his nation and its religion. But that only
set him in a life that was not open to the hearing of God's word
spoken and active in Jesus. The attitude of Jewish authority, and the
incomprehension of the mourners, make that plain. Yet Jesus, by
the very act of commanding Lazarus to 'come out', showed that the
life which he gives is one that is open, not only in this mortal
existence of man, but in the life that lies beyond man's mortality.
And that is clearly a greater miracle than any simple resuscitation of
the dead could ever be. That miracle within the miracle of Lazarus
remains the substance of the good news of 'what goes on' in
everything that takes place, as God uses events to order all things to
work his will for his creation.

The consequences of raising Lazarus were predictable. Some of
those who saw what took place saw also what was going on, and
'believed in Jesus'. Others failed to do so; and they, understandably,
reported what had taken place to the authorities in Jerusalem. For
to witness the miracle and not believe was to observe the action of a
possible false Messiah – and that was certainly a proper matter for
report, especially at a time when Jerusalem itself would soon be
greeting the Passover crowds. A Messianic disturbance at that time
would be highly embarrassing to the Jewish authorities in their
relationships with Rome, and a real danger to the interests of the
nation.

The Sanhedrin was summoned to a meeting to consider the
situation. It was far from promising. There were rumours of more
than one possible source of trouble. It was already clear that Jesus
could not be an authentic Messiah, for he had shown that he was a
law-breaker (John 9.16); he was also known not to have come from
Bethlehem, but from Galilee (John 7.41f.). Yet he was performing
many miracles, and if this continued there could easily be public
disturbances; the Romans would then act, and the Temple itself

could well go, together with whatever relative independence had been carved out for the Jewish nation. But Caiaphas the High Priest pointed out that, instead of letting things slide until matters came to such a head, it would be better that one man should suffer for his wrong-doing than that the whole nation should suffer instead of him. There was nothing that could be done immediately, however, so the Sanhedrin kept a watchful eye on the developing situation, with a view to action at the appropriate time.

But Jesus did not go directly to Jerusalem, but went with the Twelve for a time of retreat in the country bordering on the desert where his earliest and most lonely struggle had taken place.

On to Jerusalem

From their brief retreat into peace and companionship Jesus and the Twelve emerged some days later to continue their journey to Jerusalem. They inevitably, and probably with that intention, fell in with some Galilean pilgrims on their way to Jerusalem and the Passover celebrations. Nothing remarkable happened until Jesus and his company were about to enter the historic city of Jericho. Sitting begging by the roadside was the well-known figure of a blind beggar, Bartimaeus, known to all the regular pilgrims to Jerusalem. He could hear that some unusual group was coming along the road, and asked some travellers who it was. He was told that it was Jesus of Nazareth on his way to Jerusalem. Clearly he had heard of Jesus, and the Messianic status that some people thought he had. He cried out, 'Jesus, Son of David, have pity on me!' The first of the group going along with Jesus told him to be quiet, but he cried out all the more: 'Jesus, Son of David, have pity on me!' Jesus heard him, and asked for him to be brought forward. When Bartimaeus came up Jesus asked him, 'What do you want me to do for you?' Bartimaeus quickly answered, 'I want to get back my sight, sir.' Jesus answered his trust, and, evidently willing to risk some misunderstanding of his own Messianic mission in responding to a call to 'David's Son', he said to Bartimaeus, 'Receive your sight; your trust has brought you healing.'

If the sight which Jesus then gave to Bartimaeus was like the gift given to the man born blind, then at Jericho, before the last drama of his mission began, Jesus gave this man the ability not only to see what took place in the days ahead, but also to discern what was going on in the fateful events of the coming Passover.

The Pilgrim company went on to Jericho, where the news had swiftly come that Jesus was about to pass through the town. The narrow streets had quickly filled with curious citizens eagerly waiting to see the by now notorious figure of a suspected, and possibly false, Messiah. There was in Jericho a certain tax collector named Zacchaeus, diminutive in height, but colossal in his capacity for using his office in the Roman administration as a means for his own financial gain. He was hated by every loyal patriotic Jew, as all such 'Quislings' were. Zacchaeus wanted to see Jesus; probably they had met previously, for later that same day Jesus greeted him spontaneously by name. (There may well have been some dealings between them previously on some problem of tax or customs.) What is clear is that on that day Zacchaeus was frustrated as he tried to find a convenient place from which to see Jesus. No citizen of Jericho would make an inch of room for him. But Zacchaeus did not give up. He went well ahead of the build-up of the crowd, climbed a wayside tree, and waited. Jesus came along the street, stopped right in front of Zaccheus, looked up at him, and said, 'Zacchaeus, get down from that tree, and be quick about it! I intend to come and stay with you today.' Zacchaeus climbed down as quickly as he could, and greeted Jesus warmly. The crowd was disturbed by the manifestly unpatriotic, not to say irreligious, action of a supposed Messiah, and murmured that Jesus was going to the home of a man he must have known was rightly and publicly branded as a scoundrel and evildoer. But they followed Zacchaeus and his guest home, and waited to see what would happen next. They were certainly not prepared for what took place. Zacchaeus stood up and said, 'Look sir, I want you to know that I am making over half my possessions for the benefit of the poor; and I am willing to pay anyone I have defrauded or cheated four times the sum which he has lost to me.' In his response Jesus pointed out what had been happening to Zacchaeus that fateful afternoon. 'Today,' he said, 'salvation has come to the house of Zacchaeus; for he is, and has shown himself to be, a true "son of Abraham". And it is the mission of the Son of Man to seek out and save the lost sheep of the house of Israel.' So ancient and modern disciples alike may learn how ready the merciful kindness of God is to cross the divisions that men erect between themselves.

The King comes to his city: the 'triumphal' entry

Neither the healing of Bartimaeus nor the dinner with Zacchaeus was part of what Jesus had planned for his coming approach to Jerusalem. But what he had planned had already disclosed to the scripturally discerning Jew what he meant by his journey to share in the Passover of 32 A.D. As Malachi had conceived of the coming Messiah, he had 'sent his messengers before him'; and as he came to enter the Temple, so, in Malachi's words, would 'the Lord suddenly come to his Temple'. But could such a plan really be carried out?

Any approach to Jerusalem at Passover time which in any way savoured of Messianism would be suspect, dangerous and, to put it very mildly, officially discouraged. Yet, if Jesus were to renew the proclamation of his basic message – 'The time has come. The kingdom of God is upon you. Repent and believe the good news' – he could not avoid arousing Messianic expectations, even though his own ideas of Messiahship were vastly different from those of any of his contemporaries. The prospects were not encouraging. Already in Galilee his mission had attracted official suspicion and an investigation from Jerusalem. Further, he had learned as he left Galilee for this Passover journey that if he stayed there, or ever returned there, he would bring upon himself the same fate as that of John the Baptist. Herod intended to arrest and execute him. The forebodings he had already expressed to the Twelve were looking more justified than ever.

Yet he was profoundly convinced that the opposition to himself and his teaching rested on a basic misunderstanding of his message and his mission. Men saw in his actions and heard in his words the sort of claims he would never himself make. If his public appeal to Jerusalem at Passover time was to succeed it was therefore of the utmost importance that he should state unambiguously what he believed his mission and destiny to be. That involved making two things clear. First, he had to present himself to the nation in such a way as to make it absolutely clear that he was not the Messiah of popular expectation. He was not to be a successor to the great warriors like David or Simon Maccabeus, but would eschew all reliance on military power. Second, he had to make it plain if he were accepted as the real centre of the new people of God there would have to be some great changes in Israel's social, political and, above all, religious life. This could be stated in words, and words he would use. It could also be stated in action, and actions he would do. Perhaps an acted message would convey his meaning better than the spoken word.

To state in action that he was not a military Messiah Jesus chose to enact an oracle from the prophet Zechariah. A scripturally minded people like the Jews would surely see what he wanted to say to them if he quoted scripture to them in quite plain action. So he decided to make his entry into Jerusalem at the beginning of the week of the Passover in the terms of the prophecy which said:

> Rejoice greatly, O daughter of Zion!
> Shout aloud, O daughter of Jerusalem!
> Lo, your king comes to you;
> triumphant and victorious is he,
> humble and riding on an ass,
> on a colt the foal of an ass.
> I will cut off the chariot from Ephraim
> and the war horse from Jerusalem;
> and the battle bow shall be cut off,
> and he shall command peace to the nations;
> his dominion shall be from sea to sea,
> and from the river to the ends of the earth.

It was when Jesus and the Twelve reached the village of Bethphage (meaning House of Figs) near to Bethany and Jerusalem that the plan to act out the prophecy of Zechariah was put into operation. From there he sent two of the Twelve on what was obviously a well-prepared errand. 'Go to the village opposite,' he said, 'and you will find just as you enter it a colt tied up at a door in the open street. Untie it, and bring it here with you. And if anyone asks you what you are doing, all you need say is, "Our master needs it, and will send it back right away." ' The two went, and things turned out just as he had said, even to their being asked what they were doing, and giving the suggested and satisfying reply.

It is almost impossible to suppose that by this time Jesus had not made it perfectly clear to the Twelve what he was about to do, and what he meant to say so emphatically to the people by enacting the oracle from Zechariah. Yet, even as the Twelve joined in the kingly entry, they found means of expressing their doubts about a Messiah-king whose stated policy it was to forswear all resort to military action. We do not know whether the crowd that went along with Jesus, probably for the most part Galilean pilgrims to the

Passover, rightly understood the acted words of the oracle. Though they were exultant about a new Messiah, and gave the entry all the appearance of a great triumphal occasion, they contrived to perform actions themselves that pointed in the opposite direction from that which Jesus had taken care to announce. When Jesus was about to get on his beast, the disciples threw their cloaks on the ass, and on the ground where Jesus was to ride. In so doing they echoed the actions of the supporters of the militant Jehu who, as he set out to exterminate the whole house of Ahab, threw their cloaks on the steps where he would tread, in pledged loyalty to such a warrior king. The crowd with Jesus behaved similarly. They pulled down branches from trees growing at the roadside, and waved them in triumph, just as in 141 B.C. the crowd had welcomed Simon Maccabeus as he entered Jerusalem in triumph as their great military deliverer. Nor did the crowd stop at this. They sang their excitement thus:

> Hosanna!
> Blessings on him who comes in the name of the Lord!
> Blessings on the coming kingdom of our father David!
> Hosanna in the highest!

That song of blessing for the coming kingdom of David was hardly compatible with Jesus's assertion that he was a king of peace. The crowd may have been supporting Jesus as the Messiah, but it seems clear from their words and actions that they were not in their own view committing themselves to his pacific declarations, culled though they were from scripture.

The procession wound its way down to the Kidron valley, up the hill on the other side, and entered Jerusalem. There Jesus and the Twelve visited the Temple, returning to Bethany for their overnight lodging.

As for the Jerusalem authorities, they had witnessed what looked dangerously like the beginnings of a movement that might cause rioting, even perhaps revolt, during the feast. The fears they already had about the effects of Jesus's words and deeds were by no means quietened.

The following morning, Monday, Jesus and the Twelve left Bethany again for Jerusalem. On the way Jesus felt hungry, and was happy to spot a fig tree in full leaf. It was not yet the time for figs, which did not normally mature until June. But while the main crop came then, there were some trees in certain favoured locations which yielded a crop of what were known as 'early figs'. These figs were well known both for their good eating qualities (Isa. 28.4; Jer. 24.4-7) and for their easy picking, for they would drop off the tree into the mouth of the picker at just a slight shaking of the tree (Nah. 3.12). Jesus went forward to see if the tree was as fruitful as it looked. But there was nothing on it but leaves. How right, he reflected, were the prophets of old who likened the people of Israel to a fig tree. And how accurate a parable of present Israel was this particular fig tree. For Israel, like the fig tree, had all the appearances of a community that was sufficiently advanced to be able to be a source for those who were hungry in her emergency. In her worship at the Temple, and in the general practice of her religion, Israel gave the impression of being able to give her people the spiritual nourishment and strength that would be needed in the crisis that was about to come. Yet, when put to the test, Israel had substantially nothing to offer. She did not know how to meet the crisis of having her true king coming to her. So, speaking to Israel in the symbol of the tree, he said, 'Nobody shall ever have nourishment from you after this.' The little company continued on their way to Jerusalem and the Temple.

The Lord comes to his temple: the Temple cleansing

Jesus and the Twelve went on to Jerusalem and entered the Temple. What memories and reflections would have crossed his mind on this, which he knew would be a critical day. There were the days when as a lad of twelve years he had sat listening entranced to the doctors of the Law, and put his questions to them. There were many Passovers and other feasts he had spent in the Temple, with memories solemn and social. He could recall the talk with the Samaritan woman to whom he had voiced the inadequacy of both Gerizim and Zion as the proper temples of God, and had spoken of the day which had already dawned when true worshippers of God would worship him in spirit and truth. And he could reflect that through what he was about to do men would be asked to worship God not through rituals of animal sacrifices, but in spirit and in truth; not in a closed nationalist religion that one people used to 'keep God for itself', but in an open, universal and international religion in which all men could share.

Jesus led his company into the Temple precincts, and stepped into the Court of the Gentiles. All the usual sights were there: Jewish Passover pilgrims from all over Palestine and from settlements abroad; Gentile visitors intrigued to see the religious centre of so religious a people as the Jews*; the money-changers at their tables, ready to exchange the commercial coinage of Rome for the Jewish money approved for use in the Temple by the Jerusalem bureaucracy; those selling animals for the sacrificial rituals – doves and pigeons and lambs; the Temple guards appointed to watch over and preserve the peace. And among the Gentiles there were almost certainly some ununiformed Roman security officers, ready to report and act upon any serious threat of political or religious disturbance, especially at this festival time. It was all very much the accepted order. But Jesus had to expose it for what it really was.

At one moment the scene was quite normal; the next, there broke out a grave crisis for Judaism – though not so physically disturbing as to demand action from either the Temple guards or the Roman security officers. Jesus began to drive out of the Temple everyone engaged in the buying and selling that was going on. It was at such a moment that his innate authority came miraculously to his aid, for although he seized some cord which could have served him as a whip there was no eruption of violence as he went on to overturn the tables of the money-changers and the seats of those who sold doves. He insisted that no one should use the Court for any other purpose than the strictly religious and liturgical. The crowds were amazed at Jesus's effrontery, and in the silence that naturally ensued Jesus spoke: 'Don't you remember,' he asked, 'that in our holy scripture it is said, "My house shall be called a house of prayer for all nations." But what have you done with this house of God? You have made it nothing more nor less than a sort of Zealots' headquarters, where, as you know, the contemporary guerillas store up and share out their booty, sharing out among themselves what doesn't belong to them in the first place.' Even to have a 'Court of the Gentiles' was to deny the universality of true religion; to use it as a barrier to universal sharing in the worship of God was to turn divine bounty into robbers' booty.

The day before Jesus, by enacting an oracle, had claimed to be the peaceful king of Jerusalem, the Messiah who would achieve his

* Gentiles were allowed into the First Court of the Temple, and so gave it its name of 'Court of the Gentiles', but were not allowed beyond that on penalty of death.

kingdom without resort to military power. Now he had acted in a way that a mere word from scripture would clarify to state his second concern in his mission, the need for a new life for Israel as the true people of God. His challenge had been made. He had come to the centre of the religious life of the old Israel to make clear what the coming of the new people of God involved. The question was whether either the Jerusalem authorities or popular opinion as represented in the festival crowd would understand what he had done, and be ready for the consequential changes. In the Court of the Gentiles he had very appropriately condemned the failure of official Judaism to share with all the nations the good news of God's universal kindness, and had exposed the nation's exclusiveness as being precisely equivalent to the Zealot guerilas who gathered all kinds of booty in their 'dens' just to share it out among themselves. He had also made a dramatic protest against the sacrificial cultus of the Temple, a protest which he knew was also made by the desert sectaries, of which his kinsman John had been a member. With the desert sects he realized that the religion of the new and true people of God would have to be both universal and non-sacrificial; it could hardly be the one without the other. So the Messiah of peace had shown his hand in the Temple. Indeed, 'the Lord had come suddenly to his Temple'. How would men react?

Immediate reactions were not perturbing. Fortunately the 'demonstration' went off without direct repercussions. Somehow Jesus's pacific authority had not provoked physical resistance, so neither the Jewish guards nor the Roman observers had any occasion to intervene. But it was hardly likely that the incident would stop there.

The festival crowd was spellbound by his teaching. He was evidently making a strong impression with his message. This state of affairs lasted for the next day or so. Some brought blind and lame persons to Jesus for healing, and he cured them. The reaction of the Gentiles found an interesting outlet in the approach of some Greeks to Philip, asking if they could meet Jesus. Philip discussed this with Andrew, and the two of them went and told Jesus about it. It is not known whether the desired meeting took place, but the comment of Jesus on the request is significant. He said, 'The hour has come for the Son of Man to be glorified. The solemn truth is that a grain of wheat stays a solitary grain unless it falls into the ground and dies; but if it dies, then it can bear a good harvest.' In other words, just to know 'Jesus in his lifetime', 'in the flesh', was not really to know him. The 'historical Jesus' was not the 'real' Jesus; the real Jesus could only be known when his story was complete, and he had suffered a sacrificial death upon the cross.

The Jewish authorities had the Temple cleansing incident reported to them. They at once saw the incipient dangers of the situation, and began to look for some convenient way of removing Jesus.

The following day, Jesus and the Twelve were up early, left Bethany where they had stayed overnight, and returned once more to Jerusalem and the Temple. On the way there, Peter looked at the fig tree that had disappointed Jesus the day before. He saw that it had withered from the roots, and remarked on that extraordinary fact to Jesus. Jesus made a very topical reply. Indicating with a sweep of his arm the hill on which the Temple was built, he said, 'Trust God! I can assure you that if anyone says to this mountain, as I said to it yesterday in what I did, "Get moving and throw yourself into the sea", without any doubt in his heart, but believes that what he says is actually happening, so it will happen for him. So if you ask for anything in your prayers, believe that you will get it, and you will. And if, whenever you stand up to pray and have anything against anyone, you are forgiving, that will enable your heavenly Father to forgive you the wrongs you have done' (Mark 11.22-25). Clearly the moral of this last response is that while it is perfectly right for the citizen of the kingdom to work for the abolition of wrong forms of religion and its false rituals and pieties, it is never right to harbour wrongs done to oneself. Forgiveness is the cement that holds the community of the kingdom together.

Official reactions to the Temple cleansing became clear when Jesus and his followers reached Jerusalem and re-entered the Temple. They were met by a delegation from the Sanhedrin, which asked him, 'What is your authority for doing what you have done? Who gave you the authority?' Jesus was not seeking a confrontation, and he replied indirectly: 'Let me put a question about authority. If you answer my question, I will answer yours. The baptism of John: was it offered on divine authority, or only on human authority? Tell me that.' This was a very searching point to put to the authorities, for John had by his baptism symbolized the formation of a new people of God. The Sanhedrin members were embarrassed, and argued among themselves. 'If we say his authority was from God, he will reply, "Then why did you not believe him?" But if we say his authority was just human, then we've got to face the popular opinion that John was a prophet sent from God.' So they answered Jesus by saying, 'We don't know', at which Jesus said, 'Then I won't tell you what my authority is for acting as I have done.' If that seems evasive, it must be pointed out that to have claimed divine authority at this stage of his stay in Jerusalem would have given the authorities the chance to act against Jesus, and so forestall any further opportunity he might have of taking his message to the Passover crowds.

But though his answer might seem evasive, he went on to tell a very pointed story. There was once a man who planted a vineyard, fenced it round, excavated a winepress, and built a watch tower for it; he then let it out to some tenants, and went abroad. At harvest time he sent his own servants to get his share of the produce; they beat one, killed another, and stoned a third. He then sent more servants, but the same thing happened again. The owner then had but one possibility left: to send his only beloved son. 'Surely they will respect him,' he thought. But when the tenants saw him arriving, they said, 'Here comes the heir. Let's kill him, and then we can take the property for our own.' So they killed the heir, and threw his body outside the vineyard. 'Now what do you think,' said Jesus, 'the owner of the vineyard will do to those tenants?' The hearers answered, 'Surely he will put them to death, and lease the vineyard to better tenants who will let him have his proper share of the produce at the proper time.' Jesus responded to that by citing scripture. 'Don't you remember the text,' he said, 'which says, "The very stone which the builders rejected has become the head of the corner; this was the Lord's doing, and in our eyes it is a miracle." ' Tenants may reject the 'beloved son', builders may reject a certain stone, but God will work his will all the same. The Jews had been defective tenants of God's vineyard (Isa. 5.1-7). But their tenancy would be brought to an end, and passed on to new and properly dutiful tenants in the community of the new people of God.

This was but the first of several encounters planned for Jesus by the authorities that day. The next one came when he was approached by some Pharisees and members of the Herodian party. They met him with flattering words. 'Sir,' they said, 'we know that you're an honest man, who speaks his mind entirely without fear or favour. Tell us then, whether it is lawful to pay the Roman poll tax or not? Ought we to pay it, or should we withold payment?' Jesus at once spotted the trap. The poll tax was payable by all the population of the province. It was particularly obnoxious to the Jews, as even making the payment ministered to the resentment they felt at the Roman occupation of their homeland. Having to pay it, as was required, in silver coinage bearing Caesar's image, was an additional affront to a people in whose traditions likenesses and images were avoided. Moreover, the question was evidently addressed to Jesus as a man from Galilee, for it was there that the imposition of the tax in 6 A.D. had led Judas of Galilee to his revolt, which in turn had led to the beginning of the Zealot movement. The trap for Jesus lay in the fact that whatever answer he made would put him in the wrong with some of the crowd. If he said, 'Yes, it is lawful', he would cut himself off from both popular and the more extreme forms of nationalism, and even deny the zealous patriotism in which he had been brought up. But if he answered 'No, it is unlawful', he would put himself into the hands of the authorities or anybody else who wanted to report him to the Roman administration as someone likely to revolt against Rome. It was therefore a brilliant out-manoeuvring of his opponents when he replied, 'Why are you trying to catch me out? Bring me a coin used to pay the tax.' So he was handed a coin. He then asked his questioners, 'Whose image and inscription is on this coin?' They could only say, 'Caesar's.' 'Then give to Caesar,' said Jesus, 'what belongs to Caesar, and give to God what belongs to God.' They were astounded as if he had performed a miracle, so sure had they been that they had him in an inescapable trap.

The next interrogation came from the conservative Sadducees, who laid a trap in resurrection theology, or rather resurrection casuistry. It was somewhat uncharacteristic for them to do so, for they rejected the whole notion of resurrection as a dangerous neo-radical error. They began by telling Jesus a story based on the Mosaic regulations of levirate marriage, which required that if a man's brother died and left his widow childless, it was his duty then to marry her and beget children for his brother. The story was that the first of seven brothers married a wife, and died, leaving her childless. So the second brother married her according to the law; but he also died and left her childless. The same misfortune befell them all; having had seven husbands she was still childless. The question which the Sadducees then put to Jesus, who shared 'Pharisaic' views on resurrection, was this: 'At the resurrection, when they all come back to life, whose wife will she be?' Jesus avoided the trap. 'You've got it all wrong,' he said. 'In the first place, you fail to recognize what God's power can do; for in the resurrection he does not just renew men to the conditions of earthly life, but raises them to a new and heavenly life where, like the angels in heaven, there is no marrying or being given in marriage. In the second place, you need to know even the scriptures you acknowledge as authoritative better than your question implies, for when God spoke to Moses out of the burning bush, he declared that he was the "God of Abraham, of Isaac, and of Jacob". God is not the God of dead men, but of living beings. So you are greatly in error!' The Sadducees' question wrongly conceived the nature of God and of resurrection. Some of the doctors of the Law who had been listening were impressed. 'Well spoken, sir,' they said; while the crowd that had been attracted by the open controversy was just as astounded as if he had performed another miracle.

One of the doctors of the Law then put a friendlier question to Jesus. 'Which do you believe, sir, to be the greatest commandment in our Law?' Jesus responded quickly and confidently, 'There are two. 'The first is "Hear, O Israel, the Lord, our God, is the one and only Lord; you must love him with your whole heart, mind, soul and strength." The second is parallel to it, "You must love your neighbour as yourself." All our laws, and the messages of all our prophets, are but a commentary on these two commandments.' The doctor of the Law replied, 'You're quite right: there is but one God, and we must love him, and we must love our neighbour as ourselves. And I would agree that this is far more important than regulations about burnt offerings and sacrifices.' Jesus sensed the fundamental unity of understanding between himself and his questioner, perhaps the result of his Temple cleansing, and said to him, 'I have been proclaiming the arrival of the kingdom of God: you are not very far away from it.'

That was the end of the questioning. But Jesus took the opportunity of a crowd having gathered to say something very relevant about the greeting he had received from the crowd the Sunday before, which had been repeated by a number of children in the Temple on Monday. On both occasions he had been welcomed as the 'Son of David', i.e. as a military Messiah, who would liberate the Jews from their Roman masters. Jesus now posed a question himself: 'How can the learned doctors of the Law hold that the right title for the Messiah is "Son of David"?' Whatever may be thought by scholars today of the sort of argument that was then offered, it seemed valid enough to those who heard it then. David had written the Psalms, it was held, and under divine inspiration had said, 'The Lord said to my Lord, "Sit at my right hand until I put your enemies under your feet." ' 'But,' Jesus said, 'if David so calls the Messiah "Lord", how can the Messiah at the same time be his son?' The argument was conclusive; but the fact that he advanced it at all at that point is what is really significant, for it indicates that even in these last days Jesus was aware of the critical importance of having the title 'Son of David' ascribed to him. It was one that he utterly rejected. The crowd, and his critics among them, were stunned into silence.

As the little group of Jesus and his disciples moved round the Temple they paused at one point to watch the people passing the Temple treasury, and how they reacted to its presence. There were some who ostentatiously placed large sums into the chest set outside for donations. But as they watched an old widow came along and dropped two tiny coins into the chest as unobtrusively as she could. Jesus told his disciples, 'That poor widow has given a larger gift than anyone else; for the others have so much to start with that their large gifts are no trouble to them. But this poor widow, who really hasn't got enough to live on, has put into the chest all that she's got.'

Soon after this Jesus and his disciples left the Temple for the day. As they walked away, one of the disciples turned round and looked at the noble set of buildings. He exclaimed, 'Teacher, look at those huge stones in the Temple, and see what wonderful buildings they are.' Jesus said to him, 'You see all these grand buildings? Well, there will soon be nothing left of them, not so much as one stone standing on another. Everything will be thrown down.' So convinced was Jesus that the policies of the Jewish leaders would lead to a great disaster. When they had gone away as far as the Mount of Olives, Peter, James, Andrew and John asked him, 'Tell us more about what you said just now. When will it all happen? How shall we know that is has begun when it all starts?'

Jesus's eschatology: beginning, centre and end

In fashioning his material into a gospel each evangelist has made use of the same literary device in introducing the narrative of the passion, arrest, trial and crucifixion of Jesus.

Each has used prophetic and apocalyptic material in order to show that, whatever future historians may find to relate, the real 'end of all things' was actualized at the time when Jesus died upon the cross. So the cross is more than an historical incident; it is an eschatological

event, an end-event, as well. But it is more than an eschatological idea;
it is actual history too.

Each evangelist has used two Jewish literary devices to assist him in
this task. First, a 'foretelling' prophecy, foreseeing the future, not by
special psychical powers of divination, but by a profound moral and
spiritual examination of present trends and policies, and their
inevitable consequences; and, second, the strange but powerful
eschatological habit of writing the history of the present and the most
recent past as if it were foreseen long ago, and then linking it with the
end of all things as its immediate future, when the final kingdom of
God would arrive in events and through figures comprising a special
mythology of their own.

In what has been called the 'Little Apocalypse' in Mark (as in similar
material in Matthew and Luke, and in somewhat different material in
John), Jesus speaks of the impending and ineluctable destruction of
Jerusalem, and of the imminent end of all things, in such terms that,
as the story is told, the reader cannot but recognize that with the
crucifixion of Jesus the final end of all things has been reached and
revealed.

Jesus answered the disciples' question about when it would all
happen in three phases, one concerned with themselves and their
own integrity; one to do with Jerusalem and the destiny of Israel,
and the last dealing with the end-events themselves. There is not a
little overlapping.

The disciples had to realize that all he had to say concerned them,
and that their integrity as his disciples would be severely tested. If in
describing the woes that might precede the 'end' Jesus spoke of
phenomena already within the experience of the disciples, that only
served to underline the strangely present quality of his eschatology.
In a world where rebellions, wars and rumours of wars were rife (a
very good description of the world in which Jesus had grown up),
there would be, as they knew from their own experience, not a few
false Messianic claimants. But they must not give way to alarm.
Moreover, discomforts consequent upon human folly and wrong
would not be the only calamities; even the natural order would
seem to share in the tragedy of man's destiny – there would be
earthquakes and famines. But none of these would be separately or
together the ultimate event itself. In the midst of all this they would
find that their mission would bring them into danger; they would
be targets for arrest and persecution. But there was no need for fear,
for the Holy Spirit would give them the right words to answer their
accusers and persecutors at the required time. The preaching of the
good news of the kingdom would continue to cause many heart-
breaking divisions among men. Children would be estranged from

parents, and young people from young people. Jesus's disciples could well come to feel that the whole world had turned against them. But there was no need to despair or give up. To endure to the end would bring the great reward.

As for Jerusalem, the present policies of the Jewish leaders could only result in new disaster. Jesus foresaw that present trends could only lead to another desecration of the Temple, such as the Jews had known under Antiochus Epiphanes in the days of the Maccabees. But by the time that came, terrible things would have happened to Judaism, and Jewish lives would be in great danger. It would be then that there would rise up some foolhardy 'Messiahs', who would prey upon the people's fears and even mislead the really wise, if that were conceivable. The disciples must be always on their guard.

As for the 'end-events' themselves, their cosmic character would be displayed in the darkening of the sun and moon, and the shaking of the very heavens. Then would be seen the Son of Man coming with the clouds of heaven in great power and glory. He would send out his messengers and gather his people from the four corners of the earth. The disciples must learn that when all this began to take place the Son of Man had arrived at the very door. The final events would have begun. He could say no more, save that all of which he spoke would take place in the lives of those who were about him. Their one great responsibility was to be always on the watch.

It is not improper to see in the various ingredients that Jesus used in this apocalyptic discourse elements that were drawn from his actual present, so giving even the area of the historical an eschatological quality. Since the rebellion of Judas of Galilee in 6 A.D. there had been a number of false claimants to Messiahship. The same period had seen a number of revolts, wars and rumours of wars, and earthquakes and famines as well. His own mission had occasioned the very divisions he now spoke of, as it had drawn to itself the suspicion and hostility of the authorities. Like John the Baptist, he was himself now a target for arrest, trial and death. Yet the disciples need have no alarm at the prospects before them. The Holy Spirit would put into their minds the right words for each occasion. It is more than probable that Jesus foresaw the eventual destruction of Jerusalem and its Temple as the inevitable outcome of current Jewish policies; it would be surprising if he had not. As for what he said about the Son of Man, that may be left for further consideration when his own reference to it at his trial is examined and evaluated (see below, p.215).

But Jesus sometimes stated his eschatology somewhat differently, as for example in the parable of the Sheep and the Goats. This tells of the coming of the Son of Man, whenever (as Matthew puts it) that may be. The real point is that whenever the Son of Man comes, he will bring about the final separation of evil from good, and that, as already seen (p.50), is part of the effect of the apostolic preaching of the good news.

Christians must live in the world and be concerned with its duties, i.e., be 'secular' (=live in the present age). In that secularity their vigilance for the kingdom must be exercized, and the separation take place. If that separation be extrapolated for emphasis' sake on to a chronological dimension it takes the form of a 'last' or 'final' judgment, with the Son of Man as judge. How different he will be from earthly judges! The 'sheep' will be told of their ministry to the Son of Man when he was hungry, thirsty, lonely, naked, sick and in prison; but they will protest their innocence of any such virtuous service. 'The 'goats' will be told of their failure to minister to the Son of Man in the same set of circumstances; they too will protest their innocence of any such neglect. To both sheep and goats the Son of Man declared that it was in their secular life that he lived with them, that he was in need of ministry in normal human relationships. Response to such need will not take a man from the secular to some other realm, but it will transfigure secular life with the glory of the heavenly kingdom. Hence the ultimate separation of men turns on their alertness to the hidden presence of the Son of Man in their ordinary lives. The separation of the sheep from the goats is 'aeonian' or 'eternal'. Men live in one of two worlds, where mercy and pity reign, or where they do not. The boundary is strictly closed, save for the miraculous act of salvation in which the Son of Man visited the world and called men to repentance, which is one with divine forgiveness, begetting entry into the kingdom of Heaven, the realm of the eternal even in the midst of the secular, temporal order. This is the judgment, the separation, that accompanies the Son of Man as he now lives in self-identifying solidarity with the world's unfortunates. He is hidden in the world's needs, proclaimed in the gospel story, and experienced in the worship of the Church.

The last days

Peaceful planning

It was now Wednesday. The Sanhedrin had a session to consider safety and security during the festive days ahead. The notorious guerilla Barabbas was already in prison for murder committed during a recent rebellion, but now there was news of the man Jesus, who remained an enigma. The authorities had been trying to get him to declare his intentions ever since he arrived on Sunday, but he had very adroitly avoided doing so. They knew that the Galilean crowd which had come into Jerusalem with him on Sunday had hailed him as the 'Son of David', which meant that they believed him to be the military Messiah of Jewish hopes. But he had himself said, in clear actions if not in so many words, that he was a 'pacifist' Messiah, if that was a possible thing to be. Nevertheless, were he to claim Messiahship during the festival itself, there would at the least be a disturbance, and one that would almost certainly assume riot proportions. Were that to happen, Pilate would certainly act with swift severity to restore order.* The city would suffer damage, the Temple too would be badly damaged or even destroyed, and the Jewish people would be deprived of their few remaining liberties. That could not be seriously contemplated by any responsible Sanhedrin. There seemed but one course of action certain to preserve the peace of Jerusalem: to get Jesus at least out of the way until the feast was over. That could be done by arresting him on some charge and holding him in custody. And if events moved too swiftly for that, then, they thought, remembering the advice of Caiaphas, it was better that one man should die for the whole people, than that the whole city and nation should perish. But one

*Pontius Pilate was the Procurator of Judea from A.D. 27-37. When Herod the Great died in 4 B.C., his kingdom was divided between three of his sons: Archelaus, who received Judea, Samaria and Idumea; Antipas, who took over Galilee and Perea; and Philip, who governed the north-west territories. Archelaus proved a bad and unpopular ruler, and in 6 A.D., after two deputations, the emperor Augustus banned him from his throne. He decided to bring the difficult province under direct rule from Rome, and appointed a 'Procurator' to take charge and be responsible to him. The Procurator had his official residence at Caesarea, and also a residence in Jerusalem, where he resided at times when trouble might arise, the major Jewish feast being the chief such. Pilate was apparently very tactless in his dealings with the Jews, and alienated some Jewish funds to help to build a new aqueduct for Jerusalem. He was severe in his reactions to trouble, no doubt fearful for his own standing in Rome. After dealing brutally with a Samaritan revolt, he was banned from his office in 37 A.D.

thing remained clear even so: the arrest must not be in front of the festival crowd, for that would only be an incitement to riot. So the matter was left for the time being.

A woman's prophetic farewell

It was Wednesday, and the day passed without special incident. But it ended in revealing fashion. Jesus had been invited to dine at the house of Simon, the leper in Bethany, and he had gone there. Presumably Simon had recovered from his leprosy, possibly through Jesus's healing power. In any event Jesus's acceptance of the invitation showed that at the end of his ministry he was as ready as at its start to break down the barriers that social or religious custom, prejudice or prudence erected between men.

The company had gathered, the feast had started, and the guests were reclining at table. Then a woman entered, carrying an alabaster phial of costly oil of pure nard. She went up to Jesus, and poured it over his head, in full view of all the guests. Some of the diners were indignant, and showed their disapproval by voicing the question, 'Why such a waste as this? This expensive oil could have been sold for some thirty pounds, and the money given to the needy poor!' And they openly criticized the woman. But Jesus intervened. 'Let her alone,' he said. 'Why make a scene out of what was a remarkably beautiful action? There will always be poor people for you to help, after I am gone. But you won't always have with you the Messiah appointed to die; indeed you still haven't accepted that you have got with you a Messiah who has been appointed to die. But this woman has. And she has done all that can be done for such a Messiah as I am: she has anointed my head, as the heads of God's anointed are rightly treated. She has at the same time as it were prepared my body for burial. And that is why, you may be sure, wherever the good news of my Messiahship is preached, this woman will be linked with the good news, and she will be remembered for her beautiful and prophetic tribute.' Indeed this unnamed woman has become the first of many who have paid a tribute of love to their crucified Messiah.

The activity of Judas

'Then Judas Iscariot, one of the Twelve, went to the chief priests to betray Jesus to them. They were delighted to hear this, and promised to give him money. So he watched for an opportunity to hand him over' (Mark 14.10).

So Mark continues his narrative of the Passion after telling the story of the dinner party at Simon's home. It raises a number of questions, but leaves them unanswered. What passed between Judas and the chief priests? How did Judas 'betray' Jesus? Was his betrayal simply the act of 'handing him over'? Why did Judas go to the priests at all?

The general impression left by the evangelists about the crucifixion of Jesus is not that it was the product of the plans of evil men. Rather it was the tragic and misguided actions of good men, acting for perfectly good reasons, that brought it about. The Jerusalem authorities were sincerely concerned about the Temple, the city itself, the Jewish state, and what liberties still remained to the Jews. Pilate was certainly a severe Procurator, but he was responsible to the Emperor for the peace and safety of a province that was notorious for disturbances, rebellions and guerilla activities. The crowds, Galilean and Jerusalemite, were concerned both for the triumph of the true promised Messiah and for the peaceful conclusion of the Passover and the consequent safety of the city, Temple and Jewish state. Jesus was caught up in the centre of these good intentions, and suffered. Was Judas the one really evil figure in the drama?

The name 'Judas' has become a synonym for treachery and betrayal. It is therefore important to note that the one Greek word used can mean both 'betray' and 'hand over'. Which meaning should be applied to Judas's action? Did he 'betray' and then 'hand over'? Was he acting all through as one ready to 'hand Jesus over' for some reason not yet disclosed? It is important to review the situation in which Judas approached the chief priests. The Twelve and many of their fellow-countrymen believed that Jesus was about to establish a new political kingdom of Israel. The Twelve were encouraged, as they thought, by some things that Jesus said, to suppose that when the kingdom was established, they would have places of power and authority as a reward for their services (Mat. 19.28; Luke 18.29f.). Luke tells his readers in Acts that this political expectation even survived the resurrection (Acts 1.6).

There were, of course, differences between Jesus and the Twelve on this point. Peter had said at Caesarea Philippi that Jesus was the Messiah. Jesus had accepted the title, but went on to talk about his Messianic destiny as that of a suffering Son of Man. When Peter expostulated with him he was told that he was acting as the very advocate of Satan. And though there were no further verbal exchanges after the 'inner group' had been on the Mount of Transfiguration with Jesus, there had been only the Sunday before a difference of expression in actions. Jesus had affirmed that he was entering Jerusalem as its rightful and peaceful king, to found a universal empire without recourse to arms. But the Twelve and the pilgrims had said in effect, 'Here is the beginning of the Messianic revolt.' And this very night, in Simon's house, Jesus had reaffirmed his strange notion that he was about to suffer and die, even though – or rather because – he was the Messiah. However right this woman had been to 'anoint' his body beforehand for his burial, his death now would certainly involve some disturbance of a major kind, which the authorities were understandably trying to avoid. So what did Jesus intend? Was he after all going to start a Messianic rebellion? How otherwise could his life be at stake? For such reasons it is worth asking what it was that made Judas go to the chief priests to 'hand him over' or 'betray' him. What did he say to the priest, and why did he say it?

By this time the Jerusalem authorities would have acquired quite a large 'dossier' on Jesus. He had been interrogated and investigated and informed on ever since he first began his work in Galilee. There was very little information, if any, that Judas could have given them that they did not know already – except that Jesus had accepted the title of 'Messiah'. It would already have been known to the authorities that certain 'demon-possessed' people had called him by that title, but Jesus had always commanded the demons to be silent. Sick people had also sought his help by using the title, but Jesus had told them not to use it. Was the information that Judas 'leaked' to the authorities that he could tell them when and where Jesus had accepted that he was the Messiah? This would have given them a proper reason for arresting him as a dangerous figure for Jerusalem during the present Passover, for a Messianic rising would be a critical danger to the peace of Jerusalem and the Jewish state at such a time. But if this is what Judas told them, it is hard to understand why there was so much difficulty at Jesus's trial in getting evidence on the point. Judas may have extracted a writ of immunity from appearing as a witness, but it seems improbable. He was available throughout Jesus's trial until sentence was passed, for it was not until then that his remorse brought him to suicide (Mat. 27.3). If the admission of Messiahship was the one thing that Judas betrayed to the priests, he could have done so in the belief (and hope?) that the arrest of Jesus would force him to show his hand, one way or another. If he decided to fight, then the days of the Davidic Messiah would have begun; if he decided not to fight, then the day of the Son of Man, as conceived by Jesus, would have dawned. Perhaps it seemed to him better to precipitate events than just to let them drift.

Judas shared with all Jerusalem and the visiting Passover pilgrims the knowledge that Jesus was liable to be arrested, but that the authorities were reluctant to do so in the presence of a crowd of Passover pilgrims. Nothing must be done that would cause a riot of the dimension that would provoke Roman intervention. It would therefore have been a piece of valuable information were Judas to have told the priests of a garden outside the city walls where Jesus and the Twelve went each night to meditate and pray together. If Judas had already given information about Jesus's Messiahship, it would have been sensible also to name a place where an arrest could be made 'quietly'. As we have seen, being arrested might serve as a pressure on Jesus to declare his intentions. In any event, this was the right time for getting the matter settled once and for all. Passover was the feast at which Israel celebrated her deliverance from the slavery of Egypt under Moses; let this Passover be the one when Jesus led Israel to freedom once again, this time from the slavery of Roman occupation, whether by force of arms or by the suffering and death of the Son of Man.

There is evidence that Jesus knew of the 'betrayal' of Judas, and that he did not shrink from what it implied (Mark 14.20; Mat. 26.24f.; John 13.26f.). It is not easy to understand why Jesus should have 'let things go' in that manner. But at least an arrest such as Judas contrived avoided his appearing in court as a Davidic Messiah.

The last Passover

On Thursday morning, the day when, as usual, the Passover lambs would be slain, the Twelve approached Jesus to ask what arrangements he wanted them to make for celebrating the Passover in Jerusalem, the proper place for eating the meal. Jesus sent Peter and John into Jerusalem to get things ready. He had already made the preliminary negotiations. When they entered the city they would be met by a man carrying a leather bottle. He would greet them, and they were to follow him home; there they should say to the householder, 'The Teacher has sent us to ask "Where is the guest room you have reserved for him, so that he may eat the

Passover tonight with his disciples?" ' 'He will show you,' said Jesus, 'a spacious upper room, with all the necessary furniture for the celebration. Get everything ready there.' So Peter and John went to Jerusalem, and had a busy day seeing to the killing and roasting of the Passover lamb, and buying the necessary unleavened cakes, wine, water, bitter herbs and sauces, and oil for the lamps. They returned to Bethany before evening.

With evening came the beginning of Passover Day itself. Jesus and the Twelve made their way to the reserved room, and were joined by others, disciples of Jesus though not of the Twelve. Everyone present felt that this would prove a most unusual Passover meal; each one knew how very delicately balanced the situation was, and what menaces threatened the liberty and even the life of Jesus himself. And that meant danger for the Twelve as well.

Passover was, and still is, a very 'ritual' occasion; identical words and actions are reproduced every year in every household. Jesus, all the Twelve, and every other guest present would have known the whole liturgy off by heart, and even the slightest deviation would have been extremely conspicuous. So it was a great surprise when Jesus twice interrupted the set traditional order with words and actions of his own. First he spoke to them as they were eating, and said, 'Honesty demands that I tell you now in all seriousness that one of you is going to hand me over to the authorities.' This left the Twelve speechless; when their tongues were loosened a bit, they stumbled out, one after another, 'But surely I won't be the one to do that!'

How was Jesus able to make this statement? No doubt his own perceptive insight into the different characters of the Twelve would have enabled him for some time to have spotted a possible agent for the role. But what he had said evidently rested upon actual knowledge that Judas had made some agreement to hand him over. Jesus had friends in the highest circle of Judaism; – Nicodemus (John 3.1; 7.50; 19.39) or Joseph of Arimathea (Mark 15.42f.), might well have let Jesus know the danger he was in, hoping that he would frustrate Judas's intentions. It is possible, if not very probable, that Judas himself informed Jesus of his plan, in the hope that he would be encouraged to declare himself as the militant political Messiah that the people expected and desired. What remains significant is that though Jesus knew of the agreement to hand him over, he took no steps to avoid it. On the contrary, he prepared himself to meet it, and in meeting it to overcome its evil.

The second intervention was in its way even more surprising. It affected the Passover ritual itself, giving it a new direction of meaning, by focussing it not on the Exodus from Egypt and the march to the freedom of the land of promise, but on the exodus of Jesus (the 'son' or people of God) from the captivity of man's sinfulness to the eternal freedom of the kingdom of God.

While the Passover meal was still being eaten, Jesus took one of the unleavened loaves, and offered thanks for it in the words familiar to them all: 'Praise be to thee, O Lord our God, king of the universe, who bringeth forth bread from the earth.' He then symbolically broke the loaf, and, without eating any himself, gave the pieces to the disciples with the words, 'Take this and eat it. It is my body.' So at this Passover meal where Jesus presided, there was a body for slaughter, and a body for eating, other than that of a Passover lamb; instead of an animal sacrifice to be offered year after year, Jesus was offering his body once and for all. And as the eating of the lamb (or any other sacrificial item at other rites) was a pledge to the worshipper that he would share the benefits of the sacrifice, so now the eating of the bread Jesus had broken became a symbol and pledge to those eating it that they would share the benefits of his death. The benefits of the new Passover paralleled as they exceeded those of the old. The eating of unleavened bread in the old Passover symbolized that the participants each year were truly part of that Israel which God had created through the Exodus from Egypt. The eating of the broken bread in the new Passover meant that those who shared in it were part of the new Israel of people of God which God was creating through the new exodus under Jesus.

Later in the festival meal, at the third cup to be ritually drunk, the 'cup of blessing', Jesus continued his modification of the old Passover. He poured out the wine, raised the cup and gave thanks for it. Then he passed it to be circulated among the disciples, with the words, 'This is my blood of the new covenant, poured out for many.' Then after a slight pause, he added, 'I tell you simply and straightforwardly, I shall not drink any wine again until I drink it anew in the kingdom of God.'

Wine – blood – covenant. Passover lambs were not regarded as sacrificial offerings, but as a means for God's people to give thanks for the great divine deliverance from Egypt under Moses. That deliverance had led to the making of a covenant incorporated in the Mosaic law. Moses had impressed that upon the people when, having reached freedom, he had animals sacrificed and then sprinkled the people with their blood, saying, 'This is the blood of the covenant that God has made with you in accordance with all the words of the Law' (Exod. 24.8). But the lambs slain on the first Passover night certain had some sacrificial efficacy, for their blood was sprinkled on the doorposts of the Israelites, so that God's avenging angel should not take the lives of Israel's firstborn. Now, on the night of the new Passover, the blood of the slain lamb would have efficacy again. The whole idea of a covenant was familiar to the Jews, for their prophets had often chided them for 'not keeping the covenant' that God had made with them. But even in the Old Testament there was a new understanding of the covenant between God and his people. It found its best expression in Jeremiah: ' "This is the covenant that I will make with the house of Israel," says the Lord. "I will put my law in their minds and write it on their hearts. I will be their God, and they will be my people. No longer will a man teach his neighbour, or a man his brother, saying, 'Know the Lord', because they will all know me, from the least of them to the greatest," says the Lord, "For I will forgive their wickedness, and will remember their sins no more" ' (Jer. 31.31-34).

No doubt Jesus realized that Jeremiah's attitude to the Law expressed in that oracle was embodied in his own teaching in the Sermon on the Mount. But both now, and in that sermon, Jesus was concerned with more menacing alien powers enslaving Israel than even the might of Rome. His deliverance would lead Israel from thraldom to the powers of evil and rebellion against the love and wisdom of God. The final exodus from that land of bondage was to take place in the events of the immediate future. The new ritual of the new Passover was meant to symbolize and proclaim the forgiving mercy of God, which was about to establish the final kingdom of God upon earth. When that had been accomplished, he would no longer be a lamb waiting to be slain, but the triumphant king of the new kingdom, and so would be able to celebrate with his community the new Passover thanksgiving for what would take place that night.

Before the meal was over, Jesus handed to Judas a piece of unleavened bread dipped in the Passover sauce, saying to him quietly, 'What you have to do, you had better get done quickly.' No one else present guessed what was happening; some of them thought that Jesus was asking Judas, as the treasurer of the group, to go and buy something that had been forgotten, or even to take an offering for the poor-box. But Judas knew what was ahead. He rose from his place, and went out into the night.

Supper was over, the formalities finished, and everyone was able to relax and talk. The disciples' thoughts fastened on the kingdom Jesus had proclaimed from the beginning, and mentioned again at the table. The discussion took an uncomfortable but very human turn as the eleven began to argue among themselves who would have the highest office in the kingdom once it had been securely established. Jesus quickly intervened. He reminded them of what he had already said to them about the relative greatness of serving and being served. 'Through all the difficulties we have been through,' he said, 'you have stood by me loyally. And now it is my turn to assure you that you need have no fears about your places in the kingdom. For I make a covenant with you that you shall be the "patriarchs" of the new Israel, and you will exercize its authority, the authority that belongs to serving, sharing it with me; and you shall eat and drink at my table in my kingdom.'

But Jesus added a warning: immediately ahead was the stiffest testing yet, and the adversary, Satan, would treat them like the chaff that gets blown away as the farmer threshes his wheat. Jesus knew that Peter was particularly prone to fail in such a testing, and so spoke to him in specially intimate terms: 'Simon,' he said, 'Simon Peter, Satan has wanted to get all of you. But I have prayed specially for you, that your faith will not fail. And when you come out of it all, pass on the strength you will have received to your brothers.' Peter gave a brave if over-confident answer. 'Lord,' he said, 'I'm ready to go with you, even if it means imprisonment and death.' But Jesus, knowing Peter better than Peter knew himself, replied, 'I tell you Peter, that before the cock crows in the morning you will have denied me three times.'

Jesus then told them a little more clearly what lay ahead. 'Do you remember,' he asked, 'when I sent you out in Galilee, and told you to travel as light as possible – barefoot and no purse or pack. It is quite a different situation now. Take a purse, if you've got one, and most certainly take a pack with you. And if you haven't got a sword, buy one somehow, even if you have to sell your cloak to get it. For you are about to see how what has been written about me in scripture will find fulfilment. One text says "He was counted among the criminals" – and that will be fulfilled in me.' The disciples answered, 'We've got two swords.' And Jesus said, 'That will do.' It is impossible to think that in giving this advice Jesus was going back on his pacific conception of Messiahship so clearly stated by his ride into Jerusalem. But it could well be that he sensed that the Twelve would be in danger that night if Judas were to effect his arrest. If they tried to get back from their meeting place on the Mount of Olives to Bethany or Jerusalem, their lives might well be in danger. In that case, it might be best for them and for the movement that they had means to ensure that they 'got home'.

Yet for all the menace of the future Jesus spoke also of peace. 'Peace' was, and remains, one of the great words of the Hebrew language. '*Shalom*' or 'peace' means far more than the absence of conflict. It is a very positive state of total well-being of persons in a community where not only personal relationships are amicable, but all the conditions for a good life flourish – physical, mental, moral, legal and spiritual. Jesus had already made it clear that following him would involve his followers in a life that, in normal terms, would seem far from 'peaceful'; on the contrary, simply being his disciples would bring them into conflict. Yet he still had a peace to offer them, a peace that could transcend all earthly conflicts, be with them in all earthly situations, even though it seemed as if none of the constituents of '*shalom*' were present. 'Peace,' he said, 'is what I am leaving with you. And it is my peace that I give you. My peace is not the peace of the Pharisees who think that it can be won only by strict obedience to the law. Nor is it the peace of the Zealots who think that it can only come by the use of armed force. Nor is it like the peace of the desert sects who think it can be found in retreat from the world. My peace is one of a kingdom that has been established without a war; it is one given absolutely and entirely freely. It is one to be found while you are in the world with all its menaces and threats. So you have no need on this or any other night to have troubled hearts, or to be afraid in any circumstances. I have said all this to you, so that in the community of the kingdom you may have to the full those conditions of body, mind, heart and spirit that constitute real peace. Without doubt in this world you will have to face trouble and tribulation of all kinds. But you can face them with courage and cheerfulness, because I have overcome the world.'

Before the company left the upper room, they sang the Passover hymn, which consisted of Psalms 115 to 118. The whole four psalms repay reading in the light of this particular Passover, but some verses may well be cited here:

Our God is in heaven;
He does whatever pleases him.
O house of Israel, trust in the Lord –
he is their help and shield.
It is not the dead who praise the Lord,
those who go down to silence;
it is we who extol the Lord,
both now and forevermore.
The Lord protects the simple-hearted;
when I was in great need, he saved me.
For you, O Lord, have delivered my soul from death,
my eyes from tears, my feet from stumbling,
that I may walk before the Lord
in the land of the living.
How can I repay the Lord
for all his goodness to me?
I will lift the cup of salvation
and call on the name of the Lord
in the presence of all his people.
Precious in the sight of the Lord
is the death of his saints.
Let Israel say
His love endures for ever.
The Lord is with me; I will not be afraid.
What can man do to me?
I was pushed back and about to fall,
but the Lord helped me.
I will not die but live
and will proclaim what the Lord has done.
The Lord has chastened me severely,
but he has not given me over to death.
The stone which the builders rejected
has become the capstone;
the Lord has done this,
and it is marvellous in our eyes.
Give thanks to the Lord, for he is good;
His love endures for ever.

The last day

The last prayer

The hymn-singing over, the little band left the city and made its way to the nearby Mount of Olives. On the way Jesus again underlined the severity of the testing they would shortly be asked to undergo. He said, 'You will all find that what is coming to you will be too much for you. There's a scripture text which puts it well: "I will strike the shepherd, and all the sheep will be scattered" ' (Zech. 13.7). 'Yet,' he added, 'when I have risen, I will go before you to Galilee.' Again, they all expressed confidence in their ability to face with complete loyalty whatever the night might bring.

So they reached an olive grove on the hillside, named Gethsemane. Here Jesus told the disciples to sit down while he went on to pray; he took with him Peter, James and John (who had watched him raise Jairus's daughter, and had seen him in his transfigured glory). He began to be stricken with horror and almost overcome with grief. He said to the three men, 'My soul is well-nigh bursting with sorrow, so that it seems that I must surely die from the pressure of it. Stay here for a while, and remember to keep watch and stay awake.' So he went forward a bit, fell to the ground, and prayed that if it were possible, the critical hour might pass him by'. He said, 'Abba [=Father], everything is possible to you. Take this cup away from me, so that I do not have to drink it. Yet do what is your will, not what is mine.' He came back to where Peter, James and John were, and found them asleep. 'Simon,' he said to Peter, 'are you asleep? Couldn't you manage to keep watch for just one brief hour? Watch, and pray that you may be spared the testing. I know how willing your spirit is; but you must remember how weak the flesh is.'

So Jesus went away again and prayed in the same words as before. Then again he came to find the three asleep; and when he spoke to them they had no idea what to say to him. So he went away again to pray alone, and for a third time returned to find them sleeping. But now he had something new to say to them, for there were signs that the testing time was very near. A good number of people were approaching through the olive grove; their identity needed no speculation. Jesus woke the sleeping three. 'Are you still asleep?' he asked, and then added, 'Well, you've had your full now. The time has come. The Son of Man is now about to be handed over to sinful men. So get up, and let us be going. Look, the man who is going to hand me over is coming up.'

The arrest of Jesus

It was quite clear that something unusual was afoot. Quite a little crowd had appeared in the olive grove. They could now be both seen and heard. The three disciples who had gone forward with Jesus had been wakened. Those left behind had already seen the intruders, and had come up to see what would happen. The crowd, headed by Judas, consisted of some Jewish Temple guards, armed with swords, and some Roman soldiers, who were there to make sure the arrest was not used to stage a riot at festival time. There were also Pharisees and scribes, and a number of Jerusalem citizens, armed with clubs – altogether a somewhat formidable company to arrest one man. Yet the size of the expedition reflected the official expectation that Jesus would resist arrest when the time came, and that he would be supported by his followers.

Judas was in the lead. He had arranged to indicate which man to arrest by greeting him with the 'kiss of peace', for it would be difficult for some official who did not know Jesus well to pick him out in the comparative darkness, even when it was illuminated with torches and lanterns. Judas went up to Jesus, and kissed him. Jesus commented, 'Judas, what does it mean that you should hand over the Son of Man by giving him a kiss?' When he had been so identified, the Temple guards took hold of Jesus to arrest him. But even if Jesus was prepared to submit to arrest, some of his followers were not going to let him be taken without at least some token resistance. One of them, perhaps in the hope, or even expectation, that this might be the first blow in the final Messianic war, drew his sword, slashed at the ear of the High Priest's slave, and cut it off. Jesus at once intervened. 'That's enough,' he said. 'Put your sword back into its sheath. Remember that those who take to the sword are those who perish by the sword.' He then put his hand on the slave's ear and healed him. This is a fine example of Jesus's 'natural' authority; on the very point of arrest he took charge of the whole proceedings. Jesus then turned to his captors, and said, 'Why have you come out with swords and clubs to arrest me as if I were a militant and murderous guerilla? You know very well that I've been teaching every day this week in the Temple. But you made no attempt to arrest me there. But I know that in all that is now taking place something is going on which the scriptures can reveal. So let things take their course. They are under God's control, and I am quite content.' The disciples, seeing their Master arrested, left him, every one of them, and escaped arrest. But there was one exception:

a young man, who had left home (the house with the 'upper room'?) hurriedly in the night and followed Jesus, tried still to go along with him. The guards went up to arrest him – a sure sign that they would have arrested the eleven – but he slipped out of the only garment he had had time to put on as he left home, a linen cloth. So he left a piece of linen cloth in the soldiers' hands, and ran through the olive grove naked.

As the crowd left the olive grove and marched Jesus to the city, it was clear both to him and to the authorities awaiting his arrival in Jerusalem that it was now a fight to the end. That they had decided to arrest him meant that they believed there was a proper charge for him to answer in either a Jewish or a Roman court, or possibly even both. The charge could be religious, to be answered in a Jewish court, or political, in which case a Roman court would be involved as well. All the indications were that it would be political. Jesus had sensed that in his arrest it seemed that he was being treated as a guerilla leader, as if he were the crisis-maker, and not the authorities themselves. But if a political charge were made the case would have to be stated and sentence passed by the Roman resident Procurator, Pontius Pilate.

Legal administration in Palestine was divided between Jews and Romans. In admirable respect for its vassals, Rome had permitted certain privileges to the Jews, known to be the great religious people of the ancient world. They were allowed to deal with most minor and all religious offences in their own courts. But major crimes, especially against the state, were the prerogative of the Roman courts, and certainly no death sentence could be passed by a Jewish court. That had to be done, after careful examination of the case, by the Procurator himself. Pontius Pilate, the present Procurator, alone could pass a death sentence and order an execution.

As Jesus walked back with his captors to Jerusalem he was the most composed and serene figure in the crowd. His beliefs were to be put to the test. He was sustained and fortified by the conviction that he was the 'son' of the Father, in whom the new Israel had been constituted; it had been enlarged by the incorporation of his followers, and was now to be finally established as an indestructible reality by his own submission to death. His certainty in these matters was based both on the voice that he had heard at his baptism, and by the way in which, as he believed, the scriptures showed that all that was taking place was but the historical enactment of what had been said long ago. Because of this he could

still know that God's favour rested on him, as he had heard on the
day of his baptism.

The trial of Jesus before the Jews

Once safely inside the city gates, Jesus was taken to face the
Supreme Council of State, the Sanhedrin. It was almost certainly
not in full session at that hour of the night. But, as Professor Baruch
Kanael suggested to the present author, after his experience as
minister responsible for public order in the state of Israel, during
religious festivals there could well have been a group of Councillors
reserved for festival night duty, to deal summarily with minor
breaches of order, or to prepare a proper dossier on more serious
cases, to expedite proceedings when the full Council met the next
day. Even if that were not the custom then, and it remains purely a
suggestion, it would seem more than likely that, having sent out a
posse of Temple guards and others to arrest Jesus 'quietly', some
arrangements would have been made to have a 'quiet' hearing of
the case immediately on the arrival of the prisoner, so as to prepare
a sufficient document for the later meeting of the Council to be
brief and uncontentious. That would prevent undue public interest
being aroused, and avoid such clamour as would disturb the peace
sufficiently to provoke procuratorial action.

Jesus now faced his accusers. The proceedings were not, and
evidently did not need to be, formally correct. But they would be
inescapably decisive. The authorities were relying on a number of
voluntary witnesses, but they proved unsatisfactory in that the
legally required agreement of at least two witnesses could not be
found. Some testified that Jesus had said, 'I will destroy this Temple
that is man-made, and in three days I will erect another, not man
made.' But even on that allegation no two witnesses agreed fully. In
the absence of progress, and under the pressure of time, the High
priest took an unusual line. He stood up himself and asked Jesus,
'Haven't you got anything to say for yourself? [a very genuine
attempt to be fair?] What is it that these witnesses are trying to say
against you?' But Jesus kept quiet, perfectly composed. Then the
High Priest put to Jesus what would now be termed a 'leading
question'. He said, 'As you speak before the presence of the living
God, tell me if you are the Messiah, the son of God'. (It is
noteworthy that the High Priest used the two terms 'Messiah' and
'son of God', which Jesus had to some extent made public, and did
not mention the term 'Son of Man', which had been used by Jesus

alone.) Jesus then spoke for the only time in this trial; with serene composure he said, 'I am. And from this time on you will be able to see the Son of Man seated on the right hand of power [=God], and coming with the clouds of heaven.' Both Jesus and the High Priest knew the source of Jesus's reply, for it came from the prophet Daniel, when he was telling how God would destroy the kingdom-beasts that rejected him, but would give an imperishable and universal kingdom to the Son of Man, who would come into heaven from the earth, borne on the clouds of heaven, and be 'presented' to God, as an ambassador is presented at the court of a monarch. There he would receive for the 'kingdom of the saints of the Most High' a universal and unending sovereignty.

So the confrontation had reached its climax. The High Priest had put the life-and-death question to Jesus, who had made the astounding reply that even if his answer led to his death, that would only take him to the presence of God, where he would be assured of the inviolability of his kingdom at all times and in all places. So the substance of his first preaching, that the kingdom of God had come upon Israel, would be confirmed as true. Not surprisingly the High Priest was angry. 'Do we need to call any more witnesses after that?' he called out. 'You have heard for yourselves the blasphemy of his claiming to be the son of God. What sort of sentence does he deserve?' And the unanimous response was that Jesus was guilty of blasphemy, and should be put to death.

The story of this part of the proceedings against Jesus is manifestly incomplete. The greatest difficulty is that the charge of blasphemy was not applicable to anything that Jesus is recorded as saying during the hearing, for the name of God had not been 'railed against' or 'spoken against', as blasphemy was then defined. The best solution is to accept the suggestion that this 'trial' was not conducted by a fully constituted session of the Sanhedrin, but rather by an important 'emergency committee' (how important is signified by the presence of and the part played by the High Priest) charged with the preparation of papers for the later meeting of the full Council. By that meeting the charge of blasphemy had been dropped in favour of one concerning insurrection and public order. The transition could have developed from two points already made public. Any Messianic claimant (and Jesus now technically was one) was inevitably involved in being 'King of the Jews', for that was part of the Messianic office. And a threat to destroy the Temple would powerfully support the accusation that Jesus was a danger to public peace and safety.

It is important to restate the application of the prophecy of Daniel 7.13 to the response Jesus made to the High Priest. No doubt the High Priest knew the text of Daniel quite well, as Jesus clearly did. Little doubt either that the High Priest was familiar with the figure of the Son of Man as portrayed in the Book of Enoch, where he is a heavenly being who will descend 'on the clouds of heaven' to act as judge of all the earth at the last day. It has been the dominant tradition in the Church to think of the Son of Man as coming in the future. The present writer thinks that is wrong. First, it seems so patent that Jesus was quoting Daniel 7.13 at this point in his trial that if that quotation makes sense of the situation it should be taken as the basis of exposition, as has been done above on p.197. Second, the passage from Daniel fits the situation of Jesus at his trial in a way that the figure of the Son of Man in Enoch cannot possibly do. For Jesus was on the earth. If he was to be put to death, and was thereafter to go to the 'Ancient of Days' to receive his kingdom, then he would be going from earth to heaven, which is precisely what the figure of the Son of Man does in Daniel. But the Son of Man in Enoch is firmly in the heavens, and so cannot undertake any journey from any situation of Jesus in his lifetime, and certainly not from the place of his trial, when where the 'glory' of the heavenly Enochian figure is totally absent. Third, accepting Daniel as the basis of a proper exposition of the record of the trial makes coherent sense with the general eschatological teaching of Jesus about himself and his kingdom that is reported in the gospels.

At the earliest possible moment on Friday morning, a full session of the Sanhedrin was held. The result of the night's transactions were made available. There is no record of the discussions at this point, but the outcome is quite clear. Jesus was to be sent forward to the Procurator, no longer on a charge of blasphemy, but on a charge under his sole jurisdiction, subversive activity and planned insurrection.

The trial of Peter

Jesus was not the only person on trial during these fateful hours. In quite another way, so was Peter. Indeed, he and the rest of the eleven had already been 'tried' once, when Jesus had been arrested, and he and the others had all 'forsaken him and fled' from the olive grove. Indeed, flight was certainly the wisest course for them. Jesus was being arrested as if he were a guerilla leader, and it was only prudent that his followers, actual or suspected, should keep out of the way, avoid arrest, and so survive to continue the struggle at a later date, when the present crisis was over.

By the time Jesus was brought to the city, Peter was placed so as to be able to follow at a discreet distance. He was lucky enough to get inside the High Priest's courtyard, and even to find a place among the attendants round the night fire which they used to keep themselves warm. He had been there for a while when one of the maidservants saw his face in the glow of the flames, and exclaimed, 'You were there with that man Jesus from Nazareth.' Peter rejected the accusation, and said, 'I don't know what you're talking about!' He moved to the gateway, where he could more easily make his escape if it became necessary. He had not been there long before the same girl came by and spotted Peter; she said to the group by the gate, 'This man is one of them.' Again Peter, fearful of what it might mean to be identified as a member of a guerilla band, said that he was not. So Peter stood and talked further with the group by the gate. Then suddenly one of them exclaimed, 'Surely you must be one of them; your accent is pure Galilean!' At this obviously cogent identification Peter was really frightened; fear produced anger, and he swore that he had no knowledge of or acquaintance with the man of Nazareth at all. Just then, the cock crew, and Jesus, who was being prepared for despatch to the Procurator, turned round and saw Peter. Peter remembered what Jesus had said when he had spoken so bravely of his readiness for 'imprisonment and death'. It was too much for him. He burst into tears, and went out into the city as the last day dawned.

The trial of Jesus before Pilate and Herod

Jesus was sent on quite specific charges when he appeared before Pilate. It was necessary to go to Pilate since the offence involved the death penalty, and that could only be given by the Procurator. He could consult with others before passing sentence, but the responsibility remained his alone.

The hearing began with an outline of the charges to be brought: 'We found this man to be a perverter of our nation. He said that we must not pay taxes to Caesar, and he says that he himself is our Messiah, a King.' Pilate asked Jesus, 'Are you the king of the Jews?' Jesus asked Pilate what put that idea into his mind, and Pilate told him that it was information provided by the authorities of his own people. He went on to ask what exactly Jesus had been doing. Jesus's response was to the point, but not very helpful to Pilate. 'My kingdom,' he said, 'is not of this world. If that were the case, my followers would even now be fighting to prevent my arrest, but my kingdom is not really a political entity.' 'But you are a king,' repeated Pilate. 'That is the way you have put it,' said Jesus.

At this stage of the interrogation Pilate made a preliminary report to the waiting members of the Sanhedrin. He told them, 'I can find no crime in this man.' But they restated their accusation vigorously, saying, 'But he has been stirring up the people all over Judea; he began his work in Galilee and has repeated it all the way down to here.' When Pilate heard the word 'Galilee' he decided to send Jesus to Herod, who was in Jerusalem for the Passover period. He knew Herod would appreciate being consulted, and Herod had expressed an interest in seeing and questioning Jesus himself, and even hoped to see him perform some miracle. So Jesus was taken to Herod, and many of the Sanhedrin went too. Herod asked Jesus many questions, but received no reply. This angered Herod, who deemed it insolence, and began to treat Jesus with mockery and contempt. He ended by dressing Jesus as a king; he then sent him back to Pilate. By such a strange action Pilate and Herod healed a long-standing enmity, and sealed a new friendship that day.

The trial of Judas

It was by this time quite clear what would eventually happen to Jesus. His appearance before Pilate in itself meant that a death sentence was more than likely. His return from Herod without any word to alleviate the weight of the accusations against Jesus from Judean sources made it a virtual certainty that he would be crucified. Judas had been following events as best he could. He realized that Jesus's death was now inevitable. He bitterly regretted what he had done, and tried to make some amends. He had received thirty pieces of silver for laying the information against Jesus, and he now took it back to the Council offices. He said, 'I've committed a great sin in handing over to you a perfectly innocent man.' The officials were not moved. They said, 'That's nothing to us. It's entirely your own affair.' So Judas threw down his silver in the Temple, went out, and hanged himself. He had certainly made Jesus 'show his hand', but in so doing he had accomplished his death. It was more than he could bear. Better for him, as Jesus had once observed, that he had never been born.

Jesus is condemned to death

Jesus was taken back to Pilate, who called the Sanhedrin together, and told them, 'You brought me this prisoner as a subverter of your nation. I examined him in your presence, and there was no charge on which I could have found him guilty. Neither could King Herod. The man has done nothing to merit a death sentence. So I will simply have him beaten, and then set free.' But the members of the Council were dissatisfied with that; they called out, 'Get rid of this man! If you want to exercize your prerogative of mercy, then set Barabbas free.' Barabbas had already been committed to prison for fomenting a rising in the city, in which he had committed murder. Pilate argued with them in a conscientious attempt to have Jesus released as an innocent man. But the task proved difficult. While this heated debate was going on, a messenger came from his wife, who wrote that her husband should have no part in the sentencing of this innocent man. She had suffered a lot that very day in a dream she had had about him. But even with that plea and support Pilate found that he was fighting a losing battle against the Council, which was rapidly becoming more clamant. Finally he said to them, 'Very well. Which of the two men do you want me to release to you –Barabbas or Jesus?' (There are some old manuscripts of the gospels which give to Barabbas the fuller name of 'Jesus Barabbas' – and Barabbas means 'son of the father'.) The reply came quickly and loud; 'Barabbas!' Pilate then called for a basin of water, and in full view of the Sanhedrin washed his hands, saying, 'I am innocent of this man's blood; the responsibility is entirely yours.' He received the response, 'We know that. We are acting for our own good, and for the good of our children.' So Pilate released Barabbas, and handed Jesus over to the soldiery for the beating that was always administered before a crucifixion.

Jesus is crucified

The guards took Jesus inside the Praetorium, the Procurator's residence, and there called the whole squadron together. They joined in stripping Jesus, and putting a cloak of royal purple on him. They plaited a crown of thorns and put that on his head, and made him hold a staff for a mock sceptre. Then they went up to him one by one and bowed before him and said, 'O king of the Jews, live for ever!' Then they spat on him, and took the staff from his hand and beat him on the head with it. The official beating also took place. When it was all over, Jesus was once more dressed in his own clothes, and led out for crucifixion.

The grisly procession set out. The soldiers detailed for the duty of execution surrounded Jesus, who was obliged, like all condemned criminals, to carry his 'cross'. But this was not the cruciform shape so familiar to Christians in the cruciform symbol of their saviour, but simply the 'cross piece' – which was a heavy enough burden for a man, like Jesus, who had just endured the regulation beating, and the additional mockery of the soldiers. It soon became evident to the soldiers that Jesus would never reach the place of execution if he had to carry the cross all the way without any help. So they requisitioned aid from one who was probably a visitor to Jerusalem for the feast, a certain Simon of Cyrene, who must have been well enough known to the early readers of the gospels not to have required any further introduction. As the procession went along the narrow streets of the city it was watched by growing crowds, who had heard that the night's proceedings had ended in a death sentence for Jesus of Nazareth. In the crowd were some women supporters, who wept and wailed for him. Jesus, with the serenity that had marked his bearing all through the night, stopped and said to them, 'Daughters of Jerusalem, don't weep for me. The people to weep for are yourselves and your children. After this is over there will come times when you will say, "Happy are the barren women, the wombs that never bore, and the breasts that never gave suck!" Then, in the words of Hosea, "They will say to the mountains 'Fall on us' and to the hills 'Cover us up'." For if this is what men will do to one who is innocent of rebellion, what will they do when the real crisis gets under way, as some time it will?'

This report of something that took place on the way to execution is also an indication of what was going on in that happening. Jesus was pointing out to the women of Jerusalem what would face the Jewish state if and when it attempted a war of liberation against Rome. If they dealt with men recognized as innocent, as Pilate had recognized him as innocent, by crucifying them, what horrors would have to be faced when a real national rising began. Jesus's own way of 'pacific' kingship, which he had dramatized the previous Sunday, was the way that accorded with his own preaching, 'Repent, and believe the good news that the kingdom of God has come upon you.' Jesus's way was the only way that accorded with the will of the forgiving God whom they worshipped. Jesus was the serene innocent prisoner marching to his death. He was about to die, and the whole people would be saved, at any rate for the time being. But unless the Jewish authorities learned the real meaning of what was happening to Jesus, the whole Jewish people would not be able to avoid destruction. His ministry had not affected the policies of the authorities. Would his death do what his life had not?

So at last, at about noon on Friday, the place of execution, known as 'Golgotha' (the skull-place), was reached. Its permanent gaunt uprights seemed to be waiting eagerly for the decoration that would make them a centre of public interest. There, in the view of the crowd of gaping sightseers, the three men were prepared for crucifixion. They were made to strip. Their clothes passed by right of custom to the soldiers on duty, who would later gamble for their choice of various items. They were then made to lie on the ground while their arms were stretched over the cross pieces they had been carrying, and nailed to them. Then they were hoisted up, and the cross pieces fixed to the uprights, their feet being nailed to a small projection of wood, which gave them a minimal and precarious support for their bodies, for as long as they had strength to make use of it. When all this was done, their heads would have been just above the height of the bystanders. Nothing could have been easier than to talk to the dying men, or, if preferred, to mock them and spit in their faces in contempt.

It was at this moment that Jesus once more showed his own distinctive power and personality (Luke 23.34). 'Father,' he prayed, 'forgive them; they don't know what they're doing.' This was, as Luke's careful setting of it shows, much more than a prayer just for those who were executing him, more than for Pilate, the Sanhedrin, the soldiers and the rest, that they should be pardoned for unwittingly crucifying the 'son' of God. It was a prayer for all those who are officially or by duty bound to oppose wrong-doing by the infliction of punishment. It raises the question whether anyone knows what he is doing when he punishes another person, whether as parent, teacher, official, magistrate, or high court judge. When Jesus first began his ministry he proclaimed a baptism of repentance for the forgiveness of sins. He taught his followers that forgiveness was the cement that held the divine community together. He taught them not to oppose evil with evil, but to overcome evil with good. He made it clear that failing to forgive was something that by its very nature excluded men from the kingdom of God. Now, in his last hour, he invoked the forgiveness that is the creative principle of God's sovereignty to come to this misguided punishment of crucifixion and by forgiveness transform it.

Regulations required that every crucified criminal should be labelled with a visible note of his offence. This was printed on a card and either nailed to the cross over the offender's head, or tied round his neck. For Jesus Pilate prepared a 'titulus' which read: 'Jesus of Nazareth, King of the Jews'. When some Sanhedrin members saw this, they went and remonstrated with Pilate on the grounds that Jesus was not the 'King of the Jews'. But Pilate was not to be moved. He replied, 'What I have written, I have written, It must stand.' But the 'king', who had ridden into his city the previous Sunday, seemed to have failed completely to obtain, as Zechariah's oracle had promised, a rule extending over the whole earth.

Crucifixion was a cruel death to die. There were severe physical discomforts: public nudity and the inability to control bodily functions; the swarming of flies on untreated wounds; the fierce unrelenting heat of the sun at a high Palestinian noon. It was not surprising that Jesus cried out, 'I thirst.' Whatever serenity he possessed did not exempt him from the physical agony of crucifixion. He was certainly not less than a normal human being in that respect. The crowd heard his cry, and a sponge was dipped into a jar of sour wine, fixed on a stick of hyssop, and lifted to his lips. He took what meagre refreshment the gesture provided.

Intolerable as was the heat of the sun, darkness would have been felt as an even greater evil. The records, in their desire to make an utterly clear identification of this day with the 'last day' of Jewish apocalyptic (see above, pp. 195,197), report that there was a period of complete darkness for some three hours. This, at a time of a full moon, could not have been due to an eclipse; it is clearly an example of the use of a statement of 'what took place' to indicate what was really going on, to show that the final judgment was being made on man's religion, politics, justice and patriotism. Jesus's judges had found him guilty of a crime deserving death, and he was now suffering the penalty. But, strangely, the whole situation was being turned upside down: Jesus the dying criminal was judging his judges, and prayed for their forgiveness.

Crucifixion was a cruel death to die. There were severe social discomforts: taunts from a hostile crowd; the sight of friends or family coming to catch a last glimpse before the end came; the stigma, particularly for an innocent man, of dying publicly as a common murderer. But Jesus faced and bore it all triumphantly.

Some Council members derided him: 'Well now, you who said you'd destroy the Temple and rebuild it in three days, perform your miracles now and come down from your cross!' Others, more theologically, said, 'He's saved others; let him do it again and save himself this time! If you really are the son of God, come down from the cross, and then we'll really believe in you!' Jesus heard it all, and in his ears there sounded an echo from his battle in the wilderness after his baptism, when the adversary had said, 'If you are the son of God, cast yourself down from the Temple . . . ' 'Down from the Temple – down from the cross': he had rejected the temptation then. No more now than then would such a miracle produce belief in what he had come to do and to teach; it would only convince some credulous critics that he was a quite supernaturally gifted escapologist. He had not worked and was not suffering just to achieve that.

With eyes now dimmed and bodily reactions slowing down, Jesus saw his own mother before him in the crowd. With her was the young disciple of whom he was specially fond. They stood by the cross, and looked up to him in sorrow and pity. He said to his mother, 'Dear lady, there's a son for you to take care of'; and then to the young disciple, 'There's someone who will be a true mother to you.' And he knew that from that reconstituted home, from the joining of the old Israel that had given him birth with the new Israel, there would flow the life of the new people of God.

The two guerillas who were crucified on either side of Jesus proved at first to be entirely unsympathetic. Like most others on that day, they had learned that Jesus was being crucified as an unsuccessful rebel against Rome; he seemed no better than his fellow guerillas beside him, and they certainly had no reason to believe that he was the Messiah, or the son of God, or anything more than a failed rebel like themselves. So they joined in the general taunting that was going on. But for a reason undisclosed, but most probably connected with the serenity so victoriously displayed by Jesus, the situation changed dramatically. It happened when one of them said to Jesus, 'Aren't you supposed to be the Messiah? Then why don't you save both yourself and us?' The other scolded him and said, 'Have you no respect at all for God? Just remember that you're under the same sentence of death as he is, the only difference being that while we know that we're just getting the proper punishment for our crimes, this man has done nothing wrong at all.' He then said to Jesus, 'Jesus, when you do come in your kingdom, remember me.' This was, on any interpretation, an amazing thing to say to a man dying on a cross; and it seemed impossible to expect anything like a positive answer to it. But Jesus replied, 'I promise you that this very day you will join me in Paradise', which means something like, 'I promise you that on this day of our death you will join me, not, as we both realize, in a Judea liberated by Zealot guerillas from Roman occupation, but in the community of the true people of God, which includes those who trust in him, whether they be alive or dead.' Such were the words of forgiveness spoken by Jesus from his grotesque deathbed.

Crucifixion was a cruel death to die. It posed issues more sharply and bitterly than any ordinary life or any ordinary death. The dying criminal had to admit that his crime had failed. Jesus, though innocent of crime, had to face the possibility that his work had been wrecked by his crucifixion, and would come to nothing. But if it were, surely that would imply that God had deserted him. Was that possible? It was thus that a psalm came into his mind that spoke precisely to that depth of desolation. He began to recite it to himself, '*Eli, Eli, lama sabachthani?*' he began (My God, my God, why hast thou forsaken me?). It sounded to those near him as if he were naming Elijah, and some of the bystanders said, 'Let's wait and see if Elijah does come.' Other people thought that he might be asking for a drink again, and they brought some more sour wine, which he sipped off the sponge they used. As he felt the end very near, he cried out, 'Father, into thy hands I commend my spirit.' Such confidence expresses the mood of the ending of the psalm he had been quoting to himself, which goes, 'Future generations will be told about the Lord. They will proclaim his righteousness to a people yet unborn, for he has done it' (Ps. 22.31). And, continuing in that mood, and echoing the psalmist's words, he gave a last and triumphant shout, 'It is done.' Then his body sank, relaxed, upon the cross, and he died.

'It is done.' In those words the dying man did much more than a film or television producer does when he inserts the title 'The End' on to his screen to let his viewers know that the play is over, and that there is nothing more to come. The words of Jesus are much more a shout of triumph, like mountaineers who have struggled for days against rock, ice and snow, and the rarified atmosphere, but now at last reach the top of Everest, and cry out, 'We've done it!'

'It is done.' said Jesus, using the 'theological passive' so useful to the pious Jew who wanted to say that God had done something without having to offend his people's embargo on any pronunciation of the divine name. That was the final comment on his life after the awful desolation of the last hours between Gethsemane and

Golgotha, after the unimaginable agony of dying upon a cross. God had 'done it' – just as, at the Exodus under Moses, he had 'triumphed gloriously'.

Jesus is buried

The life of Jesus ended ignominiously, but its extraordinary repercussion began to manifest themselves at once. Jewish law required that a condemned criminal's body should be buried on the day of his execution (Deut. 21.22f.). So before the 'last day' ended, in the late afternoon, the soldiers examined the bodies on the three crosses to ensure that the criminals were dead, and the bodies available for burial. The two guerillas were found to be still alive, so their legs were broken to ensure a speedy death. But Jesus was seen to be already dead. All that was done to him, quite superfluously, was to pierce his side with a spear. Out from the wound, tells John, flowed blood and water (John 19.34). This, in spite of some critics' objections, is not an impossible phenomenon. But whether it took place or not, John recorded it so that his readers might learn what was going on in the crucifixion, and recognize that both the wine of the eucharist and the water of baptism come from Jesus, who gave his life in sacrificial death to be 'the real food and the real drink' of men (John 6.55).

There was an earth tremor (Mat. 27.51ff.), with accompanying effects that made it more portentous than ever. Whether an earthquake took place or not, the recording of it was intended, like that of the darkening of the sun (Mat. 27.45), to help the gospel reader to identify this 'last day' with *the* 'Last Day' of Jewish eschatology.

As Jesus died outside the city, another strange event took place within its walls. The veil in the Temple separating the Holy Place from the Holy of Holies was torn from top to bottom, clearly an instance of divine activity. So it was indicated that the death of Jesus was the point at which man had no need to go to God via a temple on Mount Zion (or Gerizim), for Jesus had secured for all mankind an open access to God himself (John 4.23; Mark 11.17).

The first human reaction to Jesus's death comes from the centurion in charge of the executions. He may have been on duty when Jesus was being tried, and been impressed with his serenity. He may even have been, though it is not very likely, in Gethsemane when Jesus was arrested, and observed his composure. But he certainly knew that the reason Jesus was sentenced to suffer as a rebel 'King of the Jews' was because he had claimed to be the Messiah, or son of God. He had watched Jesus endure crucifixion and die with what seemed a supernatural dignity. And when he heard him cry out his last triumphant words he could not restrain himself from saying, 'This was without doubt an innocent man', or, according to another report, 'This man was a son of God.' So the effects of Jesus's death began to manifest themselves in the lives of men.

The crowd was also much affected by Jesus's death. At the crucifixion were some who sympathized with Jesus (Luke 23.27). Others mocked him, and others no doubt were just out for the day and enjoyed the spectacle of three captured guerillas paying the due penalty for their crimes. But at the end of the day they all realized how very different a person Jesus was from the other two crucified with him. They went home beating their breasts in sorrow, deploring that such a man had been condemned to death (Luke 23.48). Both those who had hailed him as a 'militant' and those who had been affronted by his 'blasphemous' talk about being the 'Son of Man' on his way to the Father were united in their perception that an injustice had been done, and in their forebodings as to what might come upon a people that had so treated an innocent and godly man.

Among the crowd were three women supporters who had followed Jesus and his disciples from Galilee, Mary from Magdala, Mary the mother of James (the son of Alphaeus) and Salome, the mother of James and John. They had all watched the day's events 'from a distance'; at the end of it they waited in resignation for whatever might unfold after Jesus had been declared dead by the military guard. Their state was one of shock and numbness; they felt hopelessly impotent in so tragic and desperate a situation.

Joseph of Arimathea, a well-to-do member of the Sanhedrin, now had a part to play. Known for his concern for the kingdom of God, Joseph heard Jesus' teaching about it and became one of his disciples (Mat. 27.57). When Jesus died he mustered all his courage, went to Pilate, and asked to have Jesus's body to give it a decent burial. Pilate checked that Jesus was in fact dead (a useful piece of evidence for the early Church), then let Joseph have the corpse. Joseph purchased a burial shroud, wrapped the corpse in it, put it in his own rock-hewn tomb outside the city, and rolled a large rounded stone into place to close the entrance to the grave.

The women who had been watching the day's sad happenings

'from a distance' also made sure from their own observation that they knew in which tomb Jesus had been laid. Then they went off to prepare spices for embalming his body.

Coincidentally Nicodemus, who had visited Jesus on an early visit to Jerusalem, and was also a member of the Sanhedrin, secured, possibly in collaboration with Joseph, a quite abundant supply of myrrh and aloes for the embalming of Jesus's body. So the two men and the three women waited for the Sabbath to pass, after which they would be ready to pay their last respects to Jesus and to keep what they could of his 'remains' by a careful and adequate preservation of his corpse. No one seemed in the least prepared for what was to follow once the Jewish 'Sabbath' was over.

So ends the story of Jesus in his lifetime. The evangelists tried by prologue and epilogue to show that he was a figure of more than human proportions. But they also tried to show how that was confirmed by the story itself. Jesus and John the Baptist began their work under a sense of a crisis soon to break; the axe was already at the roots of the trees. Instead of the hatred and perverted nationalism that marred even their religion Jesus offered his people entry into a new people or kingdom of God freed from such evils and ready for the way of peace. Jesus made his appeal to the nation as urgently and unambiguously as he could, but the authorities so outmanoeuvred him that he was arraigned before the Roman Procurator as one who was about to create the very crisis he wanted to avoid. So Jesus lost his fight for the soul of his people. History could not now, it seemed certain, ever vindicate what he had taught. Yet it is in the very particularity of defeat that the historical order was transcended and the vindication made. Jesus was shown to have been right, not just because in 70 A.D. the Jewish state fell in the sort of crisis he had wished to avert, but much more because the good news of the kingdom that came with him is still proclaimed, with him as its ever-present king, long after his own contemporaries have passed away.

The Epilogue

The first day

Morning

The Sabbath passed mournfully enough for the friends of Jesus. But on the first day of the new work, Sunday, they sprang into activity. As so often, the women were first. Mary of Magdala, Salome the mother of James and John, and Mary the mother of James the son of Alphaeus were up before dawn, and off to Joseph's tomb with the spices for embalming the body of the Jesus they had loved. They had marked the tomb; they knew the way to it; they knew they had the right spices in the proper quantities for the embalming; they knew how to embalm a body; they knew there would be a problem about moving the great door-stone at the entrance of the tomb. They knew everything – except what was just about to happen.

When they reached the tomb the light of a new day was breaking (in more than one sense!). They saw at once that the large door-stone had already been rolled away. They also saw some Jewish Temple guards on duty at the tomb, who told them that they were there on orders of the Sanhedrin and by permission of Pilate to prevent the tomb being desecrated. They also told the women that there had been an earthquake earlier in the morning, and that while the tremor was going on the door-stone at the tomb's entrance had been rolled away by a being who was undoubtedly a heavenly visitant. They were very awestruck and fearful about it all. The women also were scared; they looked into the open doorway, but could see nothing. Then, as they turned round, a young man in white clothes spoke to them and said, 'Why are you looking for a living person in the place for dead ones?' They were absolutely amazed at this, but the 'young man', who was to their minds an 'angel', went on, 'You are looking for Jesus of Nazareth. But he is not here. He has risen from the dead. So go back to your homes, and tell the disciples, and especially Peter, that he will go ahead of them into Galilee, and will see you all there, just as he said.' The women left the tomb, quite overcome with astonishment, nor could they find their tongues to say anything to anybody.

They were afraid. Afraid, not just because of the awesome character of their recent experience, but much more because of what the rising of Jesus might mean for all his followers. During his lifetime Jesus had spoken of his resurrection from the dead. He had also said that each of his followers must take up his cross and follow him. Did that mean that every one of his disciples would be handed over to the Roman authorities and crucified? Did discipleship mean literally losing your life, with only the hope of a resurrection to follow. Jesus had lost his life, and now was risen, as he had foreseen and foretold. But what of themselves and their fellow disciples? They were afraid, and fear sealed their lips.

But on their way home Jesus himself met them. He gave them his usual greeting, 'Peace be with you.' They fell at his feet in adoration. He told them that they had no need to be afraid. Their duty was plain and simple: to go and tell the disciples that they were to go to Galilee, and he would meet them there. So the record of the astounding ministry of Jesus after his death begins with the witness of three women; their testimony could have had no value in a Jewish court of law, but on their word Jesus was content to rely as the new chapter in his life began.

The meeting with Jesus and the close-knit fellowship of his friends soon loosed the women's tongues. The disciples were told the story, though not all of them believed it; some of them thought it nothing but 'women's gossip'. Mary of Magdala had more success with Peter and the 'beloved disciple', however, and persuaded them to go back to the tomb with her. When they got near the tomb, the two men pressed ahead. The beloved disciple outran Peter, and arrived at the tomb first. He peeped inside and just saw some grave cloths lying there. Peter, impetuous as usual, went straight into the tomb, and saw that the head cloth and the body wrappings were folded up separately and laid alongside each other. The beloved disciple then followed Peter into the tomb, and saw the same things. Both of them 'believed', though their belief was not yet integrated with all that Jesus had said beforehand about his resurrection. They were evidently still speculating which of them would play the role of the risen 'Jesus', as Jesus had played the role of John the Baptist (cf. Mat. 14.1f). The two men returned to the city, with their so far incomplete and inadequate belief.

When they left, Mary was alone in the garden; she stood by the tomb, weeping. She ventured to look into the tomb herself, and she saw two 'angels' in white, seated one where Jesus's head would have been, and the other where his feet would have been. They asked why she was crying, and she told them, 'Because my Lord's body has been taken away, and I don't know where it has been taken.' She turned from the tomb to see a man standing by her. It was in fact Jesus, though Mary failed to recognize him at that moment. She thought that he must be the gardener. The 'gardener' said to her, 'Dear lady, why are you crying? Who are you looking for?' In her misapprehension she answered, 'Sir, if it is you who have removed him, tell me where you have taken him, and I will fetch him.' Jesus simply said to her, 'Mary.' Utterly overcome, she threw herself in adoration at his feet, and cried out, 'Rabboni!', 'my Master!'. Jesus said to her, 'Don't hold on to me! I have not yet returned to the Father. So go back and tell the brethren that I am now returning to my Father and your Father, to my God and your God.' So Mary went and told the disciples the good news, and the message that Jesus had given her.

Afternoon

That same Sunday in the afternoon, two disciples, Cleopas and one unknown other, set out on a walk to Emmaus, some seven miles from Jerusalem. They talked about the melancholy events of the weekend, and as they talked Jesus came and joined them, though they did not recognize him. He asked them what they were discussing so earnestly as they walked. They said, 'You must be the only man in all Jerusalem that doesn't know what has been taking place over the weekend.' 'What things?' asked Jesus. They stood still in amazement, and in their sadness replied, 'All about Jesus of Nazareth, a man who could say and do wonderful things both in the sight of God and of our own people. But our chief priests and Council saw fit to hand him over to the Roman authorities for a capital sentence. For ourselves, we had hoped that he would prove to be the man promised to liberate our nation Israel. Today, Sunday, is the third day since he died; and this morning some of our women went very early to the tomb, but found that his body wasn't there, and instead came back with a tale that they had seen some angels who told them that Jesus was alive. Then some of our men went down to the tomb, and found that what the women had said was quite correct, though they did not see Jesus.'

'Well, how dull you are!' said Jesus, 'How slow to believe what all the prophets have been saying to you!' He began with Moses, and going through all the prophets he expounded and explained to them what had been said about himself in scripture.

By this time they had reached Emmaus. As they came to the inn, the disciples went to enter it, but Jesus made as if to continue his walk alone. But, as the disciples pointed out, the afternoon was almost over, and evening would soon be upon them, so why did he not join them for a meal in the inn? Jesus accepted. And when they were served Jesus took one of the small loaves set before them, gave thanks for it in the usual words of the Jewish prayer, broke the bread and gave it to them. There was no need for him to say, 'Take, eat, this is my body'; they knew him in the breaking of the bread. But at the moment he broke it, he disappeared. The disciples reflected on their strange but wonderful afternoon. 'We might have known it was he,' they thought, 'for while he talked with us our hearts were set on fire, as they used to be in Galilee and Judea.' Then without regard for the falling darkness, they went back to Jerusalem to tell the other disciples that they had seen Jesus.

Evening

Cleopas and his companion hurried back to Jerusalem, and reached the house where the Eleven and their friends were met. The room in which they were gathered was securely locked against possible surprise entry by a suspicious authority. The two were readily admitted. They were bursting to tell their story, but were forestalled by the Eleven reporting to them in equal excitement, 'Its really true! The Lord has indeed risen, And he's been seen by Peter.' Then the two from Emmaus told their story, especially their recognition of Jesus in the breaking of bread at their meal in the inn. They were still talking excitedly about it when Jesus himself appeared among them, locked doors notwithstanding. They were not at all prepared for such an appearance to all of them together, and thought this was some 'uncanny' experience, like seeing a 'ghost'. But Jesus said to them, 'Peace be to you all!' They recognized the greeting that Jesus had given and explained at the Passover – 'It is my peace that I give you' – and began to accept the reality of their present experience. Jesus then showed them the marks of his crucifixion, in his hands and feet and side, and their perplexity passed into true joy. He shared some fish with them, and then spoke again. 'Peace to you all,' he said. 'I am now going to commission you and send you out, just as the Father commissioned me and sent me out.' With that he breathed on them, and said, 'Take this breathing on you as the gift of the Holy Spirit [=Breath], the life of your spirit, as breath is the life of your physical frame. You are going out as I have already told you, on a mission which effects the final separation of good from evil. So if you forgive wrongs done, the wrongdoers will be forgiven; but if you cannot forgive a wrong you know to have been done, the wrongdoers will remain unforgiven. In this way you will really be the judges of the new Israel of God.' Then he did for the whole group what he had earlier done for the two walkers to Emmaus, taking them through the scriptures and pointing out to them how his whole destiny was there. In Jesus and his destiny the whole history of the true Israel was centred and enacted.

He then invited them to walk with him back to Bethany, where they had stayed for some days before the Passover began. They gladly went with him. When they reached their destination, he lifted his hands in blessing, and left them. They returned to Jerusalem, and day after day went to the Temple and gave thanks to God.

The eighth day: evening

One of the Eleven, Thomas, who had been so bravely resigned to the untimely end of Jesus's mission when they were asked to go to Bethany at the time of Lazarus's illness, was not with the rest on the first Sunday. When the rest told him what had happened, he was utterly sceptical. 'I can't believe it,' he said. 'The only thing that could make me believe it would be seeing and touching his wounds myself, and putting my hand where his side was pierced, and feeling that.' On the following Sunday, the faithful company had gathered again in the locked room. Jesus came, as he had done a week before. 'Peace be to you all,' he said. Then he went up to Thomas and said to him, 'Thomas, put your finger here, and look at my hands; and reach out with your hand and touch my side.' All that Thomas could do was to blurt out, 'My Lord and my God.' Then Jesus said to him, 'Thomas, you thought yourself unfortunate because the others had seen me, and you had not. But now, like them, you have seen me, and you believe. Don't you realize that the really fortunate people are those who don't see me, and yet believe?' Then Jesus left them and they treasured his words for the help and comfort of those to whom they would bear witness. The reality of their new experience of Jesus, they were beginning to see, did not lie in visual or auditory experiences, but in the spiritual fellowship which the

resurrection had renewed, and which was enabling them really to
be with their own beloved, crucified and risen Lord.

A later day: Galilee again

It was some time after the end of Passover week that the company
of Galilean disciples left Jerusalem and returned to Galilee. They
were uncertain about their future commitment to the mission of
Jesus, and it seemed wise to wait on events for direction. So Peter
said to some of them, 'It's no use doing nothing. I'm going to get on
with some fishing.' The others in the group – Thomas, Nathanael
of Cana, James and John, sons of Zebedee, the 'beloved disciple',
and one other follower, all said, 'We'll come with you.' So, they set
out at dusk for a night's fishing, but had no luck at all.

Early in the morning Jesus came to the shore, though the men in
the boat neither knew nor expected him. As he saw them heading
for the shore, he called out, 'Have you caught anything?' They
shouted back, 'Not a single fish.' He then called out, 'Cast your net
on the right side of the boat, and you'll catch some.' This they did,
and made a good catch.

With the perceptive eye given by true intimacy, the beloved
disciple said to Peter, 'That was the Lord talking with us.' At that,
Peter put on his tunic (he had removed it for greater freedom of
movement in the boat) and went ashore ahead of the others. He
wanted to put things right with Jesus, whom he had so cowardly
denied at his trial, before his six friends came ashore. But they were
too close behind. When they did leave the boat, they saw a fire
burning on the beach; some fish was being cooked on it, with bread
by the side. Jesus asked for some of the fish from the catch to cook
with what was already there, and Peter went back and hauled the
catch in – a great haul of 153 fish. (This was the total number of fish
species that was believed to exist, so this number suggested that the
Messiah's fishermen would catch the whole of mankind.) None of
the seven had dared to ask Jesus who he was, for they all knew by
now who had come to them. Jesus invited them to break their fast
with him, and they did. Jesus took the bread, and gave it to them;
likewise the fish. So these seven also came to know him 'in the
breaking of the bread'. And each of them would have recalled
another meal of bread and fish on a Galilean hill; and each of them
would have had the memory of the broken bread at the Passover
meal a few weeks before.

When breakfast was over, Jesus turned to Peter and said to him, 'Simon, son of John, do you, as once you implied, really love me more than these other six?' Peter, by now fully realizing how little he could trust himself, and how much better Jesus knew him than he knew himself, could only make the halting answer, 'Yes, Lord, you know that I care for you.' Jesus told him, 'Then feed my lambs.' But Jesus knew that the spiritual wound was not yet fully exposed, and so could not yet be fully healed. He repeated his question, but dropped the reference to 'the other six'. He said to Peter, 'Simon, son of John, do you really love me?' Peter, still overcome by memory of his denials, could only answer again, 'Yes, Lord, you know that I care for you.' Jesus responded, 'Then tend my sheep.' Jesus then put the question a third time, as Peter had put his denial a third time, but this time he said to Peter, 'Simon, son of John, do you really care for me?' It hurt Peter (as may well have been the therapeutic intention) that Jesus should now have asked him in his own terms, 'Do you really care for me?' All his old self-confidence gone, trusting only what Jesus knew and could say of him, he blurted out, 'Lord, you know everything, everything about me. You must know that I care for you!' Jesus said to him, 'Feed my flock.' He then told Peter that the day would come when, like his Lord, he would lose his freedom and be made to suffer and die. He then repeated the call he had first made to Peter at Capernaum, 'Follow me!' By this time Peter knew what was meant by being Jesus's disciple and being ready to 'take up his cross' to follow his Lord. He had at last entered into possession of that peace which Jesus alone could give.

The Last Day: the universal and imperishable kingdom

After an unspecified period the Eleven went to the mountain which Jesus had arranged for their meeting. The scene, as Matthew saw, formed a fitting climax to the story of Jesus, particularly in those terms in which he had himself talked of his own destiny, as that of the Son of Man. He had said that some of his own disciples would, in their own lifetime, see that the kingdom of God had come with power (Mark 9.1). He had stated that when he was put to death he would go with the clouds of heaven and be presented to the Ancient of Days, and be given for the saints of the Most High a kingdom that would be imperishable and universal. He had also declared that when the Son of Man appeared he would come with power and glory, and send out his messengers to gather in his chosen ones from every corner of the world (Mat. 26.64; 24.31).

Now the 'messengers' had arrived. Now the Son of Man came as well (Mat. 28.16ff). He came, as he himself put it, 'with all authority, heavenly and earthly alike'. But that was not at once apparent to all the Eleven; some worshipped him while others were doubtful. Perhaps the latter had been expecting more of the 'trappings' of majesty such as are found in monarchs' courts, in any event a more glorious figure than one who still looked like a criminal who had been crucified. But their doubt dissolved as they entered, or re-entered, into their fellowship on the hillside.

Jesus, the Son of Man who had been to the Ancient of Days and received his kingdom, said, 'Since all authority, heavenly and earthly alike, has been given to me, you can now confidently continue and complete our mission for the kingdom of God. So go and teach all nations, for God's kingdom is universal. Remember your message is primarily for all communities to repent of their godlessness and to believe in the present power and goodness of God. But you will have much to say to the individual about personal repentance as the real way to the joys of the kingdom of God. Tell the world's peoples all that I have told you, and lead them to do all that I have commanded you, in every aspect of their corporate and individual life. You are to baptize them, as John and ourselves used to baptize into the life of the new people of God. But from now on your baptism must be a threefold reality. Baptize men in the name of the Father – that will ensure that they, yourselves and the world will realize that you have been sent on your mission by him who sent me. Baptize them in the Son, and remind them, yourselves and the world that in joining us they are being incorporated into the life of the new "son" of people of God created in and through me. Baptize them in the name of the Holy Spirit who, as you well know, is the power that animates us all in our membership of the one divine community. And my last word: you can be sure of this one thing, now that I am risen from the dead, I shall be with you all through your lives, and with all my people everywhere, to the very end of time.'

The Resurrection:
A Supplementary Study

The four gospel epilogues of the New Testament have been collated to yield one continuous narrative for the one epilogue of this book. This is a procedure which scholars will justifiably dislike, for it fails to expose certain difficulties in the gospel records themselves. Did one or two 'angels' appear at the Tomb? Did the early morning visitors see one 'young man' or 'two men'? Were the first appearances of Jesus in Jerusalem or Galilee? These are not unimportant points. But this book has tried to conceive how what took place, say on Easter Day, could be told to help a modern reader to perceive what was then going on. Moreover, the difficulties noted have been fairly exhaustively treated in a number of gospel commentaries as well as in special studies of the resurrection in the New Testament as a whole. Meanwhile the centre of debate has shifted significantly. Bultmann has put the modern issue concisely: 'If the event of Easter Day is in any sense an historical event additional to the event of the cross, it is nothing else than the rise of faith in the risen Lord, since it was this faith which led to the apostolic preaching'. (Bultmann, *Kerygma and Myth*, p 42). Did events that took place on Easter Day create the resurrection faith, or did a 'resurrection faith' create, as it were, the events that are reported to have happened on Easter Day?

Interestingly enough the statement of the modern dilemma by Bultmann can be seen to echo a tension even among the evangelists themselves. Mark and Matthew seem to tell the story of the end of Jesus's ministry as if its headlines were 'From Defeat to Victory' or 'From Humiliation to Glory', while John's story could be headed 'Defeat IS Victory' or 'Humiliation IS Glory'. In this, as in other matters, Luke stands midway between Mark/Matthew and John. The 'synoptic' story depicts Jesus as contrasting his death by crucifixion with his subsequent rising on the third day (Mark 8.31), whereas John tells that he saw the hour of his crucifixion as the hour of his glorification (John 17.1). In the one tradition the disciples appear throughout as men awaiting the arrival of a political kingdom, with themselves in places of prominence and power

(Mark 10.37, 41; Luke 22.24), while John presents Jesus as confident that his disciples were not ready to fight for him because they knew that his kingdom was not of this world (John 18.36). The synoptists tell of the agony of Jesus in Gethsemane as he contemplates his death (Mark 14.33-41), while John portrays him as very much, even if quietly, in control of the situation (John 17.1-5; 19.11). Mark and Matthew relate that the last words of Jesus were a cry of desolation, 'My God, my God, why hast thou forsaken me?', whereas in John they were the triumphant cry, 'It is done!' (Mark 15.34; John 19.30). In the synoptic story the disciples are quite sure that they will not 'let Jesus down' or desert him on the night of his arrest (Mark 14.29; Mat. 26.35; Luke 22.33), but John has no such detail, save for a special warning to Peter in response to his expressed willingness to lay down his life for Jesus (John 13.37f.). Both traditions tell of the attempt to prevent Jesus from being arrested, and Jesus's immediate reaction (Mark 14.47; John 18.10).*

To return to Bultmann's dilemma. Between the historical event of the cross and the historical event of the apostolic preaching, was there another historical event, to be called 'the resurrection', which would account for the preaching of the apostles? Was there a 'resurrection event' other than the actual preaching of the resurrection faith? Four points at least need consideration.

First, the evidence available must be used for what it was meant for, and not asked to serve purposes for which it was not intended. All the testimony contained in the gospels, and for a relatively obscure event of its time it is considerable, was concerned to witness to Jesus risen; there was none, nor any evidence that there ever was any, to Jesus rising. The Church, the critics and the world must come to terms with that.

Second, the ideas about Jesus's death which influenced the disciples' actions up to, including, and even beyond Easter Day itself positively preclude any ungrounded genesis of a resurrection faith of the kind which the disciples came to believe in and to

* It is interesting that John names Peter as the man who used his sword in defence of Jesus. If that line is pursued, it could be held that the reason for Peter's 'denial' of Jesus was his quite new realization of his error in supposing that Jesus was a militant Messiah (so that Peter had not really 'known' him), and that his re-examination after the resurrection (John 21.15-17) concerned not just his 'loyalty', but, more fundamentally, his grave misunderstanding of the nature of Jesus's Messiahship. No doubt there are difficulties in the way of such an exposition; but it seems to make just as much sense of the available evidence as any other alternative.

preach. The women and two wealthy disciples ensured that they had a proper and adequate supply of spices to embalm the body of Jesus. None of the disciples showed the slightest disposition to think of Jesus dead as Jesus living.

Third, the idea of a personal resurrection in history was not unfamiliar at that time. It was known to Jesus, the Twelve, Herod and many others. It was believed that on the death of some significant person, it was possible that he could 'rise again' in the person of someone quite different, who would then continue his mission. On that basis Herod supposed, along with many others, that Jesus was John the Baptist 'risen from the dead', though some people thought that he was Elijah, or Jeremiah, or some other great prophetic figure (Mat. 14.1f). Knowing this conception of what resurrection was, it would have been natural for the disciples to proclaim one of their own number as the 'risen Jesus' – Peter, or John or the 'beloved disciple'. But they did nothing of the kind. Moreover, as suggested above (p.207, etc.), it is quite feasible to think that the cause of many of the disciples' disputes about who should be greatest in the kingdom of Heaven were connected with the problem of who might succeed Jesus in leading the group after he was taken from them.

Fourth, there is a positive side to the negative fact that no disciple was proclaimed as 'Jesus risen from the dead'. This is the simple fact that the entirely new and original idea that the very same person who had died had risen from the dead to continue his work was the only message ever proclaimed by the apostles. The whole testimony of the gospels is designed to convince the reader that the claim was made by men who knew Jesus both 'in his lifetime' and in the life he lived with them after his rising from the dead.

The proclamation of the risen Lord is much more than an affirmation that one unique individual has miraculously risen from the dead. Had that been all the disciples had to tell the world the information might have been passed down to the present time, but that is by no means certain, considering the plethora of miracle stories circulating in antiquity. What makes this particular piece of news important and worthy of transmission is not just the affirmation that Jesus rose from the grave, but that he was restored to, and lives with, and works through the Christian community, just as actually and as effectively as he had 'in his lifetime'.

What then may be said, in the context of modern thought, about the experiences which the biblical witnesses gave to their contemporaries, and to us, in the thought forms of their own age?

Consider first the story of the empty tomb, recounted in each of the four gospels (though with differences of detail) and therefore not to be lightly set aside. That so abnormal a phenomenon even for the first century was recorded in itself demands that it be examined carefully. The Jews of the time would not have accepted the evidence of the women (Mark and Mat.) about the empty tomb, though they could not so easily have dismissed the narratives in Luke and John. Yet despite the unanimous and unambiguous testimony of the four evangelists, the empty tomb is nowhere referred to in the rest of the New Testament. Paul either knew nothing of it, or declined to make use of it. Its fundamental value is properly negative, though even that is important in so unusual an alleged happening. A proven empty tomb means that the corpse, once laid there, is missing, and suggests that if it were to reappear it would be recognizable, alive or still dead. The fact that it is not mentioned elsewhere in the New Testament strongly suggests that had the disciples had only an empty tomb to talk about, there would have been no preaching in the resurrection of Jesus. Some 'live' appearance of a buried person is an indispensable prelude to any announcement of a rising from the tomb.

The positive evidence for the resurrection of Jesus consists of the visual, auditory and tactual experience of a number of witnesses. In the relatively unsophisticated first century A.D. that evidence would have been quite enough. But to a sophisticated modern reader of the gospels it has a very different look. For he knows that there are alternative ways of understanding the disciples' experience to that traditionally given to it in the Church. What can be said to any such alternatives to the accepted belief in Jesus's resurrection?

First, one has to acknowledge that there is no unanswerable objection to the scepticism or denial of the 'modern mind'. Yet the modern believer can continue believing with real integrity. The objects of experience – persons, things and situations 'out there' in the external world – are normally disclosed to the observer by some stimuli from the object so acting upon his sense organs that he sees, hears, touches, tastes or smells it. Unquestionably the disciples believed that their experiences of the risen Jesus came to them 'normally'. But there are some experiences of objects that appear to be 'out there' which have no detectable external stimulus at all. Such are 'ghosts', day dreams and visions, whatever may be concluded about their 'reality' in the end. It is important to remember that the gospels twice report that Jesus appeared to the disciples in a manner which they first interpreted as the appearance of a 'ghost'. The first time, in Matthew 14.26, was during an early morning storm on the Sea of Galilee, when Jesus came to the disciples in their boat and 'walked on the sea'. They were terrified, and said, 'It's a ghost!' But when Jesus spoke to them, in the authoritative way he had, they knew him for the real man he was. The second time, in Luke 24.37, was as the two disciples who had met and supped with Jesus at Emmaus reported their experience to the Eleven. At the sight of Jesus the disciples were frightened, and thought they were seeing a ghost. Jesus then asked them to touch him. He ate a piece of fish in front of them. They would then have realized that they were being confronted with much more than a 'vision'. Then Jesus spoke to them, telling how the scriptures spoke throughout of him and his destiny. They would now have been sure that their more-than-visual experience was really of the Jesus they had known 'in his lifetime'. Ghosts and visionary figures cannot achieve with real persons the lively and stimulating intercourse that authentically 'live' persons alone can share.

External objects are presented to each observer in and through a complexity of data. These are normally interpreted so immediately as to appear automatic. Yet interpretation is limited in two ways: first, by the subject's previous range of experience, what has been termed his 'apperception', that accumulation of images and ideas with which alone he can translate the sensory data presented to him in terms of an orderly and therefore stable world. No member of a primitive tribe, for example, could either generate or interpret the visual data of a television set, though he could, in the right environment, those of a tree. Second, by each person's general set of beliefs. For example, Greeks and Jews of the first century A.D. differed greatly in their beliefs about death and life beyond it. The Greek experience of 'seeing the dead' would have been limited by the Greek belief that soul and body were distinct and separate entities, united in life but sundered in death. The Jews believed that a person in any sense alive was an 'embodied soul' (or an 'ensouled body'), with both physical and psychical elements in the person. What might have persuaded a Greek that he had seen a 'dead person' alive again might have done no more for a Jew than convince him that he had seen a ghost!

The question posed by the resurrection narratives in the gospels then is this: granted that the disciples really believed themselves to have seen Jesus – the Jesus they had known 'in his lifetime' – alive after he had died and been buried, how did that 'seeing' originate? What was the cause of the visual (and other) data they experienced? Did those data originate from within the disciples themselves, or from the presence before them of an external reality? And was the 'external reality' identical with that of 'Jesus in his lifetime'?

It must first be noted that the evidence suggests that there were some differences between 'seeing Jesus in his lifetime' and 'seeing Jesus risen from the dead'. Matthew reports of Jesus's last appearance to the Eleven that 'when they saw him they worshipped him; but some doubted'. Mary Magdalene did not recognize Jesus from just 'seeing' him in the garden on Easter morning. The two disciples on the road to Emmaus did not recognize Jesus when he came up to them. More than sensory experience was needed to identify Jesus risen with Jesus in his lifetime.

It is important next to remember that however much the sensory data suggested the presence of Jesus to those experiencing them, there were some abnormal elements in the experiences themselves. The risen Jesus could enter a room with doors locked against the chance intruder. He could disappear in a similarly unusual manner, as he did from the two disciples at the hostelry at Emmaus.

These two points lead to a third and most important consideration: that the experience of Jesus risen from the dead was not conveyed by sensory data alone, but by some additional element of experience through which the real presence of Jesus could be convincingly made known. Mary in the garden heard Jesus speak her name with the care and concern he had for her. The disciples on the walk to Emmaus recognized Jesus when he broke bread, and they could recall the feedings in Galilee, and, perhaps, the breaking of bread at the Last Supper. Then they could recall the strange 'warming of the heart' which they had felt as he spoke to them in his new and revealing way about the scriptures. The frightened disciples in the locked room heard him repeat his gift of peace, his promise of the Holy Spirit, and received his commission to be his apostles. They all knew that what they were experiencing was more than a series of sensory phenomena; they were meeting with a very specific person, with the Jesus they had known 'in his lifetime'.

But sensory data seem to have been an indispensable element in all the gospel records of the disciples' experience of their risen Lord. Two questions need to be considered: what caused the sensory elements of the first disciples' experience of seeing Jesus risen from the dead? And why did later disciples not – and why do they still not – find sensory elements necessary to their knowledge that Jesus is present with them?

The sensory data that produce awareness of the presence of a person are normally caused by that person's actual physical presence. But that cannot be said of the post-resurrection appearances of Jesus recorded in the gospels. Jesus died on Friday, and his body was laid in a tomb. It is difficult to suppose that it was that physical frame that was resuscitated, even though some evidence records that the risen Jesus could show the wounds of his crucifixion. For the same records (John 20.19-29) report that Jesus entered a room that was locked to prevent any unheralded arrival! Sensory data can be stimulated by other than normal means, by some word or action functioning as an evocatory symbol, or by the objectification of an interior condition such as grief or the inability to accept the death of a beloved friend. But there is nothing in the gospels to suggest that such an external symbol acted to evoke the sensory data which formed the basis of the disciples' experience of their risen Lord. It is possible to suppose, as some critics have, that the disappointment and conflicts of the disciples at the death of Jesus in some way occasioned the sensory data that led them to affirm that they had seen him alive after his death. To adopt this account of the disciples' experiences is to affirm that they suffered, as individuals and as a group, from hallucination. This is not a palatable theory for Christian believers, but it must not be rejected on that account. It calls for rejection, however, because it cannot really account for some of the evidence given in the scriptures.

The recognition of Jesus as a living person after his death was not affirmed simply on the basis of visual (or other sensory) data themselves, but, as seen above, on what the sensory data brought anew as a possibility of experience, the continuation of intercourse with the man they had known as Jesus in his lifetime. It may well be, as some critics would hold, that within the hallucinatory experience some resumption of intercourse could take place. But it seems impossible to suppose that, if the experiences were hallucinations, the intercourse could reach beyond the realm of what had already been achieved. And it is at this point that the theories of hallucination fail, in regard both to individual and group hallucination.

It is evident from the gospels that throughout the lifetime of Jesus he had found great difficulty in getting the disciples to accept his notion of the kingdom of Heaven in which true greatness lies not in the exercize of power and the enjoyment of glory, but in being the humble servant, indeed 'slave', of all. It was on the way to Jerusalem for the last Passover that James and John asked for the key places of power and prominence in the kingdom when it came. It was at the Last Supper itself that the band of disciples argued as to who would be the greatest in the kingdom of God. And after the resurrection they were still asking whether the time had come when Jesus would 'restore the kingdom to Israel'. It is quite clear that had the gospels been written before the resurrection there would have been no mention of the teaching of Jesus about true greatness – and yet the gospels have faithfully recorded not only the disciples' grave misconceptions, but, very clearly and forcefully, the sublime teaching of Jesus. There is no place for the disciples to have been brought to their final acceptance of the teaching of Jesus except in the intercourse that was opened up for the disciples in their meetings with the risen Jesus. Such a step forward is unthinkable without the intervention and stimulus of Jesus himself. It is possible to conclude that the disciples' experience of the risen Jesus was due to the real presence of Jesus himself, that his coming evoked the sensory stimuli that in turn conditioned their renewed intercourse with their risen Lord, who was indeed none other than the Jesus they had known in his lifetime. But is that a feasible suggestion today?

Modern philosophy has a good deal to say about what are the necessary and sufficient conditions for knowing that a living human being is 'there'. The study of the senses and perception have established a proper science of epistemology. But that sort of knowledge could only be applied to the knowledge that men had of Jesus 'in his lifetime'. Something also is known of what is called 'extra-sensory perception', though, even if much more were known, it could not apply to the post-resurrection experiences of the disciples, since they all contained some excitation of one or more of the senses. What remains certain is that very little, if anything, is known about two matters basic to any judgment of the resurrection narratives: what are the necessary and sufficient conditions for a human being to continue in existence after death; and what are the necessary and sufficient conditions for a human being to know of the continued existence of some other human being after death. In the absence of any conclusive demonstration that no such conditions exist, or can exist, there seems no alternative to accepting the apostolic testimony of the presence of the risen Jesus as that is recorded in the gospels and the rest of the New Testament.

The four gospels provide the chief evidence for the life and death of Jesus, and constitute the only written near-contemporary witness to his resurrection. The resurrection testimony was, however, not an attempt to establish the occurrence of one unique event in human history, when Jesus rose from the dead, and was 'seen' alive after death by a fortunate few. That could well have been interesting and intriguing news, unbelievable to men of the first as well as of the twentieth century. The testimony to the resurrection of Jesus becomes good news for men of every age and place because:

1. It was given by those who had known Jesus well in his lifetime. What they saw of him before and after his death enabled them to say with confidence that the two persons were truly identical. The Jesus who had risen was the very Jesus who had been crucified.

2. The testimony is not simply to what was 'seen' of Jesus, but, more particularly and cogently, to the intercourse the disciples had with him after he had risen from the dead. He was still the stimulating and creative centre of the community he had created 'in his lifetime'.

3. The testimony establishes that the sensory data were not the only medium – and certainly not the permanent one – by which the presence of Jesus could be discerned. The good news of the resurrection is that the real Jesus who was known in his lifetime through the medium of sensory data remains the living, knowable and creative centre of his community or kingdom, and that his presence is a permanent possibility of experience for all who seek it in trust and hope. It is good news because the life that Jesus brought, and still brings, to his people and shares with them has already been proved to be indestructible. And that life is the gift promised to all who belong to his community.

If the Church is to share such a new and indestructible life, it needs some criteria for identifying the spiritual forces operative in its life. The gospels were written so that men might recognize that in the life of the Church of any age it is not just the 'spirit of the age', the 'Zeitgeist', that animates her to be and remain a true Church, but the presence and power of Jesus himself. The gospels tell the Church of every age that whenever she breaks bread, there the risen Lord is (Mat. 26.26-29; Luke 24.30.; John 6.53-58; 1 Cor. 10.16f.; 11.23-26); that whenever she lives by the forgiveness she has received and practises it, the risen Lord dwells in her (Mat. 9.8; 18.21f.; 28.19f.; Luke 24.47ff.; John 20.21ff.); that whenever the Church, or for that matter any secular man or society in the world, meets the hungry or the thirsty, the stranger or the ill-clad, hears of sick or imprisoned persons, they are really meeting Jesus himself, whether they recognize him or not, and whether they minister to him or not (Mat. 25.31-46); that whenever two or more individual disciples meet together 'in the name of Jesus', he will be with them in his risen power (Mat. 18.20). In such ways the Church of every age can receive those stimuli that occasion the experience of Christ's real presence with his people, and confirm the ageless confidence that Jesus is risen, and lives again for and with and in his community. So it is that Christians of all ages and cultures have been enabled to 'see Jesus' in the solemn liturgical worship of the Mass, the Eucharist, the Lord's Supper, Holy Communion, the Breaking of the Bread, or whatever name is used for the celebration of the 'new Passover' of the Christian Church. They have known him to be present with them in all varieties of group meetings, from church meetings in local churches, through to National Church Councils or Synods, and the great ecumenical meetings of the early Church, and of the ecumenical movement of the twentieth century. They have known and felt his presence in all manner of devotional groups, from 'house groups', of the early and the contemporary Church, to monastic communities. They have found him as they have served their local communities or undertaken larger enterprises for the sick, the poor, the imprisoned, the persecuted, or the outcasts and refugees of the world.

Are such claims true? The answer of the angel at the tomb is still offered to the questioner: 'Come and see!' The preaching of the resurrection is basically an invitation to begin a new experience of the world and to enter a new world of experience where, already within the bounds of the temporal, historical order, the eternal dimension of life is opened to men. Men can still 'repent' and, 'believing the good news', enter the kingdom of God. Through their life in the community of Jesus, or rather through his life in and with and through them in that community, Christians can know even in the present world the joys of that eternal kingdom which Jesus from first to last proclaimed. The Church says 'Amen' (='So it is') to the testimony that Jesus lives; and that living, he reigns.

Jesus reigns? Yes, because the Jesus of the resurrection is one and the same and continuous with Jesus in his lifetime. And in the ministry of Jesus in his lifetime he made it clear that his coming initiated a new kingdom. It was not the political kingdom that so many of his Jewish contemporaries awaited, not a kingdom of the kind that Rome had won by world conquest, and which she governed in Palestine. It was a kingdom within those or any other kingdoms (whatever the form of political organization), whose citizens he so compellingly described in the Sermon on the Mount. He was a king of the kind that he so dramatically symbolized for his contemporaries by his ride into Jerusalem on the Sunday before he died. He affirmed his real kingship to a misconceiving Pilate. On his cross his accusation stated truly but inadequately that he was 'King of the Jews'. And the kingdom that was 'lost' on Good Friday by the execution of its king was restored to new vitality on Easter Day after Jesus, to use the prophetic words from which he quoted about himself, had been presented to the Ancient of Days, and received for the saints of the Most High an eternal and universal kingdom.

> So be it Lord; thy throne shall never,
> Like earth's proud empires, pass away;
> Thy kingdom stands and grows for ever,
> Till all thy creatures own thy sway.

5

IN CONCLUSION

Finally, it is worthwhile to review the main points of this study, and to ask again whether the gospels provide a reliable picture of Jesus in his lifetime. It is also important to look forward from the gospels to what the Church has come to think and teach about Jesus. Does the gospel story really sustain the great affirmations of the creeds that Jesus is 'the only begotten son of God, begotten of his Father before all worlds'? Did he 'rise from the dead' and 'ascend into heaven'? Does he now 'reign' over all things? Will he 'come in glory to judge both the quick and the dead'? Will his kingdom 'know no end'? What has been written in this study has obvious consequences for answering such questions. Three main contentions are for this reason worth reviewing.

What goes on and what takes place

It is difficult for any twentieth-century man to take the four gospels as relating literally just what took place in the lifetime of Jesus. Of course some trustworthy information is given, but many statements appear unbelievable. Accepting that embarrassing fact, liberal theologians and later Professor Bultmann and his followers have made what they deemed to be helpful suggestions. Liberal scholars saw that the miracle worker of the gospels was hardly an acceptable figure in history. Their remedy was to explain or even explain away the miraculous element in the gospels. Thus at the feeding of the five thousand what 'really took place' was that a small boy with a lunch package offered his food for the general benefit, and this infectious generosity so affected the crowd that all were properly fed and satisfied. That is not an impossible explanation, but as it fails to penetrate to what was discerned by the evangelists to be going on, it is nothing but an emasculation of the gospel story. Better to keep the miracle and therewith the pointer to what was going on than to banish the miraculous and be blinded to what went on.

Liberal theology was thus left with a Jesus, obedience to whose unparelleled ethical and spiritual teaching, and the following of whose persuasive example of a love which crossed all boundaries in its concern, and of a humble patience that endured opposition even to the point of death, constituted a saving power in human life. But teaching and example are not 'happenings', 'events' that historically decide the destiny of men. Liberal theologians thus really lost the significance of Jesus as a man whose life achieved a new destiny for human kind. In a word, liberal theology ceased to ask what was going on in history, and instead asked what lessons could be learned from it, or from the teachers who spoke in it. That was a fatal attenuation of the good news of the gospel.

Professor Bultmann has suggested an alternative way to deal with the elements in the gospels that seem unacceptable to modern man. The gospel narratives should be, in his word, 'demythologized'. The elements in the gospels alien to modern man must be recognized as arising from the apperceptions of the first century – such as angels, demons, powers of the air, and miracles themselves – and reinterpreted in terms of the apperceptions of the twentieth century, when they will disclose themselves as influences acting upon men for good ('from above') or evil ('from below'). If such a demythologizing is radically carried through, the gospel reader is freed from having to reject (or accept) Jesus on the grounds that he operated with unrealities, and can accept or reject him only on the proper terms of facing his claim from his followers. Thus Bultmann removes the Jesus who meets us in the gospels out of his historical situation, and brings him and us into the realm of the existential, the realm of decision-making; in this way, like the liberal theologians from whom he otherwise differs so greatly, he loses the one indispensable note of the gospel message, that Jesus has done something for human kind in history and beyond it.

It is a matter for gratification that some of the more erudite and perceptive of Bultmann's disciples have begun to have second thoughts, and have initiated and persevered with a New Quest for the historical Jesus. They have realized that to meet Jesus is not to leave the realm of the historical, that the only place where Jesus meets and speaks to men is through his actions and words as recorded in the gospels.

This book differs from both the liberals and Bultmann. It proposes that the gospels be read as a record not only of what took place when Jesus lived, but also as a statement of what was going on in what he did and experienced. It recognizes how limited were the historiographical devices available to the evangelists in making such a record. The gospel reader is thus freed from having to suppose that every incident recorded took place 'just so'; instead he can see the gospels as providing him with clues as to what was going on. Admittedly this way of reading the gospels will not bring anyone nearer to 'what took place' when Jesus was alive, (though it will not take him further from it), but it will take him nearer, or keep him as near, to what was really going on. The book does not try with the liberals to explain the inexplicable, nor with Bultmann to forsake the historical for the existential. It stays in the annalist but real historical field of what took place, until the record yields its treasure, and discloses the dimension of what was going on in what took place. To gain true knowledge of Jesus in his lifetime it is but necessary to take the records as they are and ponder them. It is foolish to demythologize or rationalize the gospels, and then expect them to disclose their full meaning.

Jesus as the son of God

Some readers will have noticed that the title 'Son of God' is used in this book for the most part without a capital letter for the word 'son'. This is not because the author wishes to deny what those believe who put a capital letter for 'Son', but because he wants to restore the place that the Old Testament gave to the term as Jesus heard it at his baptism (see above, p.112f.). In the Old Testament 'son' is characteristically used to mean 'people' or 'nation': 'Israel is my first born son' (Exod. 4.22). 'When Israel was a child, I loved him; and out of Egypt I called my son' (Hos. 11.1). In the New Testament Christ is held to dwell in his people, and they in him (2 Cor. 6.16; 1 John 4.13). The Church is Christ's body, of which he is the head (Eph. 1.22; Col. 1.18). Nowhere in the New Testament is Jesus a man of divine stature without a community of men with him

to share his life and his very being. He was not the Messiah, nor did
he act or speak as the Messiah, without a people of the Messiah
about him. He did not collect a mere unordered following, but
formed his disciples into a recognizably symbolic re-formation of
the old Israel or people or nation of God. An unfortunate effect of
the great affirmations of Jesus's sonship in Christian doctrine has
been that the corporate nature of the son so dominant in the bible
(even the 'sonship' of Solomon was given him only as the representative of the whole people) has become an individual attribute of
Jesus alone. Jesus is God's son, and that is all that can be said. But
with a biblical understanding of sonship one would say, 'Jesus is
son, and so are all those bound to him in a community of faith! They
too are part of and share his sonship!' This does not lessen the
doctrine of Jesus's sonship, but gives it a proper statement in
accordance with a theme running through the whole bible. The son
of God is a corporate entity not just an individual one. That is all we
know, and all we need to know.

Jesus's sonship was decisively disclosed to him at his baptism,
though according to Luke he had intimations of it before that (Luke
2.49). Was his sonship then like that of Solomon, whose sonship was
not only disclosed to him on a certain day of his life (his coronation)
but actually began at that time? The theologians have given an
emphatic 'No' to that question, and have reinforced their stand by
doctrines of a virgin birth and an immaculate conception. They
want to make it quite clear that Jesus was Son of God quite apart
from, as well as in, the sonship he exercized in his earthly life. What
is at stake – not only for the theologian, but for the ordinary
believer? It could be put in such terms as these: God appointed or
adopted many persons in the old Israel to be his sons. They were
not so called in their own right, but only as individuals who
incorporated in themselves the whole body of the people. Hence
the king was typically God's son in the Old Testament (Ps. 2.7). But
such sons were only mortal men, with all the frailty and proneness
to sin of mortal men. Though they were God's sons, the 'heads' of a
people chosen and appointed and adopted by God to serve him and
accomplish his purposes in the world, time and again they failed
him. But the sonship of Jesus was of quite another order or
dimension (Heb. 1.2-13; 3.6). He was appointed a son before the
world was made (Heb. 1.2) and will continue in the sonship forever
(Heb. 1.8). Jesus was not a frail mortal adopted for a sonship he
could not fulfil; he was a being of a new order, a son who was not a

man of this world, though he was a man in this world. He could
fulfil God's will and purposes – and he has done so. If this were not
so, there could be no assurance that God had at last completed his
great design for his creation and its creatures. So the issue of an
'eternal' sonship is vital to those believers who see that it is in the
realities of history that Jesus in his lifetime achieved the universal
salvation that he proclaimed to men in the arrival of the universal
kingdom of God.

This examination of sonship has disclosed an inadequacy in the
traditional formulation of the Church's doctrine about Jesus. In the
fourth and fifth centuries it was important to convince the world
that God was in Christ. No less a truth than that could assure men of
the reality of the salvation that was proclaimed. Hence the
discussions at Nicaea and Chalcedon were dominated by the need
to show that Jesus was divine. This was done by expounding what it
meant to say that he was God's son. What is still needed is a fuller
and more enlightening presentation of that truth in a clear linking
of Jesus with his community on earth – and beyond – so that the
whole is recognized as the 'son' of God. Not that the people of
Christ are such on their own, individually or together, nor even that
Jesus is such on his own, but that in God's grand design both
together are his 'son', by Jesus's willing self-identification. If this
were done, the question of the person of Christ could be seen in a
wider and more fruitful perspective. The son over whose life Easter
has shown evil and death to have no further power is the bringer
and the substance of a universal salvation in the solidarity that he
has effected with his people.

John the Baptist, Jesus and political reality

The story of Jesus is not simply of theological and religious
interest. It is concerned with political realities as well. What Jesus
taught was itself a responsible critique of contemporary politics and
politicians in his part of the world. He announced that the kingdom
of God had arrived. That message differed vastly from what other
leaders of Jewish thought (except John the Baptist) were saying. It
also had very different implications for action. If the kingdom had
arrived, the Pharisees were wrong to teach that it could not come
until every Jew obeyed the Law completely. The Sadducees were
wrong to act out of expediency in relation to Rome, because they

believed the kingdom of God was still to come. The Zealots were wrong to suppose that the only way to bring about the kingdom was to fight for it, which in the context of the time meant rebellion against Rome for an independent Jewish state. The desert sectaries were nearer the truth in their conviction that it was possible to live the life of the kingdom within the present political order, though they were wrong to require an apprenticeship first, to practise a testing asceticism, and above all to declare that the coming of the kingdom would involve the fighting of a great Messianic war, in which they must be properly prepared participants. In contrast Jesus said that entry to the kingdom of God was open to all who repented of the national failure to be truly a people of God, for Israel had failed both to remove the injustices in her own society, and to take to Gentile peoples the good news of God's universal and beneficent purpose for all mankind.

Those who followed Jesus and became citizens of the kingdom of Heaven were not immediately granted immunity from all discomfort and disaster. On the contrary, his disciples not only shared with other men in suffering the 'slings and arrows of outrageous fortune' but were liable additionally to suffer just because they were disciples and citizens of the kingdom of Heaven. 'Whoever does not bear his own cross and come after me cannot be my disciple' (Luke 14.27). Yet, as the Beatitudes made clear, to be a heavenly citizen and be persecuted for it is a matter for congratulation. Such a sufferer knows, even in such life, the bliss that is transcendent in quality. To be such a citizen is not to join a political party, or become dedicated to some cause, but to live in a world where politics are real, knowing that in and alongside all the passing kingdoms of this world there is one which will never pass away.

It was into the world of 'real politics' that John the Baptist and Jesus stepped when they first announced to the Israel of their day that 'the kingdom of God had come upon them'. John's 'Red Sea' baptism symbolized the emergence at that time of a new people of God. As a result, 'the people were on the tiptoe of excitement, all wondering about John, whether perhaps he was the Messiah'. Whatever the two preachers might have meant, popular expectations connected with the Messiah were extremely threatening in the eyes of Rome. John's preaching of repentance was addressed not just to individuals, but to the nation and people of Israel as a whole. The point has been made (p.112), and need not be repeated here.

The fact that Jesus came to be baptized by John is a clear

indication that he recognized the truth behind John's baptizing: Israel's need to repent. But repentance can be demanded in all sorts of circumstances of any people. What was special and urgent about the situation to which John addressed himself? John saw (and Jesus saw with him) that the religious, racial and political attitudes of official Judaism would inevitably bring ruin and disaster to Israel in the quite foreseeable future. When some of the Jerusalem officials came to listen to John he met them with the question, 'Who told you to escape from the coming retribution? Prove your repentance by the fruit it bears.' He told them not to suppose that the fact that they were Jews would exempt them from the nemesis of their actions. 'Already the axe is laid to the roots of the trees.' John knew that the time left for any kind of manoeuvre was very short, and his message was therefore delivered with a great sense of urgency. It was that which probably made the crowds wonder whether he were not the Messiah deliverer himself.

John made a considerable impression on the general public, but aroused nothing but resentment and hostility among the authorities. For a time Jesus and he worked side by side in parallel missions. Jesus was even said to be symbolically baptizing more citizens into the kingdom than was John. When Jesus moved to Galilee, John continued his mission in Judea. But not for long. Herod had him arrested, put him in a remote prison, and eventually had him executed. Jesus remained in Galilee alone.

When Jesus heard of John's imprisonment, he decided at once to resume his own mission, but not in Judea. In Galilee there was less chance of interference from Jerusalem, and perhaps a readier ear for a message critical of officialdom. It is interesting to detect how Jesus's actions reflect a sense of urgency. The new people of God, focussed as he knew in himself, must be brought to life and activity. But if John had so soon been put to death, how much time had Jesus himself? He gathered his disciples, fashioned his little community into an order that symbolized in its twelve 'patriarchs' that the new Israel was now alive and at work, and sent them out to prosecute their mission. Time was short, so they had to concentrate on the essentials. They had to preach the good news of the kingdom of God. There was no point in talking to Gentiles who would not understand what a 'new Israel' was, or in arguing with Samaritans who would engage in endless discussions, religious and political, about Jews and Samaritans. Because the aim was a new Israel of God, the mission had to be to the old people of God, to those regarded by the 'authorities' as 'lost sheep', to recruit them, a ready-ripe harvest, represented in the persons of the patriarchs of the new Israel – four or more fishermen, partners in family businesses; at least one ex-member of the Zealot movement; one Quisling tax collector among them. It was also represented in the people with whom Jesus was willing to have formal table fellowship: tax gatherers, 'sinners', prostitutes and lepers, as well as Pharisees and scribes.

While John was still in prison he sent some of his disciples to ask Jesus whether he was the 'one who was to come' (see above, p.143). John had proclaimed before Jesus was baptized that 'the axe is already laid to the roots of the trees'; now it seems as if he was enquiring as to how the critical days were passing, whether the movement they had begun side by side was going to be in time to avert the disasters that threatened. When Jesus heard of the death of John he 'withdrew from there in a boat to a lonely place apart' (Mat. 14.13). No doubt, like many another, Jesus wanted time to wrestle with his grief alone; less certainly he may have sought an opportunity to reflect on what strategy the death of John demanded of him as the one survivor of their joint Judean mission. It is not without significance that immediately after this withdrawal Matthew records that Jesus fed five thousand followers in a formal meal, serving notice to followers and authorities alike that his movement was both sizeable and significant.

In planning his last season's activity Jesus showed a great sense of urgency (see above, p.151). He took what measures he could to ensure that the crowds and the authorities received his message of the kingdom and its king plainly and unambiguously. That is why he made his 'pacific' entry into Jerusalem on Palm Sunday, and cleansed the Temple the next day. He sensed that the crisis was about to break, and that it was desperately urgent to change policies and attitudes if it was to be avoided. 'Forswear the sword' and 'Make your religion universal' he stated in his two dramatic actions before the Passover. His lament over Jerusalem echoes his sense of crisis: 'O Jerusalem, Jerusalem, the city that murders the prophets and stones the messengers sent to her! How often have I longed to gather your children, as a hen gathers her brood under her wings; but you would not let me. Look, look! there is your temple, forsaken by God, and laid waste!' (Mat. 23.37). Jerusalem had not been willing to heed the warning that Jesus had sounded. The result would be disastrous. The same distressing ideas permeate the apocalyptic chapters of the gospels; Jesus foresees that the result of present trends will be that the sacred city and its temple will be razed to the ground. The crisis which John and Jesus foresaw broke at the Passover of 32 A.D. It did not result, as expected, in the military humiliation of the Jews, and the destruction of Jerusalem and its temple. Instead it was Jesus who died, while the nation survived. As the Sanhedrin had been advised before the Passover: 'It is better for you that one man die for the people than that the whole nation perish' (John 11.50). But that political cynicism was turned into an evangelical promise by the action of God; crucifixion was shown by the resurrection to be the historical centre of what had been going on throughout history, the demonstration of God's love and forgiveness in bringing all men to share the life that is life indeed.

In his lifetime Jesus brought and bestowed the Father's gift of 'life in the kingdom', or, in the fourth gospel's phrase, 'eternal life'. Now as the risen Lord he remains the bearer and bestower of that gift. Historically his 'lifetime' ended in 32 A.D.; but beyond the temporal and historical that life continues. 'Jesus in his lifetime' is still accessible to those who want to meet him.

For Further Reading

The following list of books includes all those I have mentioned. A few others have been added, but it is quite impracticable to give anything like a full bibliography for a subject that has been so widely discussed for so long. It would be useful for those who find the subject new to consult some good single-volume (or more extensive) commentary on the Bible, with a comprehensive and informed bibliography. Thus the *New Catholic Commentary on Holy Scripture*, Peake's *Commentary on the Bible* (revised edition) and such publications as *The Expositor's Bible* all contain very valuable references. To those who are well versed in discussions about the historical Jesus, I can only say that I have tried to write for the less advanced, and have deliberately avoided references to authorities, and my reasons for differing from them. I have done so in order to encourage believers and unbelievers alike to see both the importance of the issues involved, and one possible and positive resolution of them.

Bornkamm, Günther, *Jesus of Nazareth*, Hodder & Stoughton, 1960
Bultmann, Rudolf, *Theology of the New Testament*, SCM Press, 1952
    The History of the Synoptic Tradition, (2nd ed.) Blackwell, 1968
Dodd, C.H. *According to the Scriptures*, Nisbet, 1952
    The Apostolic Preaching and its Development, Hodder & Stoughton, 1939
    The Founder of Christianity, Collins, 1971
    History and the Gospel, Nisbet, 1938
    The Parables of the Kingdom, Nisbet, 1935
Fuchs, E. *Studies of the Historical Jesus*, SCM Press, 1954
Fuller, R.H., *The Foundation of New Testament Christology*, Scribners, 1965
    The Mission and Achievement of Jesus, Scribners, 1965
Glasson, T.F., *His Appearing and His Kingdom*, Epworth, 1953
    The Second Advent (2nd Ed.), Epworth, 1947
Hoskyns and Davey, *The Fourth Gospel* (2nd ed.), Faber, 1947
Jaubert, A., *La date de la Cène*, Paris, 1957
Kümmel, W.G., *Promise and Fulfilment*, SCM Press, 1957
Lightfoot, R.H., *History and Interpretation in the Gospels*, Hodder & Stoughton, 1935
    Locality and Doctrine in the Gospels, Hodder & Stoughton, 1938
Marsh, John, *The Fulness of Time*, Nisbet, 1952
    Pelican Commentary on John, 1968
Moule, G.F. (Ed.), *The Significance of the Message of the Resurrection for Faith in Jesus Christ*, SCM Press, 1968
Robinson, James M., *A New Quest of the Historical Jesus*, SCM Press, 1959
Stauffer, E., *Jerusalem and Rome* (*The writings of Josephus*), Meridian Books, 1960
Todt, H.E., *The Son of Man in the Synoptic Tradition*, Westminster Press, 1965

Index